1996

Evening Standard

LONDON RESTAURANT GUIDE

To Gilly

Christmas 1995

Let's choose a restaurant,
book our baby sitter and go
for a real

love

D0542065

1996

Evening Standard
LONDON
RESTAURANT
GUIDE

FAY MASCHLER

TO REG GADNEY, MY DEAREST COMPANION

First published in Great Britain in 1995 by
PAVILION BOOKS LIMITED
26 Upper Ground, London SE1 9PD

Designed by
THE BRIDGEWATER BOOK COMPANY

Wine reviews by Bruce Yardley
Additional testing and reporting by Dee McQuillan
Commissioning Editor for the *Evening Standard*: Joanne Bowlby

A CIP catalogue record for this book is
available from the British Library

ISBN 1 85793 740 6

Typeset in (Adobe Caslon 8.5pt)
Printed and bound in Great Britain by Butler & Tanner Ltd,
Frome and London

2 4 6 8 10 9 7 5 3 1

This book may be ordered by post direct from
the publisher. Please contact the Marketing Department.
But try your bookshop first.

Corporate editions and personal subscriptions of the
Evening Standard London Restaurant Guide are available.
Call us for details. Tel: 0171-620 1666

ALSO PUBLISHED IN THIS SERIES:
the *Evening Standard London Pub Guide*
by Angus McGill and the *Evening Standard
London Wine Guide* by Andrew Jefford

CONTENTS

INTRODUCTION

You are right to buy this guide. London is now the most exciting city in the world for eating out, but to get the best out of it you need explanation, elucidation, clarification and encouragement to explore new territories: you need a cryptographer, editor and demythologizer. Having been the restaurant critic for London's *Evening Standard* for the past 23 years, I feel equipped for the task. It is, of course, not a task, but for the most part a pleasure endlessly to eat out, chasing the latest good meal, the most revealing exposition of some aspect of regionality of a cuisine, the newest absurdity launched in the name of fooling most of the people's palates some of the time. It provides exercise – panting in the wake of chefs whose notions of fidelity (to their workplace) bear comparison with those of Don Juan. Never has the volatile business that is London catering been so fitful as in this past year.

This guide to about 250 of London's best restaurants is as up to date and accurate as it is possible to be. Fortunately, beneath the skittering of the divas and the driven there is a solid foundation of establishments happy in their own skin and these are recognized and appraised. Close on 40 recently opened restaurants have merited inclusion since publication of the last edition, and nine new establishments are awarded the ultimate London accolade, awarded on an annual basis, an Eros.

In assessing this guide it is pertinent to look at the Eros Awards. These are not the equivalent of stars given in recognition of the conventions of haute cuisine – they do not applaud the pointless trappings of luxury. They aim to leave in place, after the sieve has been shaken, establishments that succeed vivaciously and buoyantly in what they set out to do, and which make London such a singular place for eating out. This year, for example, a Lebanese restaurant, Al Hamra, is selected. Lebanese food is seldom given the credit it deserves for its diversity, healthiness and subtlety and the high standard of both preparation and service invariably applied. Indian vegetarian food, one of the great pleasures of London eating and one of its most affordable, deserves celebration: the Keralan cooking offered at Rasa in Stoke Newington is a revelation. Trained chefs arriving directly from India have led to a breakthrough in mainstream Indian restaurant cooking, excitingly exemplified by Star of India. Italian restaurants continue to evolve, and the names we now associate with them are those of chefs rather than owners or managers, a phenomenon apparent at Zafferano. English food has, at last, emerged with pride and brio, as you will discover in a visit to St John. The reverse colonizing taking place, with Antipodean chefs producing some of the most enticing modern menus in town, is the background of The Sugar Club. Some English chefs, having trained with the acknowledged masters, are finding their own path, as is the case at The Square. Certain restaurants have held on to their Eros since last year and among them is what I consider the cream of fine dining – La Tante Claire, Bibendum, Les Saveurs and The Restaurant at The Hyde Park Hotel – and the best of modestly priced neighbourhood places – The Brackenbury and Ransome's Dock. Glamour, an important element in eating out, as well as very good food is served at Le Caprice and The Ivy, the two best-run restaurants in London. There are more.

All the restaurants in the guide have new entries based on revisits, not every one by me, as that would be an impossibility, but some by an anonymous team of trusted inspectors to whom I am deeply greatful. Bruce Yardley has assessed the wine lists. Information as to opening times etc has been given by the restaurants and is reproduced in good faith.

Price: The price quoted, based on dinner à la carte, is an indication of the cost of a three-course meal for one, including half a bottle of modest wine, tax but not service. Eating at lunch time or from set-price menus will often be cheaper.

Service charge: Where service charge is a fixed percentage this is stated in the restaurant information. Optional service leaves it up to you: 10% is adequate, 15% is generous. There is no requirement to pay a fixed charge if truly indifferent service can be proved.

Newcomers: The list of newcomers is of restaurants which opened after August 1994.

Telephone numbers: Only 0181 numbers are prefixed: all others are 0171 numbers.

All that remains is for you to pick up the phone and make a booking!

FAY MASCHLER

MAP I • Greater London

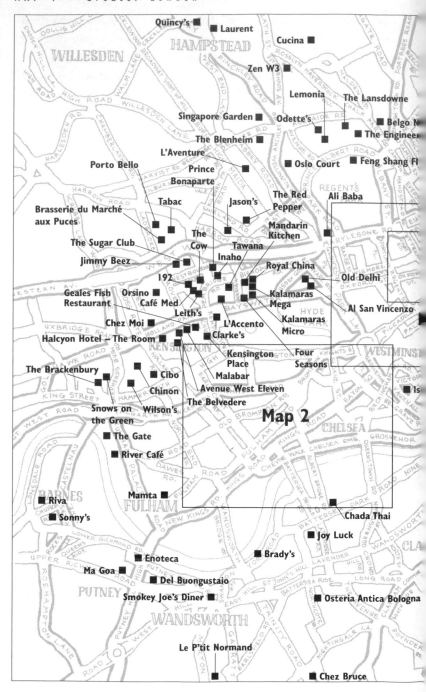

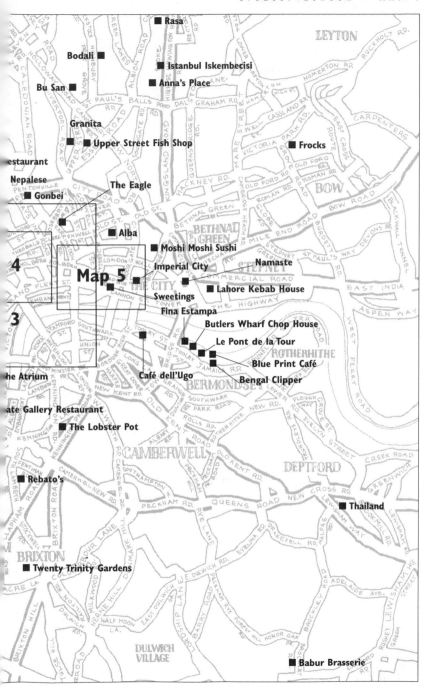

Rasa

Bodali

Istanbul Iskembecisi

Anna's Place

Bu San

Granita

Upper Street Fish Shop

Frocks

estaurant

Nepalese

Gonbei

The Eagle

Alba

Moshi Moshi Sushi

Imperial City

Namaste

4

Map 5

Sweetings

Lahore Kebab House

3

Fina Estampa

Butlers Wharf Chop House

Le Pont de la Tour

Blue Print Café

he Atrium

Café dell'Ugo

Bengal Clipper

ate Gallery Restaurant

The Lobster Pot

Rebato's

Thailand

Twenty Trinity Gardens

Babur Brasserie

MAP 2 • West London

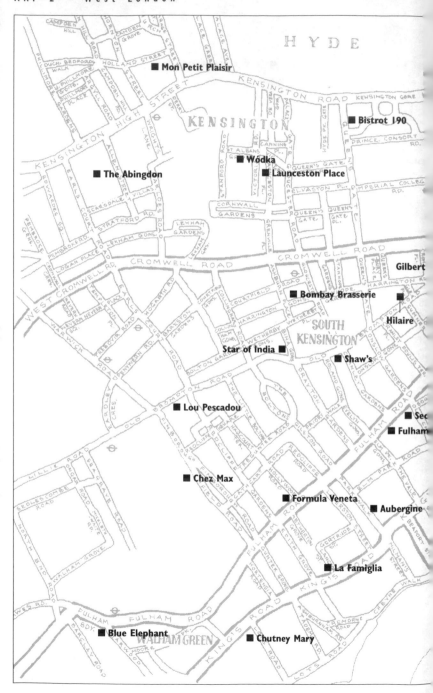

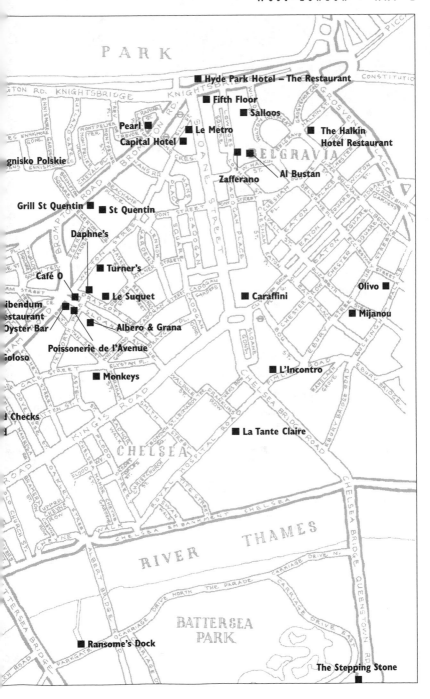

MAP 3 • Central London

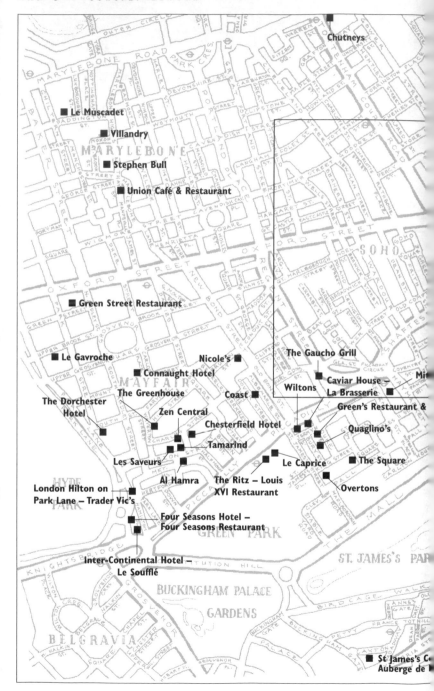

■ Chutneys

■ Le Muscadet

■ Villandry

MARYLEBONE

■ Stephen Bull

■ Union Café & Restaurant

■ Green Street Restaurant

SOHO

■ Le Gavroche

Nicole's ■

The Gaucho Grill

■ Connaught Hotel

MAYFAIR

Wiltons ■

Caviar House –
La Brasserie ■   Mi

■ The Greenhouse

Coast ■

Green's Restaurant &

The Dorchester
Hotel ■

Zen Central ■

Chesterfield Hotel ■

Quaglino's ■

Tamarind ■

■ The Square

Les Saveurs ■ ■

Le Caprice ■

HYDE

Al Hamra ■

The Ritz – Louis
XVI Restaurant

Overtons

PARK

London Hilton on ─ ■
Park Lane – Trader Vic's

■ Four Seasons Hotel –
Four Seasons Restaurant

GREEN PARK

ST. JAMES'S PAR

Inter-Continental Hotel –
Le Soufflé

BUCKINGHAM PALACE
GARDENS

BELGRAVIA

■ St James's C
Auberge de

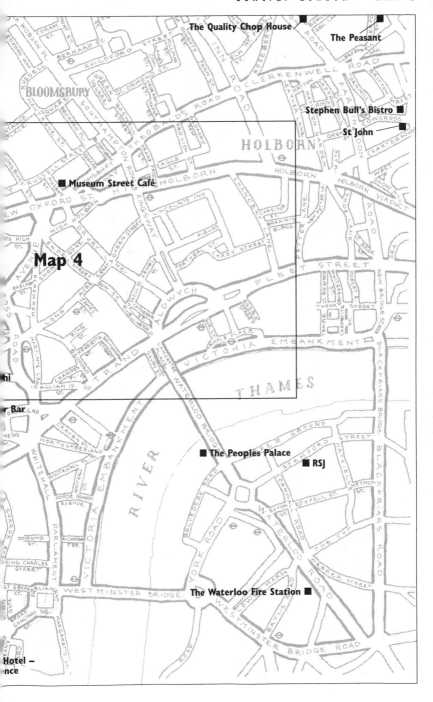

The Quality Chop House

The Peasant

BLOOMSBURY

Stephen Bull's Bistro

HOLBORN

St John

Museum Street Café

HOLBORN

Map 4

hi

Bar

The Peoples Palace

RSJ

The Waterloo Fire Station

Hotel –
nce

13

MAP 4 • The West End

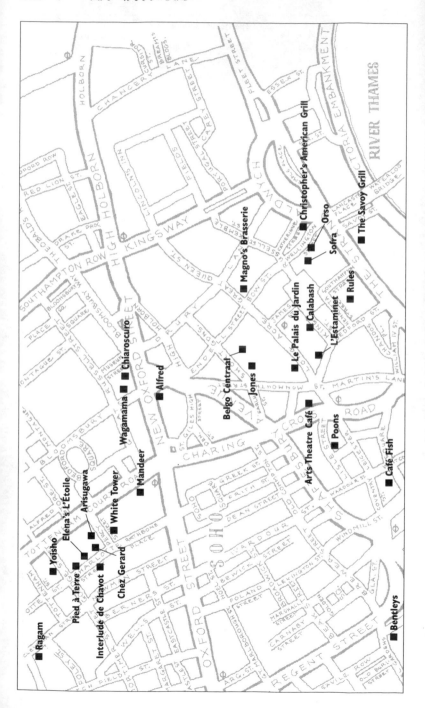

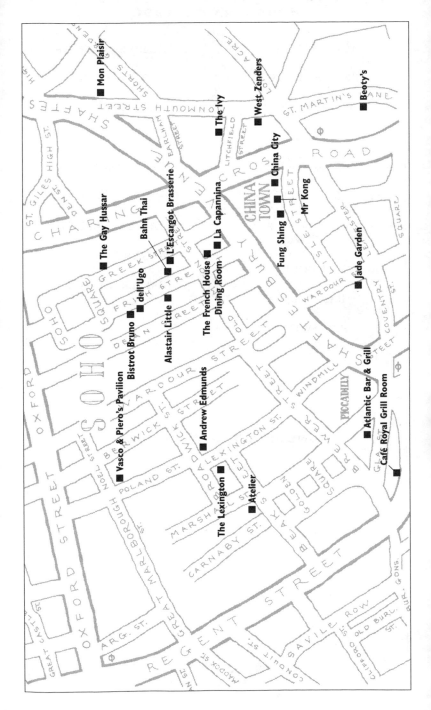

Mon Plaisir

West Zenders

The Ivy

Beoty's

The Gay Hussar

China City

Mr Kong

Bahn Thai

L'Escargot Brasserie

La Capannina

CHINA TOWN

dell'Ugo

Fung Shing

Bistrot Bruno

The French House

Alastair Little

Dining Room

Jade Garden

Vasco & Piero's Pavilion

Andrew Edmunds

PICCADILLY

Atlantic Bar & Grill

Café Royal Grill Room

The Lexington

Atelier

Eros Awards 1996

AL HAMRA W1

BIBENDUM SW3

THE BRACKENBURY W6

LE CAPRICE SW1

CHEZ MOI W11

HYDE PARK HOTEL – THE RESTAURANT SW1

THE IVY WC2

RANSOME'S DOCK SW11

RASA N16

RIVA SW13

THE RIVER CAFÉ W6

ST JOHN EC1

LES SAVEURS W1

THE SQUARE SW1

STAR OF INDIA SW5

THE SUGAR CLUB W11

LA TANTE CLAIRE SW3

WAGAMAMA WC1

ZAFFERANO SW1

London's Top Wine Lists

BIBENDUM

FIFTH FLOOR

GILBERT'S

MIJANOU

RANSOME'S DOCK

RSJ

THE ABINGDON

54 ABINGDON ROAD W8   937 3339

'Michelin-starred chef works in pub'

£25

OPEN
MON–SAT

HOURS
12.00–2.30PM
5.30–11.00PM

CREDIT CARDS
AMEX DELTA
MASTERCARD
SWITCH VISA

SERVICE
OPTIONAL

**SET-PRICE
LUNCH**
£8.95

FACILITIES
SEATS 46
TABLES OUTSIDE
SEAT 20
WHEELCHAIR
ACCESS

**NEAREST TUBE
STATION**
HIGH ST
KENSINGTON/
EARLS COURT

MAP 2

Shortly before his untimely death, Bob Payton sold his company My Kinda Town. The new owners have transformed what was previously a link in the small chain of Payton's American-inspired Henry J. Bean's into a more contemporary kind of pub conversion, putting in as chef Brian Baker who was previously cooking at The Criterion (now in the hands of Marco Pierre White). One Michelin star is nearly always mentioned in the same breath as Brian Baker's name – he gained it quite a while back at Hambleton Hall in Leicestershire – but perhaps this makes The Abingdon the first London pub with a Michelin-starred chef. With his menu Baker has taken a different route from most of the new food-conscious pubs in offering a basically French menu. It is, authentically enough, a fairly conservative list but the dishes are scrupulously prepared as was evidenced by a salad of green beans, red onions and marinated anchovies (chosen from the £8.95 set-price two-course lunch menu) where the slender green beans had been slit in half, the finely sliced onions marinated, the anchovies prepared from fresh and olives and well-chosen salad leaves rounded out the assembly. Chicken liver and foie gras parfait had, perhaps, a preponderance of the former over the latter, but otherwise was like the luxurious slabs of ambitious restaurants. Fish stew with saffron and potato aïoli had a resonant broth, an adventurous choice of fish pieces and a nicely grainy (with potato starch) aïoli. There is also rack of lamb, grilled côte de boeuf with pommes frites and grilled calf's liver with Lyonnaise onions. Home-made apple sorbet transformed a red apple and a green apple into two intensely flavoured round, icy scoops: brilliant. Seating in the front part of the pub is preferable to the red leatherette booths at the back (a relic of Mr Bean days).

L'ACCENTO

16 GARWAY ROAD W2   243 2201

'Worth quite a long walk but not a long drive'

£26

OPEN
EVERY DAY

HOURS
12.00–3.00PM
6.30–11.00PM

Open seven days a week for lunch and dinner with a set-price menu at both occasions of £10.50 for two courses (no price change in three years) means that when you open the

CREDIT CARDS
MASTERCARD VISA

SERVICE
12½%

SET-PRICE
LUNCH
£10.50

SET-PRICE
DINNER
£10.50

FACILITIES
SEATS 65
TABLES OUTSIDE
SEAT 37
PRIVATE ROOM
SEATS 25
WHEELCHAIR
ACCESS

NEAREST TUBE
STATION
QUEENSWAY/
BAYSWATER/
ROYAL OAK

MAP 1

door to this Italian restaurant in a tame side-street off cosmopolitan Westbourne Grove you are met by a roar of noise – Notting Hill thirtysomethings at their ease. The front room with its sienna and white walls splashed with unframed art has closely – too closely – packed tables and chairs. The lower back room is marginally more peaceful. On the carte each main course is announced by its main ingredient in Italian followed by a qualification in English as to how it is prepared. Thus: ARAGOSTA – basil tagliolini with lobster, tomatoes and fresh herbs; VITELLO – veal ossobucco with a saffron risotto; FEGATO – pan-fried calf's liver with balsamic vinegar. The cooking of these dishes is precise, but an all-purpose vegetable garnish can strike a jarring note, as it did in roast potatoes with grilled salmon steak with a lemony, buttery sauce. The prix fixe menu (three choices in each course) tends to start with pasta, perhaps beetroot flavour fresh tagliatelle with braised fennel, shallots and raisins, and moves on to something agreeably countrified like roast rabbit with soft polenta. There is nothing low-rent about the contents of this list, which costs for two courses much the same as a main course à la carte. Desserts are given the Italian cursory consideration. Waiters with designer stubble and ponytails serve swiftly and well.

ALASTAIR LITTLE

49 FRITH STREET W1   734 5183

'In price, Alastair Large'

A decade has passed since Alastair Little's eponymous Soho restaurant caused a big stir with its dynamic, eclectic menus and no-nonsense surroundings and service. Other chefs have since been inspired (and taught) or have imitated, the menu now seems not the revelation it once was and the decor not so much nobly uncompromising as uncomfortable. To some extent these observations – or you can read them as criticisms – are related to the audacious prices charged. Little is the first to admit that he is not a businessman and I have heard some of his co-chefs mutter that, financially, they would order things differently – in every sense of the word. However, this 'godfather of modern British cooking', as he has been described by Kit Chapman in *Great British Chefs 2* (Mitchell Beazley, £19.99), has never wavered in his love for food and his enthusiasm for cooking – it does happen, oh yes – and if that means Little makes sorties to Italy in summer to teach or digresses into an

£42

OPEN
LUNCH MON–FRI
DINNER MON–SAT

HOURS
12.00–3.00PM
6.00–11.30PM

CREDIT CARDS
AMEX DELTA
MASTERCARD
SWITCH VISA

SERVICE
OPTIONAL

SET-PRICE
LUNCH
£12.50 (BAR)
£25 (RESTAURANT)

FACILITIES
SEATS
35 (RESTAURANT)
20 (BAR)
PRIVATE ROOM
SEATS 16
WHEELCHAIR
ACCESS

inexpensive neighbourhood restaurant near his flat in Notting Hill Gate (as is his plan) then it is part of the price we pay. Although menus continue to be written twice daily there is a core of dishes which appear with regularity and are dependably well prepared: pasta e ceci; potato pancakes with smoked eel, bacon, soured cream and horseradish; oysters with shallot relish and spicy sausages; roasted sea bass with parsley salad; chicken wrapped in Parma ham with Savoy cabbage; Panettone bread-and-butter pudding. Other dishes enjoyed this year were a bourride of sliced fish, scallop and king prawn with a pugnacious broth; roasted Tuscan pigeon with pancetta and polenta and, indeed, roasted Umbrian pigeon with winter vegetables and zampone; feuilleté of apple, pecans and caramel. Ribollita (bread-based soup) has been too basic, OK in Calabria perhaps but not near Old Compton Street; a pizzetta bianca too tough a disc of dough; and deep-fried rolls of filo-wrapped asparagus and prosciutto rendered greasy in the cooking. So you pays your considerable amount of money – less in the downstairs bar – and you hope to have made a sound choice. The wine list is short but well formed.

NEAREST TUBE STATION
TOTTENHAM COURT ROAD/ PICCADILLY CIRCUS/ LEICESTER SQUARE
MAP 5

ALBA

107 WHITECROSS STREET EC1   588 1798

'Always in season'

A little corner of Piedmont near the Barbican development seems an unlikely quirk of geography, but at Alba of an evening you could order a four-course menu degustazione at the reasonable price of £16.90, which started with a salad of pheasant, porcini mushrooms, celery, fennel and peppers, moved on to a risotto of artichokes, leeks and salmon, progressed to civet of hare with polenta and finished with budino (a baked cream) with nougat and hazelnuts. Revamped this year to give more spacious, clean-cut surroundings with a swop from pink to muted apricot as the predominant colour, the restaurant Alba is Italian to the tip of its boot in its insistence on regionality and also seasonality. A menu offered during asparagus season, as well as providing the spears hot or cold, folded them into risotto, into a crêpe with fontina cheese, dressed them alla Milanese with eggs, butter and Parmesan and laid them down alongside English veal. This approach to celebrating what is available or at its peak is particularly rewarding from about November to January when white truffles are

£26

OPEN
MON–FRI

HOURS
12.00–3.00PM
6.00–11.00PM

CREDIT CARDS
AMEX DELTA
DINER'S
MASTERCARD
SWITCH VISA

SERVICE
12½%

SET-PRICE DINNER
£16.90

FACILITIES
SEATS 60
PRIVATE ROOMS
SEAT 20 & 30
WHEELCHAIR ACCESS

NEAREST TUBE STATION
BARBICAN/ MOORGATE
MAP 1

imported. Meal testers this year came to the conclusion that the current chef is perhaps more of a meat cook than a farinaceous one, basing the observation on an excellent first course of slices of poached tongue spread with a judicious amount of salsa verde and a similarly fine main course of new season lamb cutlets with young artichokes and potatoes, but a slightly overcooked risotto – both in the rice and the garnish – and hard-edged meat-filled agnolotti which had a definite adhesive quality. Although nowadays there is considerable scope for eating out after a concert or play at the Barbican Centre, Alba holds its own – after doing some pioneering work – and is tremendously popular with City gents at lunch time. With impeccable logic, the wine list is Northern Italian.

ALBERO & GRANA

89 SLOANE AVENUE SW3   225 1048

'For Gaudi nights'

Albero & Grana is several things: a big, sometimes boister-ously busy bar where smartly dressed youngsters like to meet; the provider of superior but expensive tapas; and, beyond the reach of the babble and elbows, a serious Spanish restau-rant. Brilliant red-and-yellow walls, black and white table settings and paintings of monster lobsters are the dining-room decorations, along with two towers which look like architect's models by the great Gaudi. The simple-sounding menu prose (seafood stew, snails tourte Andalucian style) needs elaboration, which you are advised to seek from the maître'd, who has memorized all that is missing. But even with his exposition it can be hard to guess which recipes are close to their Spanish origins and which over-restored by the chef Angel Garcia, who held one Michelin star in Madrid. Items that sound robust can be subject to the sort of sophistries the Red Guide encour-ages: certainly the description 'stew' was misapplied to a Michelinesque medley of fish plus lettuce-wrapped lard which had taken on an unporcine and unpleasant bitterness. The huge stew olla podrida appears unreconstructed and inviting, and an admirer of Spanish food reckons the plainly served roast suckling pig 'better than in Segovia'. Fans should reserve their portion of piglet when they book, as it is popular. Surreal humour is something to which the chef seems prone. This works when the substance is there, as when sending out complete (washed) lettuce sprinkled with excellent olive oil as a

£37

OPEN
LUNCH MON–SAT
DINNER EVERY
DAY

HOURS
12.00–4.00PM
6.00PM–1.00AM

CREDIT CARDS
AMEX DINER'S
MASTERCARD
SWITCH VISA

SERVICE
12½% PARTIES
OF 7 & OVER

**SET-PRICE
LUNCH**
£15

FACILITIES
SEATS 120
PRIVATE ROOM
SEATS 50
WHEELCHAIR
ACCESS

**NEAREST TUBE
STATION**
SOUTH
KENSINGTON

MAP 2

green salad, or having langoustines burst out of seafood-filled, lightly fried peppers, an ensemble of exquisite taste. But a so-called skate salad which strings a small amount of fish along a single stick of celery, with four caper buds and pieces of peeled tomato flanking, hardly merits a hollow laugh. A shorter lunch-time menu offers three courses for £15 and may be the way to see how the style and humour appeal to you. The wine list could be wider in scope and lower in price.

THIS LIST AFFORDS a rare opportunity to investigate the wines of Spain, sherries included, but from having over-florid descriptions it now has none at all, and the customer is left to wander the country's regions – the list is arranged by region – guideless. Yet who besides a wine buff will know how different are the white riojas of Marqués de Cáceres (crisp and fruity) and Marques de Murrieta (almost sherried in its woodiness)? The house selections are all available by the glass, which takes some of the sting out of the prices – Torres' Gran Coronas 1988 at £45 is three times what one would pay at The Ivy (q.v.) and Caprice (q.v.) and six times what one would pay at Sainsbury's.

AL BUSTAN

27 MOTCOMB STREET SW1   235 8277

'Making a meze in Belgravia'

Like Japanese restaurants, Lebanese restaurants tend to be places you go to because you already know that you like that style of food. It is unlikely that people drop in casually at either, particularly when, as with the Lebanese Al Bustan, the establishment is in a side street off Belgrave Square. Perhaps because of their dedicated customer bases, both Japanese (the expensive kind) and Lebanese restaurants serve a fairly uniform range of dishes cooked to a reliably high standard. The family-run Al Bustan is no exception and the staff are anxious for their customers' enjoyment whether they be old hands or new bugs. One of the latter reported back for this year's guide, arriving at that conclusion we all do which is that Lebanese menus are far more interesting for their first courses than their main dishes. The £2 cover charge brings you a plate of raw vegetables and a dip of oil and raw garlic. Dipping a spring onion or a chilli into this mixture can be a dip too far for some. More raw garlic jabs its elbow into batarikh, a dish of cod's roe. Other first-course dishes to try are mouhamara, spiced nuts; makdous badinjan,

£30

OPEN
EVERY DAY

HOURS
12.00–11.00PM

CREDIT CARDS
AMEX DINER'S
MASTERCARD VISA

SERVICE
OPTIONAL

COVER CHARGE
£2

SET–PRICE LUNCH
£16

SET–PRICE DINNER
£20

FACILITIES
SEATS 65
TABLES OUTSIDE
SEAT 12
PRIVATE ROOM
SEATS 20
WHEELCHAIR
ACCESS

stuffed baby aubergines; fatayer, spinach- or cheese-stuffed pastry; hlaiwat, fried lamb's sweetbreads sharpened with lemon juice. Since a spread of hot and cold hors d'oeuvres (there are many more to consider) accompanied by the terrifically good breads is so satisfying, it might be worth establishing with the waiter at the outset whether or not there is a necessity to move on to dull kebabs, grills or chicken in a special sauce which is special for all the wrong reasons. You could make up a bill pleasing to the management by roaming through the over-priced wine list. For lovers of Lebanese food it is worth noting that 'in terms of courtesy and personal service, Al Bustan is a rare example of a restaurant with perfect pitch'.

ALFRED

245 SHAFTESBURY AVENUE WC2   240 2566

'You've never had it so good'

£24

OPEN
MON–SAT

HOURS
12.00–4.00PM
6.00–12.00AM

CREDIT CARDS
AMEX DELTA
DINER'S
MASTERCARD
SWITCH VISA

SERVICE
OPTIONAL

SET-PRICE
LUNCH
£11.95

SET-PRICE
DINNER
£11.95

FACILITIES
SEATS 60
TABLES OUTSIDE
SEAT 38
WHEELCHAIR
ACCESS

NEAREST TUBE
STATION
TOTTENHAM
COURT ROAD

MAP 4

The re-invention of British cuisine, an activity that kept several restaurateurs busy in 1995 – notably Fergus Henderson at St John (q.v.), Antony Worrall-Thompson at The Atrium (q.v.) and Gary Rhodes at The Peoples Palace (q.v.) – has been particularly successful at this purposefully bleakly decorated site at the north end of Shaftesbury Avenue. From a relatively slow start, insofar as numbers of customers were concerned, the joint (which includes a basement bar) is now jumping. Chef and co-owner Robert 'Bobby' Gutteridge cooks with verve and an unabashed confidence in the validity of the style. Dishes such as toad- in-the-hole and faggots are not on the menu to make some ironic statement but because, when prepared carefully, they can hold their heads high. First-course salads such as those of wood pigeon, wild mushrooms, bacon and potatoes or smoked haddock, poached egg and mustard and cress are substantial but sensitively assembled. Soups are good. Main courses come fully thought through, not really needing further garnishes except perhaps chips or mash. Favourites are the sugar-slicked braised knuckle of bacon with pickled cabbage and pease pudding; rabbit in beer and sage sauce with roast bacon, onion and mushrooms, bringing with it echoes of Gutteridge's stint at Belgo Noord (q.v.); grilled rib-eye of beef with bone marrow, greens and a Guinness and onion gravy; and a butcher's view of lamb comprising roast saddle, kidney, sweetbreads and liver served with pan haggerty – a fried potato cake – and mashed root vegetables. The faint-hearted can be reassured that there are also fish dishes and even something to suit vegetarians. Dessert is not a course to pass up, as you might infer from gingerbread with lavender custard; rhubarb Trinity College burnt cream; sticky toffee pudding with vanilla ice cream. The courage of the eponymous Fred Taylor's patriotic convictions runs on into the drinks list with its range of British beers, ciders, wines and eaux de vie. He is not so foolishly chauvinistic, however, to confine the wine selection to England. Popularity can make for noise and long waits but service on the whole stays chirpy and in control.

AL HAMRA

31–33 SHEPHERD MARKET W1   493 1954/6934

'Middle Eastern promise fulfilled'

Perhaps because, for obvious reasons, the Lebanon is not a holiday destination as is, say, Greece, the cuisine has not received the acceptance and acknowledgement it deserves. The variety, subtlety, intricacy and healthiness of a Lebanese meal are hard to better and Al Hamra in Shepherd Market is as good a place as any to conduct exploration. On a summer's day this can be done sitting outside at one of the pavement tables which provides an appropriate context. Ignoring, as is sensible, Western hors d'oeuvres such as smoked salmon and prawn cocktail, this still leaves you with 45 Lebanese small dishes, hot and cold, from which to compose a meze. Some you might reject on grounds of squeamishness, for example, fresh raw lamb's liver or grilled lamb's testicles (pity though), but the best way forward is to mix the familiar such as tabouleh and hummus with the more adventurous such as makdoue, baby aubergines stuffed with walnuts, spices and garlic; batrakh, fish roe with garlic and olive oil; nchaat pane, lamb's brains scrambled with eggs; sojuk, Armenian beef sausages. Add in some grilled chicken's wings or grilled quails, what they refer to as Lebanese pizza – minced meat, onions and tomatoes on flat bread – and you have a wonderful, diverting spread needing only something simple to follow such as shish taouk, a brochette of marinated chicken, or kibbeh meshwieh, minced meat mixed with walnuts and crushed wheat, rolled and grilled to resemble a handful of cigars, plus a salad with a spice-hot dressing. In addition, there are Lebanese dishes of the day worth checking. The cover charge brings an array of raw vegetables and excellent breads, a warm puffy one and a thicker

£26

OPEN
EVERY DAY

HOURS
12.00PM–12.00AM

CREDIT CARDS
AMEX DINER'S
MASTERCARD VISA

SERVICE
OPTIONAL

COVER CHARGE
£2.50

**SET-PRICE
LUNCH**
£16

**SET-PRICE
DINNER**
£20

FACILITIES
SEATS 75
TABLES OUTSIDE
SEAT 16
WHEELCHAIR
ACCESS

**NEAREST TUBE
STATION**
GREEN PARK

MAP 3

chunk sprinkled with poppy seeds. For dessert the waiter might suggest a selection of syrup-soaked, rosewater-fragrant pastries from the trolley but fresh fruit might be all you have energy for. Lebanese wines are the obvious choice but there is also iyram, diluted yogurt.

ALI BABA

32 IVOR PLACE NW1   723 7474

'Open sesame (as in tahini)'

£14 BYO

OPEN
EVERY DAY

HOURS
12.00PM–12.00AM

CREDIT CARDS
NONE

SERVICE
10%

FACILITIES
SEATS 55
WHEELCHAIR
ACCESS

NEAREST TUBE
STATION
BAKER STREET/
MARYLEBONE

MAP 1

A quiet backwater of Marylebone is not necessarily where you look for an authentic Middle Eastern experience, but the family-run Ali Baba, trading now for 14 years, can supply it. The front part of the premises serves as a takeaway operation with notable home-made pastries. Walk on through and you are in a converted domestic sitting room where, true to type, the television is on, Granny is minding a baby, other family members wander in. The menu is short, offering starters from which you could compose a meze and include the particularly unctuous hummus, the fresh-tasting tabbouleh, falafel and moutabal (aubergine purée). In the main course among dishes such as couscous, mousaka, bamia (okra) with meat, the Egyptian national dish of melokhia (a slightly glutinous soup made with the deep green melokhia leaf), kebabs and grills is the Ali Baba Speciality. Reminiscent of a biriani, it features slow-cooked lean lamb and beautifully prepared, seasoned rice enhanced by the glancing sweetness of dried fruit. The dressed-down dining area has as atmosphere only the food, the wine you bring yourself, cable TV and at one visit the attractive waitress whose outfit and accessories must have cost more than the entire interior design scheme.

AL SAN VINCENZO

30 CONNAUGHT STREET W2   262 9623

'A singular Italian restaurant'

£34

OPEN
LUNCH MON–FRI
DINNER MON–SAT

HOURS
12.30–2.00PM
7.00–10.00PM

CREDIT CARDS
MASTERCARD VISA

When quizzing people about their favourite London restaurants, as I am tediously wont to do, I inwardly mark them highly if they include this family-run Italian restaurant off the Edgware Road. Vincenzo Borgonzolo's cooking cannot be classified under any of the ages of the Italian restaurant in London. Although inspired by the southern Campania

Al San Vincenzo

RESTAURANT
30 CONNAUGHT STREET,
LONDON W2 2AE
TELEPHONE: 13/1/96
0171-262 9623

VAT REGISTERED NO. 577 3018 29

COVERS 2   6   TABLE NO.

2 Starters   15·00

2 Main Course   33·00

2 Dessert   10·00

2 Coffee   3·90

½ Chianti Classico   8·95
Mineral water   2·25
Sambuca   4·50
                    ⌐77·60

SERVICE IS NOT INCLUDED

region of Italy, the cooking has scant reference to that of the trattorie owned and run by chaps from Naples which evolved in the Sixties, nor in its combinations and complexity does it have much in common with the currently fashionable pared-down presentations content to let prime ingredients speak for themselves. Borgonzolo's menu is short, singular and fluid enough to render the place an ideal restaurant du quartier suited to regular, unpretentious eating out, a role also signalled by the simple warm decor of the small dining room which is under the direction of Elaine Borgonzolo. Those discerning eaters who earn my respect rarely have prejudices about food or, indeed, allergies or intolerances. They do not recoil from sweetbreads – especially when served with Carnaroli rice and Savoy cabbage, nor pussyfoot around fresh snails – especially when served with cannellini beans in a chilli-hot sauce, nor find it anything but delightful that a pig's trotter should be stuffed with spiced forcemeat to make zampone and be accompanied by slices of cotechino (another coarse sausage) and braised lentils. In season these same folk demonstrate an Italian's enthusiasm for furred and feathered game. The restaurant also provides lighter assemblies, for example, carpaccio of fish either raw or smoked; smoked duck with rocket salad and mostarda di Cremona; prawns and a warm slice of foie gras with a citrus dressing. Pasta might appear as a first course or main course but is not always the best choice, viz. stodgy gnocchi dressed (imaginatively) with caviar, chives and nutmeg and a very workaday spaghetti con pomodoro with no sunshine in the sauce. However, if the robust little 'ears', orecchiette, are offered dressed either with green leaves or fresh tomatoes, do not omit to try them. Bread-and-butter pudding made with Panettone is the dessert speciality but also notable is semifreddo of chocolate served with a mess of raspberries. The brief, wholly Italian wine list sports some interesting choices and some welcome half bottles.

SERVICE
12½% GROUPS OF 5 OR MORE

FACILITIES
SEATS 22
WHEELCHAIR ACCESS

NEAREST TUBE STATION
MARBLE ARCH

MAP 1

ANDREW EDMUNDS

46 LEXINGTON STREET W1   437 5708

'Raffish charm'

An early eighteenth-century shop-window façade leads you to a small, deliberately scruffy ground-floor restaurant and bar and then downstairs to a low-ceilinged dark-green-painted basement with wooden banquettes of eighteenth-century

£24

OPEN
EVERY DAY

HOURS
12.30–3.00PM
6.00–11.00PM

CREDIT CARDS
AMEX
MASTERCARD
SWITCH VISA

SERVICE
OPTIONAL

FACILITIES
SEATS 48
TABLES OUTSIDE
SEAT 4

**NEAREST TUBE
STATION**
PICCADILLY
CIRCUS/
OXFORD CIRCUS

MAP 5

discomfort. Andrew Edmunds – the eponymous chap also owns a print shop next door – exerts a pull on a faithful clientele of faintly rakish customers who like its clubbiness and presumably also the food, vividly responsive to the market and the moor, and certainly the wine list (see below). Irishman Paul Croal is chef and his daily-changing menu can deliver some treats such as first courses of a chilled pea soup in summer, roast parsnips with cumin mayonnaise in spring. There are always imaginative salads and well-thought-out accoutrements to bought items such as charcuterie. Main courses might include rare cold meat with warm vegetables or vice versa, a habit conceivably explained by the diminutive size of the kitchen. There is always a vegetarian dish, often jollied with Eastern spicing and game in season. Chocolate mousse cake is something of a speciality and when plum and almond tart is on offer it runs out fast. Strong, confident women run the floor and brook no nonsense.

THE WINE LIST IS a bizarre little assortment which looks as if it has been picked up at auction following the death of a rich crank, with surprisingly grand bottles available at bargain prices. Sassicaia '1982 or 1985' – both vintages which wine enthusiasts would kill for – is offered for £50 – £5 more will buy you Mouton '83, and at the other end, below £20, are decent burgundies from Domaine de l'Arlot and Roger Lassarat.

ANNA'S PLACE

90 MILDMAY PARK N1   249 9379

'A little corner off Newington Green that seems forever Swedish'

The old-fashioned food of Northern Europe easily deteriorates into god-fearing plainness. Quite what can be achieved instead with fastidiousness and flavouring is demonstrated at Anna's Place, where Swedish cooking minus the usual meat balls and Jansson's temptation is offered. Mustard, mild horseradish, dill, caraway and spices are used to intriguing effect so that one realizes that the various and delicious cured appetizers have received a lift, but would be pushed to identify the culprits (allspice, pepper black and white, clove and bay leaf are the basis for the pickled herrings; Madeira and pepper for the excellent gravad oxfile, a Swedish bresaola). In the sauces and pickling there is a fine appreciation of piquancy, how it stimu-

£26
OPEN
TUE–SAT

HOURS
12.15–2.15PM
7.00–11.00PM

CREDIT CARDS
NONE

SERVICE
10%

FACILITIES
SEATS 42
TABLES OUTSIDE
SEAT 20
WHEELCHAIR
ACCESS

**NEAREST TUBE
STATION**
HIGHBURY &
ISLINGTON

MAP 1

lates, but must not be pushed. Main courses are mountainous, whereas starters are small. Biff Strindberg (August's raffish brother?), cured salmon grilled with creamed leeks, and huge and very crabby crab cakes are commended main courses, though the waitress said as she took the orders that Anna had been trying to get the popular Biff (he is mustard-marinated and pan-fried) off the menu for ages. Her chef is allowed to vary the routine with daily specials including vegetarian options such as excellent guacamole with waffle-cut potato crisps or sweets like a lemon and raspberry Swedish Swiss roll. The restaurant is a town house with conservatory, decorated with an assortment of art; there is a garden for good weather; but, please note, no facility for paying by plastic. Anna Hegarty says with mock regret that the twentieth anniversary of her Place is next year. Congratulations are definitely in order: it is rare to find such liveliness in restaurants half the age.

ARISUGAWA

27 PERCY STREET W1   636 8913

'Few concessions to the West'

Entering this restaurant through an unremarkable doorway in a modern block just off Tottenham Court Road and descending the staircase you are faced by a scene almost hallucinogenically Japanese. You might think you were in Tokyo. It is difficult to define the exact atmosphere, but the essential components are a) groups of businessmen chainsmoking, b) no women sitting at the tables, c) waitresses crawling about on their hands and knees, d) lots of loud laughter, e) bottles of Chivas Regal reserved for particular customers, f) low-slung tables, g) men eating seven or eight courses, h) staggering prices. The clientele tends to be predominantly Japanese but Westerners are made to feel at their ease in various ways including a dug-out space beneath the low tables which obviates sitting cross-legged. Chef Mr A. Takeuchi has had 42 years' experience in traditional Japanese cuisine, making choice from the carte rather than settling for a set-price menu the savvy way to order. Sashimi gleams in exactly the way it should. Beef teriyaki is made from tender Scotch beef but, perhaps as a special concession to round-eyes, arrives with the odd accompaniment of roast potatoes and peas. The table-cooked dish of mixed fish in broth comprises a huge earthenware bowl of subtle aromatic stock in which immaculately fresh fish, shellfish

£40

OPEN
LUNCH MON–FRI
DINNER MON–SAT

HOURS
12.30–3.00PM
6.00–10.00PM

CREDIT CARDS
AMEX DINER'S
MASTERCARD
SWITCH VISA

SERVICE
15%

SET-PRICE LUNCH
£7–12

SET-PRICE DINNER
£20–38

FACILITIES
SEATS 110
PRIVATE ROOM
SEAT 20 & 12

NEAREST TUBE STATION
TOTTENHAM
COURT ROAD

MAP 4

and vegetables are poached. In general, standards are high in both cooking and presentation, and discoveries can be made by the gastronomically intrepid and flush customer. At a test meal a couple accompanied by their children were approached by the manageress who suggested the children might like to go to Japan with her children, which seemed an extraordinarily friendly gesture. It turned out she also had an interest in a travel agency. At ground-floor level there is a sushi bar, busy at lunchtime, and teppanyaki – cooking on a hot plate – is also available.

ARTS THEATRE CAFÉ

6–7 GREAT NEWPORT STREET WC2   497 8014

'Proving that cooking is also one of the arts'

£20

OPEN
LUNCH MON–FRI
DINNER MON–SAT

HOURS
MON–FRI
12.00–11.00PM
SAT
6.00–11.00PM

CREDIT CARDS
NONE

SERVICE
10%

SET–PRICE
LUNCH & DINNER
£10 & £12.50

FACILITIES
SEATS 35

NEAREST TUBE
STATION
LEICESTER
SQUARE

MAP 4

The history of restaurants in theatres is not an entirely happy one, the more successful operations being small-scale ones such as those at The Traverse in Edinburgh and The Everyman in Liverpool. The Café beneath the Arts Theatre triumphantly proves this point. One chef and one remarkably efficient and accommodating waitress cook and serve an oft-changing Italian menu which, like the best Italian food, comes across as delicious home cooking. The popular set-price meal changes on a daily basis. It tends to start with an imaginative soup such as potato, chorizo and Savoy cabbage or Primavera based on beans and fresh peas or perhaps the option of crostini, the Italian version of something nice on toast, moves on to a robust main course such as pot-roast pheasant with cloves, coriander and honey or beef stew with carrots and potatoes garnished with grated fresh horseradish, and ends with a relatively wide choice of dessert. Chilled zabaione made with vin santo served with whipped cream and a raspberry sauce is one temptation. On the carte there is usually an enterprising salad such as Sicilian style spring vegetable with broad beans, peas, artichokes and seared scallops, a terrine, a pasta of the day and daily fish specials as well as a meat-based casserole and a grill such as rabbit or calf's liver. There are also daily vegetarian specials. It is a commendable operation, steadier this year in the high standard of cooking. Candles flicker on the rickety tables even at lunchtime. Surprisingly, you are barely conscious that there is a busy street just above your head, but the interval crowd at performance times hammers home the point that you are attached to a theatre.

LES ASSOCIÉS

'Old-fashioned values'

O ne of the associates has changed at this north London restaurant beguilingly lodged in a time warp. Chef Gilles Charvet has been replaced by Mark Spindler, but the menu continues to offer the sort of food you might find in the local serious restaurant of a small French town and owners Dominique Chéhere and Didier Bertrand still work the room formally dressed in white shirts with black bow ties. They do so with considerable practised Gallic charm, but it is important to realize at the outset that it is they who decide the (stately) pace of the meal. The assumption is, reasonably enough, that dinner here is your evening's entertainment. The premises occupy the ground floor of a house among other houses, i.e. not in a parade of shops, which requires careful noting of road numbers when driving to find it. Decoration has changed little over the years – ears of wheat remain the pattern on the cream Anaglypta wallpaper – but a few of the paintings now point to someone whose role model is Van Gogh. Actually, so bizarre is the collection that you wonder if some Crouch End customers have tried to pay for their meal with a picture the way they have heard Picasso used to do. Old favourites such as la charteuse d'escargots à la crème d'ail, le millefeuille de turbot aux epinards frais and – celebrating the peculiar liking for pairing meat and fish – le filet de boeuf en crustaces stay on the main menu but the more alluring list, to my mind, is the one headed Today's Specials. From it have been enjoyed la salade de St Jacques au croustillant d'échalotes; les asperges blanches sauce vinaigrette; le lapin au senteur de Provence; le canard de Barbarie rôti a l'ail. Eating those along with some scrupulously cooked fresh vegetables provided le nice time. Cheeses are well bought and well kept. The popular way to approach dessert is via la selection providing tasters of the range. Tarte Tatin, hazelnut cake and chocolate mousse would all be worth ordering in larger quantity. Anyone tired of ponytailed waiters shoving bruschetta their way should head for Les Associés twinned with Elizabeth David circa 1960.

£28

OPEN
LUNCH TUES–FRI
DINNER TUES–SAT

HOURS
12.00–2.00PM
7.30–10.00PM

CREDIT CARDS
MASTERCARD
SWITCH VISA

SERVICE
OPTIONAL

**SET–PRICE
DINNER**
£16.95

FACILITIES
SEATS 36
WHEELCHAIR
ACCESS

**NEAREST TUBE
STATION**
FINSBURY PARK/
HIGHGATE

ATELIER

'Not an artist's studio quite yet'

£34

OPEN
LUNCH MON–FRI
DINNER MON–SAT

HOURS
12.00–2.30PM
6.00–10.45PM

CREDIT CARDS
AMEX DELTA
DINER'S
MASTERCARD
SWITCH VISA

SERVICE
10%

SET-PRICE
LUNCH
£14.50 & £17

SET-PRICE
DINNER
£14.50
£10 & £12.50
(6.00–8.00PM
ONLY)

FACILITIES
SEATS 45
PRIVATE ROOM
SEATS 16
WHEELCHAIR
ACCESS

NEAREST TUBE
STATION
PICCADILLY
CIRCUS/
OXFORD CIRCUS

MAP 5

Joanna Shannon, co-owner and manager, and Stephen Bulmer, co-owner and chef, met while training at Le Manoir aux Quat'Saisons. Joanna Shannon, formerly an advertising executive, holds a special place in the *Evening Standard* pantheon for having won our Gourmet Competition in 1987. Atelier – the name was chosen in recognition of the fact that Canaletto was once resident in the West Soho building – further emphasizes artistic connections through the furnishings, some of which are specially commissioned one-off pieces. The decoration has a sort of 'moderne' battyness admissible and even welcome in commercial rather than domestic settings. Since opening in autumn '94, set-price menus at both lunch and dinner have been introduced in addition to the carte, presumably in order to lure more custom to this somewhat unprepossessing street. Raymond Blanc, chef of Le Manoir, has sent out into the world seven British chefs who have subsequently gained one or more Michelin stars. Bulmer is not one of them, but his cooking has some of the characteristics of having been Blanched; culinary similes and metaphors teased out from the main ingredient to a point where you can lose sight of the original definition. However, many of the dishes are splendid. There has been special mention of field mushrooms filled with chicken mousse topped with Provençal breadcrumbs and served with a rosemary jus, managing to be both rich and light with flavours distinct; pan-fried médaillons of monkfish, a difficult creature to cook well, served with crab tortellini made fragrant with ginger – crab and ginger going together like a horse and carriage – in a gentle, limpid lemongrass jus; fricassée of fresh morel mushrooms with home-made pasta and a Noilly Prat jus, a supremely harmonious dish starring beautifully made pasta. Hot pancakes with blueberries and walnut and maple syrup ice cream featuring un-leathery pancakes, rich, crunchy ice-cream and a trace of blueberry sauce needed only crisp Canadian bacon to render it an American glutton's breakfast. Dishes on the menu change regularly, resulting in a completely new menu every six weeks or so, but the style can be reliably inferred from the above. There is a prudently chosen but not uninteresting wine list.

ATLANTIC BAR & GRILL

20 GLASSHOUSE STREET W1   734 4888

'Proof that fashionable and edible are not incompatible'

Make a booking for dinner and go straight to the head of the queue, which is mostly of dressed-up twenty-to-thirtysomethings who are jockeying for a place at the hugely popular, late-licensed bar. In case of difficulties, which have been known to occur, be sweetly insistent. In the early days chaos reigned and entry was barred to various famous folk, but now that entrepreneur Oliver Peyton has stolen a bit of his own thunder by opening Coast (q.v.) the weather system at the Atlantic should be calmer and food lovers should not be deterred from sampling Richard Sawyer's chic menu. Chef Sawyer's menu prose is precise about provenance and processes, yet what arrives tends to be less fancy than it sounds, for hipness has been tempered with restraint so that the dubious excess of tortellini filled with foie gras turns out to be cut with the mineral taste of the watercress purée with which it comes. The steak frites or tournedos Rossini needed to please the banker backers who like to hang out here are meticulously done. A mixed vegetable platter and the sashimi have also been enjoyed. All in all there is an appealing combination of neatness and inspiration in the cooking. With its high ceilings, dark colour scheme and deco touches, the huge space may call to mind a cinema building which has been invaded by a load of lubricated Londoners. Lunch is the much quieter time. With last orders for food at 11.30pm, the Atlantic is an interesting new option for eating after the theatre. Quibbles have been the calibre of the service and the company one is forced to keep: the former is now brighter and more professional, the latter a matter of pot luck.

WHAT SEEMS TO BE a holiday brochure (electric blue waves swirl over the cover) turns out to be the wine list, and very sharp it is, with especially good, varied house selections. If you are celebrating a lottery win you have a straight choice between Pétrus 1979 and La Tâche 1942 (£285 apiece) but these are the only loopy price items and there is plenty to admire between £15 and £30, including Thévenet's superb Mâcon-Clessé, Michel's Cornas, and Qupé's Syrah.

£33

OPEN
LUNCH MON–SAT
DINNER
EVERY DAY

HOURS
MON–SAT
12.00PM–3.00AM
SUN
6.00–11.30PM

CREDIT CARDS
AMEX DELTA
MASTERCARD
SWITCH VISA

SERVICE
12½% PARTIES
OF 8 OR MORE

SET-PRICE LUNCH
£11.90

FACILITIES
SEATS 152
PRIVATE ROOM
SEATS 80
WHEELCHAIR
ACCESS

NEAREST TUBE STATION
PICCADILLY
CIRCUS

MAP 5

THE ATRIUM

4 MILLBANK SW1   233 0032

'Wozza goes back to his roots'

£25

OPEN
LUNCH MON–FRI
DINNER MON–SAT

HOURS
MON–FRI
8.00AM–11.00PM
SAT
7.00–11.00PM

CREDIT CARDS
AMEX DINER'S
MASTERCARD
SWITCH VISA

**SET-PRICE
LUNCH**
£15.95

**SET-PRICE
DINNER**
£18.95

FACILITIES
SEATS 150
TABLES OUTSIDE
SEAT 100
PRIVATE ROOM
SEATS 25
WHEELCHAIR
ACCESS (ALSO
WC)

**NEAREST TUBE
STATION**
WESTMINSTER/
ST JAMES'S PARK

MAP 1

Antony Worrall-Thompson, having colonized most of the world's cuisines, has here, in a Millbank office block down from the Houses of Parliament, turned his attention to English food or, as he puts it, Anglo-Irish cooking. But for colcannon and champ appearing as a garnish on the main menu the Irish element seems rather fugitive but, as with many of Wozza's wheezes, it sounds good. You can, however, start the day with an Irish breakfast, served 8am–11am on weekdays for £5.95. Heartiness seems the guiding principle of the dishes on the main menu and most are served pre-diet Soames size which doubtless pleases the targeted audience. Cooking under chef Harry Greenhalgh has improved since the opening (Spring 1995), becoming sharper and tidier and with fewer elements in each composition. Dishes of the early days, such as pan-fried duck breast with roast beetroot, crispy cabbage, potato cakes and gooseberry compote, are replaced in a later menu by the simpler – and doubtless more successful – pot-roasted salt duck with braised cabbage and wild mushrooms. Each day there is Roast or a Pot, the latter title including items such as fish pie and chicken and leek pie, which makes sense, but also deep-fried breaded plaice with chips and peas and grilled sea bass with sorrel and artichoke mash, which does not. Thus do best-laid plans gang aft agley, or however you say that in Anglo-Irish. Puddings are good: fresh raspberry jelly with lemon curd and candied peel and rhubarb and ginger crumble with vanilla ice cream let you know you have moved on from your school-days. Savouries are also offered, a nice touch. Some tables are on the terrace beneath the lofty atrium incoporated into the Legoland building, others are in two dining rooms which flank a bar. A café menu is available and in the evenings, when trade is slower, there is a £10 three-course set menu.

AUBERGINE

11 PARK WALK SW10   352 3449

'Frothing at the mouth'

£40

OPEN
LUNCH MON–FRI
DINNER MON–SAT

HOURS
12.15–2.30PM
7.00–11.00PM

Steven Terry, chef of Coast (q.v.), made an interesting point in an interview when he said something to the effect that kitchens in the US were so much healthier as chefs didn't live in fear of the judgements of the Michelin guide. Certainly what Michelin looks for and rewards and what the average customer wants can be poles apart. Michelin-tremor seems palpable at last year's feted newcomer, Aubergine, where hovering waiting staff are apt to address you in French whatever your nationality and the menu continues the practice with a ridiculous hodge-podge of the French and English languages, or, as it would doubtless be put, hodgepoché. My other reservation about this otherwise truly excellent restaurant is chef Gordon Ramsay's uncontainable delight in the gadget that froths up a soup or sauce. Whilst admissable in his signature first course of 'cappuc-cino of haricot blanc with sauté morels', foam is otiose on most other dishes and around 'caramelized calf's sweetbreads, etuvée of carrots, jus Sauternes with curry' just looks like toxic scum on a stagnant pool. Ramsay is currently writing a cookery book and I asked him how home cooks would manage the foaming. He said that the appropriate gadget would be on sale at Peter Jones. Be prepared for the South Ken dinner party frothé. However, many dishes demonstrate Ramsay's undeniable talents: for example, salad of roasted langoustine with candied aubergine; salad of tuna with the ideal foil for the cold fish displayed in its sauce aigre-doux (from a lunch-time menu); a perfect filet of beef with shallot confit, sauce Hermitage (also lunch time); a sublime 'poulet Bresse pochée-grillée, tagliatelle of mushrooms, sauce foie gras (légère)', served for two, one of the best dishes I have had all year. Basil being one of the flavours in the dessert of three crème brûlées might make you a touch wary of that course but it can be satisfactorily explored via the Assiette de l'Aubergine. Long lead-in times for bookings can result in customers taking flash photos of each other eating, which is a pity. Lunch time fields a livelier crowd as well as being cheaper. The sommelier is commendably approachable and full of good suggestions.

AUBERGINE'S wine buyer has done a professional job in recruiting good producers to its Franco-centric list – Jean Thévenet in Mâcon-Clessé, Charles Schleret in Alsace, Alain Graillot in Crozes-Hermitage, and Domaine de Triennes in Provence. The presentation is less professional. Among the whites, the eight bottles from the Loire are divided into sub-regions, while the 27 bottles from Burgundy are all lumped together; Sauternes are accorded their 1855 classifications, but clarets are not; producers are dignified with a 'Mr', even though some are clearly institutional rather than personal names, while

CREDIT CARDS
AMEX DELTA
DINER'S
MASTERCARD
SWITCH VISA

SERVICE
OPTIONAL

SET-PRICE LUNCH
£19.50

SET-PRICE DINNER
£34 & £44

FACILITIES
SEATS 50

NEAREST TUBE STATION
SOUTH KENSINGTON/ GLOUCESTER ROAD

MAP 2

spelling, capitalization and accenting show a disregard for French nomenclature which is too great to be explained away as native familiarity. None of this would matter in a less ambitious setting, of course.

L'AVENTURE

3 BLENHEIM TERRACE NW8   624 6232

'Un petit coin de Provence au bois de St Jean'

£32

OPEN
MON–SAT
SUN (MAY–SEPT
ONLY)

HOURS
12.30–2.30PM
7.30–11.00PM

CREDIT CARDS
AMEX
MASTERCARD VISA

SERVICE
OPTIONAL

**SET-PRICE
LUNCH**
£18.50

**SET-PRICE
DINNER**
£25

FACILITIES
SEATS 50
TABLES OUTSIDE
SEAT 30

**NEAREST TUBE
STATION**
ST JOHN'S WOOD

MAP 1

Blenheim Terrace in St John's Wood is one of those side streets of vitality you can stumble on occasionally however well you think you know London. Suddenly here is a group of restaurants, all with terraces, one French, one Italian and on the other side of the road a pub/café full of incredibly loud young people. Beyond the restaurants are some stately, Georgian terraced houses. On a warm night it is a creamy, dreamy, middle-class eco-climate all of its own. The French restaurant L'Aventure has been in existence in this street for 15 years. Trees and bushes have grown to shelter the terrace and in the evening they are discreetly, romantically spotted with fairy lights. In colder weather you retreat behind glass. Meals are set price and offer four options in each of the three courses, plus there are specials of the day described by the waiter. The style of the cooking is genuinely Provençal, and if the same food were served in, say, a restaurant in Aix, it would attract the same sort of enthusiastic clientele. Dishes enjoyed on one balmy evening – obviously weather has a part to play – included an artichoke dressed with olive oil, balsamic vinegar, chopped peppers, tomatoes and pine kernels; coquille St Jacques sizzling from the grill napped with a light cream sauce; steak described as pièce de boeuf poêle au cardamom served with a roasted onion whose interior had liquified to a brilliant jam; tian d'agneau on a bed of tomatoes and courgettes. Desserts were good but served in the style of an icing sugar explosion all over a big plate. A deconstructed crème caramel and strawberries and ice cream were both surrounded by a scatter-gun firing of pistachios, almonds and icing sugar. Wines are expensive, the house wine, La Cuvée Ropiteau, £14.50. Service can be slow at busy times, a fact which, in that style peculiar to French waiters, the customer is encouraged to take on board as his own fault rather than that of the establishment.

AVENUE WEST ELEVEN

157 NOTTING HILL GATE W11   221 8144

'Eclecticism contained'

This Notting Hill restaurant, brother of Brasserie du Marché aux Puces (q.v.), started life with an eclectic menu which was not so much varied as all over the place. With the arrival of chef Mark Broadbent in the summer of 1995, the food has improved enormously. Broadbent's dishes stay more or less completely faithful to Europe and a penchant for Spanish recipes and ingredients is an agreeable aspect. Menus change daily but representative dishes are tostadas of Cornish crab, guacamole and coriander; Mantuan capon salad, roast peppers, pinenuts and basil; Spanish charcuterie, ripe peaches, almonds and piquillo relish; griddled rump of lamb, couscous and apricots; calf's liver, melted onions and mostarda di Cremona; tranche of rare wild salmon, asparagus, fennel and almond aïoli. Presentation is free-form tending towards the school of early Frank Auerbach, but ideas and flavours are good. The impetus does not flag in desserts. Blueberry jelly with Devonshire clotted cream and shortbread was memorable. There is a Moroccan theme to the decor, using found-in-nature colours and rough textures. A recent development is the opening up of the downstairs bar where a lighter menu is served. Prices have gone up since last year but so have food standards.

£30

OPEN
LUNCH SUN–FRI
DINNER EVERY
DAY

HOURS
12.30–2.30PM
7.00–11.00PM
SUN
7.00–10.30PM

CREDIT CARDS
AMEX DELTA
DINER'S
MASTERCARD
SWITCH VISA

SERVICE
OPTIONAL

**SET-PRICE
LUNCH**
£12.50 & £15.50

FACILITIES
SEATS 65
WHEELCHAIR
ACCESS (ALSO
WC)

**NEAREST TUBE
STATION**
NOTTING HILL
GATE

MAP 1

BABUR BRASSERIE

119 BROCKLEY RISE SE23   0181-291 2400

'Festive Indian food'

There is a palpable feeling of more effort than usual being made in the look, the style and the service of Babur Brasserie. The long menu includes, in a fairly haphazard manner, various regional specialities of India, some the consequence of the restaurant's regular food festivals. Legacies of the Raj Festival linger on in the menu in first courses such as rostos-crab, devilled crab served in its shell; regimental cutless, a breadcrumbed patty of minced chicken with a coconut sauce; and in the main courses of pheasant Darjeeling and salmon kedgeree. However, there is much else that is indigenously Indian. Dishes enjoyed this year include chingri meerchi, a first course of notably fresh prawns tossed with chillies, ginger, garlic

£20

OPEN
EVERY DAY

HOURS
12.00–2.30PM
6.00–11.30PM

CREDIT CARDS
DELTA DINER'S
MASTERCARD
SWITCH VISA

SERVICE
OPTIONAL

FACILITIES
SEATS 54
WHEELCHAIR
ACCESS

**NEAREST BR
STATION**
HONOR OAK PARK

MAP 1

and spring onion; aloo choff, a cashew-nut-studded fried ball of vegetables and mashed potato; sali jardaloo, a Parsi dish – there goes another festival – of lamb cooked with dried apricots and sprinkled with straw potatoes; badak xec xec (pronounced shek shek), shards of duck in a piquant sauce, an assembly that persuaded a vegetarian to fall off the wagon. This is saying something given the range of enticing vegetable dishes, some quite out of the ordinary, for example, subze tandoori, marinated vegetables including red pumpkin, okra and carrots cooked in the tandoor, and oonbhariu, a mix of bananas, sweet potato, aubergine and shallots spiced with lovage seeds, cumin seeds and puréed asafoetida. The use of whole spices in the cooking is unusual and done to good effect.

BAHN THAI

21A FRITH STREET W1   437 8504

'Give yourself time to explore Thailand'

'The Original home of true Thai Food in London since 1982' is the sub-head on the front of the menu. Owner Phillip Harris takes his mission to explain very seriously indeed; it is worth allowing yourself time to study and absorb the two pages of guidance notes and the ten pages listing savoury dishes complete with symbols to indicate temperature, spiciness and suitability for vegetarians. For £1.95 the restaurant will provide a basket of prawn crackers and dipping sauce for nibbling while you do. Now 14 years since the inception of Bahn Thai in a Kensington basement, with Thai ingredients sold in supermarkets and Thai restaurants flourishing above pubs and on practically every high street, exoticism, carved vegetables and the naughty sweetness of some dishes are no longer reasons enough to gratify the interested eater. For him or her, careful and, to a certain extent, fortuitious selection from the Bahn Thai anthology/menu can demonstrate the width and depth of the cuisine. First courses which show how the same items can be traduced elsewhere are spring rolls, crab cakes and fried marinated chicken skin served with a spicy sweet plum sauce. As the guidance says, it is then worth assembling a curry, a fried dish with chillis, a fish dish (perhaps steamed), vegetables, a soup, an omelette and rice – all to be shared. Frog's legs, calf's liver, venison and wild boar are some of the more unusual starting points. Interesting assemblies are listed under the heading Speciality Dishes, where you find freshly steamed mussels

£29

OPEN
EVERY DAY

HOURS
MON–SAT
12.00–2.45PM
6.00–11.15PM
SUN 12.30–2.30PM
6.30–10.30PM

CREDIT CARDS
AMEX DELTA
DINER'S
MASTERCARD
SWITCH VISA

SERVICE
OPTIONAL

FACILITIES
SEATS 120
TABLES OUTSIDE
SEAT 8
PRIVATE ROOMS
SEAT 28–50
WHEELCHAIR
ACCESS (ALSO
MEN'S WC)

**NEAREST TUBE
STATION**
LEICESTER
SQUARE/
TOTTENHAM
COURT ROAD

MAP 5

cooked in batter with beansprouts; steamed sea bass; a curious fusion of Chinese and Japanese flavours in roasted marinated duck served with pickled ginger and soya sauce; and Pad thai, the favourite noodle dish, which is done well – as it should be at £6.95 (with prawns). Prices generally are, how shall we say, confident. The wine list is notable in its efforts to find bottles that do not cower in the face of spices. I suspect this is the only Thai restaurant to list Roederer Cristal.

BELGO CENTRAAL

50 EARLHAM STREET WC2   813 2233

'A beer hall directed by Luc Besson'

As more large restaurants open or are projected, it crosses my mind that one day the supply of customers must run out. But anyone planning a huge enterprise could take heart from Belgo Centraal, a 400-seater basement in the heart of Covent Garden which has been packed since day one (in late April 1995). Not only is the restaurant/beer hall full, but there are stories of putative diners weeping with frustration as they try to get through on the phone to someone who can work the state-of-the-art computer that deals with bookings. Of course the venture is based on a formula already successfully tested in north London (see below). The scope of Belgian food, which until the advent of Belgo in Chalk Farm had been a secret carefully guarded from Londoners, is shown in Covent Garden to be even wider than you might have thought. Mussels – better in pots than on a platter – chips and mayonnaise remain at the heart of the menu but it is embellished with spit-roast chicken – nice served à l'estragon – a variety of choucroutes, croquettes, marinated herrings, grilled lobsters, salads, beer-based assemblies, stoemp (a sort of bubble and squeak), waterzooi (light, creamy soup-stews of fish, shellfish or chicken) and tartines (rye bread with toppings). It is laudably ambitious and only sad when humankind buckles under the strain, as can happen – to beer-filled customers as well as fraught staff. On the whole, reports are good, although you must be young or young at heart to bear the cacophony. Ron Arad and Alison Brooks have achieved a thrilling design best appreciated as you approach the roaring, bawling open kitchen via the wire-mesh cage of a lift. Half the space, dedicated to no booking and quick turnover, is open all day. So wipe your eyes and get ready to eat at tea time.

£20

OPEN
EVERY DAY

HOURS
12.00PM–12.00AM

CREDIT CARDS
AMEX DELTA
DINER'S
MASTERCARD
SWITCH VISA

SERVICE
OPTIONAL

SET-PRICE LUNCH
£5

SET-PRICE DINNER
£10
FOR PARTY
BOOKINGS £10,
£14.95, £19.50 &
£25

FACILITIES
SEATS 400
PRIVATE ROOMS
SEAT 25 EACH
WHEELCHAIR
ACCESS (ALSO
WC)

NEAREST TUBE STATION
COVENT GARDEN

MAP 4

BELGIUM AND BRITAIN may dispute which offers the greater range of beer styles, but good cask-conditioned British ale can only really be drunk in pubs. Nearly all of the most characterful Belgian beers, on the other hand, are also fermented in the bottle, which makes them suitable for the restaurant trade. Belgos Noord (q.v.) and Centraal have a good spread of all the main styles: tart, refreshing wheat beers, sweet-and-sour fruit beers, and heavy, alcoholic after-dinner sipping brews. And you can either settle your stomach or chase your beer with a colourful range of genevers and fruit brandies. The rudimentary tasting notes (all the beers are 'smooth', 'fruity' or 'malty') could be sacrificed in favour of some more background information, but the alcohol content of each is probably the single most relevant item of data. Oh, and there's some wine from Belgium's large, southern neighbour.

BELGO NOORD

72 CHALK FARM ROAD NW1   267 0718

'Mussels on the Northern line'

The opening of Belgo Centraal (see above) seems to have taken some of the pressure off the Chalk Farm premises. At least a test lunch was a relatively calm affair when the premises – much enhanced by the Ron Arad/Alison Brooks addition with its glazed ceiling sectioned by curved pieces of wood reminiscent of boat keels – took on something of the feeling of a canteen for people who work locally. The welcome from young chaps in monks' habits is friendly and easygoing and how much or how little you eat seems of no great import. The menu is a shorter version of the one described above, with oysters, mussels and lobsters plus the various set deals covering one side of an A5 page; on the other are asparagus, other starters including various croquettes and Belgian main-course specialities. Demi coucou de Malines rôti is an eminently satisfying, very un-English dish of roast chicken, celeriac purée and a beer-based, Dijon-mustard-flavoured sauce. The half lobster at £10 is a diminutive creature but a pile of good chips acts as makeweight. Another page the same size lists the many beers available (also sold in an adjacent shop). The impersonality of the thundering Centraal makes the Northern branch seem almost homey.

£20

OPEN
EVERY DAY

HOURS
MON–FRI
12.00–3.00PM
6.00–11.30PM
SAT
12.00–11.30PM
SUN
12.00–10.30PM

CREDIT CARDS
AMEX DELTA
DINER'S
MASTERCARD
SWITCH VISA

SERVICE
OPTIONAL

SET-PRICE LUNCH
£5

SET-PRICE DINNER
£10

FACILITIES
SEATS 110
WHEELCHAIR
ACCESS (ALSO
WC)

NEAREST TUBE STATION
CHALK FARM

MAP 1

THE BELVEDERE

OFF ABBOTSBURY ROAD W8   602 1238

'Needs to take care that it does not become Belvedrear'

This restaurant in an old orangery in Holland Park is the prettiest and most substantial of our park restaurants. Those who like both parks and food may laugh a hollow laugh, for the competition is not exactly stiff. There seems to be bureaucratic resistance to making buildings available to enterprising restaurateurs. As Johnny Gold and his team at the Belvedere have gained such an elegant foothold, perhaps they should use the space more inventively, turning the ground floor into a café or bar and thence more profits? Mostly when eating at the Belvedere you eat upstairs, with the possibility of trying for a place (difficult to secure) on a small balcony when the weather is welcoming. The menu is the familiar modern mix. Standards of cooking have been, at the time of writing, inconsistent: heavily oily in the case of a goat's cheese fritter and sweet and sour sole fillets served with French fries and deep fried spinach, of unfathomable flavour in the case of a 'homemade' sorbet as against inspired, prettily presented dishes like a tuna gravadlax with avocado mousse, squid with spiced couscous and sweet pepper and herb oil, or a princely pear soufflé with pear ice cream – no lack of flavour there. Stricter supervision in the kitchen seems to be called for.

£28

OPEN
LUNCH EVERY DAY
DINNER MON–SAT

HOURS
12.00–3.00PM
7.00–11.00PM

CREDIT CARDS
AMEX DELTA
DINER'S
MASTERCARD
SWITCH VISA

SERVICE
OPTIONAL

SUNDAY BRUNCH

FACILITIES
SEATS 150
TABLES OUTSIDE
SEAT 40
WHEELCHAIR
ACCESS

**NEAREST TUBE
STATION**
HOLLAND PARK

MAP 1

BENGAL CLIPPER

31 SHAD THAMES BUTLERS WHARF SE1   357 9001

'Putting imported spices to good use'

There is a seemliness to the presence of this Indian restaurant at Butlers Wharf – it having been the chief importing wharf for spices coming from the East – which the outlets of Conran's self-styled Gastrodrome lack, but sadly the ground floor of the Cardamom Building is denied a view of the river. Some compensation may be found in the wood-panelled decor, which reminded one visitor of a P & O liner in the fifties. Certainly the food provides diversion, and its setting and service, as well as the cooking, are reminiscent of the restaurants of grand hotels in India. As far as the kitchen is concerned the Bengali theme is tenuous, with most of the seafood dishes based on giant prawns or, in one rather odd case, Dover sole, rather than freshwater fish such as hilsa so beloved of Bengalis.

£23

OPEN
EVERY DAY

HOURS
12.00–3.00PM
6.00–11.00PM

CREDIT CARDS
AMEX DELTA
DINER'S
MASTERCARD
SWITCH VISA

SERVICE
OPTIONAL

COVER CHARGE
£1.50

**SET-PRICE
LUNCH**
£12.95

**SET-PRICE
DINNER**
£18.95

However, there is tiger fish hara massala, based on the river fish marinated and then prepared with a sauce flavoured with coriander, tomatoes, ginger, chillis and lemon juice. Goan spicing informs quite a few of the dishes, such as the starters of kakrar chop, based on crabmeat mixed with mashed potato, and golda chingri nizami roll, chopped prawn deep-fried in spicy poppadoms, and the main courses of xacuti chicken, tangy and vibrant in its coconut-based sauce, kali mirch murgh spiked with roasted black peppercorns, and crab vindaloo. Duckling (hass) is also served with a vindaloo sauce. Mustard seeds – a typical Bengali spice – appear in the aubergine dish bagari begoon, and in tarka massor dal made from orange lentils. The tandoori mixed grill is doubtless popular with the element of the clientele who look like snooker or boxing promoters from Chigwell. They too make the Bengal Clipper distinctive in this somewhat doctrinaire development. A pianist plays in the evenings. Very P & O.

BENTLEY'S

11–15 SWALLOW STREET W1   734 4756

'More suited to the Walrus than the Carpenter'

Bentley's has been serving oysters and fish at this Piccadilly site since 1916. The attractive ground-floor oyster bar and the club-like dining rooms on the first floor, where tables are well separated and the walls covered with Spy prints, comprise a significant part of the attraction of eating here. Bentley's enjoyed a relatively brief fling with chef Stephen Corrigan: now he's gone to Hackney Stadium, and something of his innovative style stays on in the menus of Keith Stanley, previously chef at The Ritz. Unfortunately, it is where Stanley tries to be hip with dishes such as tempura crab claws with black bean sauce and grilled prawns with chilli salsa that the cooking can falter. A more sure-fire way to enjoy yourself here is to stay with items like smoked Scottish salmon or a classic shellfish bisque followed by grilled Dover sole or roast lobster. Puddings are gloriously British and the expansive, three-piece-suited gents who make up a good part of the clientele enjoy, say, a treacle tart with clotted cream or an apple and rhubarb crumble quite as much as the twinkle in the eyes of the pert, professional waitresses. Set-price menus are relatively very good value and perhaps the safe way to enjoy this piece of fishy history.

FACILITIES
SEATS 175
WHEELCHAIR
ACCESS

NEAREST TUBE STATION
TOWER HILL/
LONDON BRIDGE

MAP 1

£36

OPEN
MON–SAT

HOURS
11.30AM–11.30PM

CREDIT CARDS
AMEX DELTA
DINER'S
MASTERCARD
SWITCH VISA

SERVICE
OPTIONAL

SET-PRICE LUNCH
£16.50

SET-PRICE DINNER
£19.50

FACILITIES
SEATS
60 (RESTAURANT)
30 (OYSTER BAR)
PRIVATE ROOM
SEATS 14

NEAREST TUBE STATION
PICCADILLY
CIRCUS

MAP 4

BEOTYS

79 St Martin's Lane WC2   836 8768/8548

'Fifty years on'

This Greek/Cypriot restaurant celebrating half a century in theatreland proves that flexibility is perhaps one of the keys to survival. In addition to what used to be called a 'Continental' menu – La Bisque d'Homard followed by L'Entrecôte de Boeuf à la Diane would be one possible order here – there are dishes of the day which might include steak and kidney pudding or poached wild Scottish salmon, a good-value set-price deal, and a separate set-price vegetarian menu. Most targets are covered including the one that is parties of Americans who break into applause at the sight of Les Flambés à Votre Table. Beotys, with its tetchily avuncular waiters, is for those who like sedate, old-fashioned restaurants with space between formally laid tables. This would seem to include groups of Freemasons who sit in serried ranks with slim, black briefcases neatly at their feet. If you choose from the Greek menu – the name of chef Mr Ahmed El Gaulant, diplomatically enough, seems to relate to none of the cuisines on offer – you are probably playing safest. A meal of kalamarakia (squid) followed by kleftiko (braised lamb) was praised for being 'the real thing' and appreciated for its sheer quantity. Desserts ride in on the trolley. When booking, ask for a ground-floor table.

£26

OPEN
MON–SAT

HOURS
12.00–3.00PM
5.30–11.30PM

CREDIT CARDS
AMEX DINER'S
MASTERCARD VISA

SERVICE
OPTIONAL

**SET-PRICE
LUNCH & DINNER**
£13 & £15

FACILITIES
SEATS 100
PRIVATE ROOMS
SEAT 10–70
WHEELCHAIR
ACCESS (ALSO
WC)

**NEAREST TUBE
STATION**
LEICESTER
SQUARE

MAP 5

BIBENDUM RESTAURANT AND OYSTER BAR

MICHELIN HOUSE 81 FULHAM ROAD SW3   581 5817

'Still the tops'

A ripple of disquiet went through the many fans of Bibendum this year when it became known that chef and co-owner Simon Hopkinson was, as he put it, taking a step back from the stoves. However, his pedagogic abilities, as evidenced all over the Conran restaurant empire as well as at Chez Bruce, The Fifth Floor Restaurant, The Chiswick and The Square (all reviewed in this edition), have not been lost on Matthew Harris, who is now Bibendum's head chef. A meal taken after Hopkinson had left to devote his time to writing and wine appreciation revealed the same delights as ever, plus (for me) some new discoveries. One was the first course of lobster tart with saffron modelled on the tried and true combi-

**RESTAURANT £45
OYSTER BAR £24**

OPEN
EVERY DAY

HOURS
MON–FRI
12.30–2.30PM
SAT–SUN
12.30–3.00PM
MON–SAT
7.00–11.30PM
SUN
7.00–10.30PM

CREDIT CARDS
AMEX DELTA
MASTERCARD
SWITCH VISA

SERVICE
12½%

COVER CHARGE
NO

**SET-PRICE
LUNCH**
£27

FACILITIES
SEATS 72
WHEELCHAIR
ACCESS

**NEAREST TUBE
STATION**
SOUTH
KENSINGTON

MAP 2

nation in quiche aux fruits de mer, a dish Hopkinson learned at the beginning of his career when he worked for Yves Champeau at La Normandie in Birtle, Lancashire. What Champeau did not think to do was to cook a lobster claw in crisp breadcrumbs to accompany the flaky pastry tart containing soft saffron-infused custard and tender lobster pieces. In its own humbler way oeufs en meurette, poached eggs in a red wine sauce, was also eminently satisfying, and, in its extravagance with morels, the dish of pappardelle was notable as a simple celebration of ingredients, a description that also applies to cucumber salad with caviar and crème fraîche. Bold statements made with fine produce are also apparent in the main course and underlined when two decide to share a roast poulet de Bresse with tarragon or best end of lamb with aubergine, garlic and Parmesan cakes. Deep-fried lemon sole with chips and tartare sauce, and fillet steak au poivre, besides being commonplace dishes uncommonly well prepared, suit the range of clientele, having appeal to businessmen who like no-nonsense food and pop stars who feel comfortable with food they have heard of. Desserts keep up the momentum. Pithivier au chocolat is well worth the 20-minute wait by which time you might be feeling more ready for dessert. Service tends to favour rather too obviously the famous or the frequent visitor. Those who worry about whether they have got the best table have a lot to worry about here. However, the room designed in homage to the Michelin man (who idiotically withholds his stars) and the French motor industry, which brought so many good restaurants within reach (the building was formerly headquarters of the tyre company), is a delight to all. I would defy anyone not to feel a-quiver with anticipation when sitting down to eat at the handsomely laid places. It costs a lot – the set-price lunch menu (£27) ameliorates the bill somewhat – but a meal at Bibendum is a treat worth saving for.

On the ground floor behind the forecourt, where a camionette sells oysters, lobsters, crabs and caviar, is **Bibendum Oyster Bar**. It is not the most comfortable of places, a fact that you might be spitefully pleased about if queuing for a table, but can deliver a sexy little meal. A plateau de fruits de mer to share is glamorous to look at and delightful to excavate, or there are salads, crostini, smoked salmon and main courses such as spiced duck breast with red onion and chilli relish or thinly sliced rare beef with potato and spring onion salad, rocket and horseradish cream. No booking, but it is open all day, noon to 10.30pm last orders.

THE GREAT STRENGTH of Bibendum's 1000-strong wine list is the room it gives to the classic wines of the less fashionable regions such as Southern France, Italy, Spain and Germany, as well as the more predictable ones of Bordeaux, Burgundy and the Rhône. The New World selections are also bang up to date. Since the compilers quite clearly have encyclopaedic knowledge and impeccable taste it seems a pity that so much of the list is given over to showy, three-figure (sometimes four-figure) wines which will only ever be bought by a tiny handful. The price tags on the humbler offerings take some justifying, too: St Hallett's Old Block Shiraz will relieve the diner of £42.50 when it has a 'street value' of around £9. An unintended pleasure, therefore, consists in totting up the money saved by having drunk certain wines elsewhere. There are good bottles under £30 – the Mas de Daumas Gassacs from Languedoc, the brilliant Schoffits from Alsace, and Louis Belle's smokey Crozes-Hermitage – but they take some rooting out.

BISTROT BRUNO

63 FRITH STREET W1   734 4545

'Loubet's legacy'

Writing about Bistrot Bruno – an Eros award winner – in last year's *Guide*, it was noted that soon after the book was published, chef Bruno Loubet was due to open L'Odeon in Regent Street in partnership with Pierre Condou, owner of Bistrot Bruno. Due to various not unfamiliar problems with permissions and building works, L'Odeon is now due to open at about the time this edition is published (October 1995). Loubet will leave behind at the Bistrot chef Pierre Khodja, who has been working alongside him and is capable of the same vivacious style, the sort of successful daring pairings exemplified in curried 'brandade' and grilled aubergine terrine; chicken liver, bacon and Swiss chard pie with a Roquefort sauce; fresh mackerel roasted with Indian spices; grilled quail with liver crostini and hazelnut jus; roast rack of lamb with merguez sausages, spicy fennel and saffron mash. Loubet is one of very few French chefs – Joel Antunes at Les Saveurs (q.v.) is another – to realize that flavouring à l'Indienne goes far beyond a pinch of Vencat. Loubet's trick is to have maintained cooking roots in his native South-West France while letting alight in the branches many of the exciting eclectic influences which are on

£30

OPEN
LUNCH MON–FRI
DINNER MON–SAT

HOURS
12.30–2.30PM
6.15–11.30PM

CREDIT CARDS
AMEX DELTA
DINER'S
MASTERCARD
SWITCH VISA

SERVICE
OPTIONAL

FACILITIES
SEATS 40
WHEELCHAIR
ACCESS

**NEAREST TUBE
STATION**
TOTTENHAM
COURT
ROAD/LEICESTER
SQUARE

MAP 5

the loose in London. He will be overseeing the kitchen in Soho. Service at Bistrot Bruno has been known to be abrasive and it is not the most comfortable of restaurants. Café Bruno next door is popular for quicker, cheaper meals.

BISTROT 190

190 QUEEN'S GATE SW7   581 5666

'Where ingredients meet to be eaten'

£24

OPEN
EVERY DAY

HOURS
7.00AM–12.00AM

CREDIT CARDS
AMEX DINER'S
MASTERCARD
SWITCH VISA

SERVICE
OPTIONAL

FACILITIES
SEATS 60
PRIVATE ROOM
SEATS 30
WHEELCHAIR
ACCESS (ALSO
WC)

**NEAREST TUBE
STATION**
GLOUCESTER
ROAD

MAP 2

Ever the innovator, Antony Worrall-Thompson at his perennially popular Bistrot 190 has introduced a menu divided into price bands offering a reasonably wide choice within each figure. These range from £2.95 for simple starters, for example, warm salad of borlotti beans with goat's cheese and oregano, to £12.95 for the more expensive main courses featuring ingredients such as scallops, seared tuna and confit of duck. The tidy, good-housekeeping effect is slightly marred by a supplement of £2 being added to pasta dishes if they are chosen as a main course. However, value is there, as can be quickly deduced, and so is AW-T's commitment to acting as a sort of lonelyhearts' club for ingredients (c.f. dell'Ugo). However, as befits a bistro, the dishes here are relatively reined-in in terms of what is put with what, and some tried and true marriages – prosciutto with pears, Italian sausages with lentils, calf's liver with onions – are left more or less alone. A flirtation with Moroccan spicing and flavouring simmers on, and was satisfyingly exemplified in the dish of flash-fried Moroccan chicken with rice, sweet potato, mint and yogurt. It was a substantial assembly, but chargrilled squid with chilli oil and rocket was praised for its lightness of being and tenderness of squid. Lemon and lime tart managed to taste of neither and looked rather poorly. Tiramisu has been compared unfavourably to Sainsbury's version. A policy of no bookings coupled with an enthusiastic clientele means that early or late arrival within conventional mealtimes will get you seated more quickly. There is a bar adjacent where you wait in louche comfort. When the dining room cluttered with pictures and objets is full, noise and smoke rise to levels some find uncomfortable. A notably ambitious and inventive breakfast is served from 7am to 11am.

BLEEDING HEART
RESTAURANT AND WINE BAR

OFF GREVILLE STREET EC1   242 2056

'Old virtues such as cholesterol and claret hold sway'

£26

OPEN
MON–FRI

HOURS
12.00–3.00PM
6.00–12.00AM

CREDIT CARDS
AMEX DELTA
DINER'S
MASTERCARD
SWITCH VISA

SERVICE
RESTAURANT
12½%
BRASSERIE
OPTIONAL

**SET-PRICE
DINNER**
£9.95
(BRASSERIE)
£12.95
(RESTAURANT)

FACILITIES
SEATS
60 (BRASSERIE)
75 (RESTAURANT)
TABLES OUTSIDE
SEAT 28
PRIVATE ROOM
SEATS 50
WHEELCHAIR
ACCESS

**NEAREST TUBE
STATION**
FARRINGDON

MAP 3

More wine bottles on tables than is usual in these puritanical days is one of the encouraging signs at this restaurant and wine bar/brasserie on the fringes of the City, between Smithfield and Hatton Garden. Besuited men with braces over large tummies and only a token smattering of women are also pointers to its geographical location. Entrance to the restaurant is through a yard named after a legend concerning Lady Elizabeth Hatton, details of which might put you off your food. Suffice it to say that it concerned the Lady E and her jilted lover, a swarthy European ambassador with a vicious temperament and a clawed right hand. The restaurant is down some steps and situated beyond the wine bar, where a reasonably priced bistro menu offers dishes such as crumbed mushrooms with aioli; marinated herring with potato salad; omelette au choix; coq au vin; steak et frites. The more ambitious French menu of the restaurant reads rather better than it delivers, an observation that maybe should not be separated from the fact of a terrine of pheasant and partridge with a prune and Armagnac compote being offered in May. Crab on Oriental cabbage with a sweet and sour sauce was stronger on the worth of the main ingredient – crunchily fresh crabmeat – than its treatment. However, the wine list is a boon and a blessing, with 52 choices offered under £15, as well as many fine wines. And the cheese board is kept in tip-top condition thanks to the clientele's stiff upper lip in the face of the enemy chloresterol. They deal with it the way the French know how: another bottle of Pommard. Service is professional.

THIS EXTENSIVE LIST is continually being updated, and has about it an air of unfinished business. New Zealand is the current focus, a result of three buying trips undertaken in the past 12 months: try the nutty Chardonnay and jammy Pinot Noir from Martinborough Vineyards. Burgundy and the Rhône are other strengths, while claret is best at its lower end (how rarely one sees that), with sensibly chosen Cru Bourgeois. Magnums outnumber halves, which should really be reversed, and if the Black Watch are billeted upon you there is a hogshead of Springbank (360 bottles) for sale.

THE BLENHEIM

21 LOUDON ROAD NW8   625 1222

'A pub with a terrific wine list'

£24

OPEN
TUES–SUN

HOURS
12.30–2.30PM
7.00–10.30PM
SUN
12.30–9.00PM

CREDIT CARDS
AMEX
MASTERCARD
SWITCH VISA

SERVICE
OPTIONAL

FACILITIES
SEATS 65
TABLES OUTSIDE
SEAT 50
PRIVATE ROOMS
SEAT 20 & 30

**NEAREST TUBE
STATION**
ST JOHN'S WOOD

MAP 1

A handsome public house in a prosperous residential area has been converted into a restaurant and bar, although the bar plays an unusually small part in this current trend for turning neighbourhood pubs into what might be called the English equivalent of a bistro. Chef is Caroline Symonds out of The Carved Angel and Villandry (q.v.), who from a kitchen on view – de rigueur – sends out a short, modern menu designed as a list of dishes rather than divided into courses, permitting quick, light eating if that is what you want. None of the choices startles with originality, but ingredients are carefully sourced and thus an item like grilled asparagus with Hollandaise can reach unexpected heights through the quality of the 'grass' and the mustard-yellow yolks of free-range eggs used in the sauce. Typical dishes on a menu that changes in part regularly are butternut squash and apple soup; Caesar salad; pan-roasted vegetables with a Parmesan croûton; fish cakes with lemon aïoli and tomato salad; roast Gressingham duck with sage and warm grated beetroot; English cheeses; blood orange sorbet; treacle tart (excellent) with cream. The Blenheim delights with its drinks list devised by Douglas Wregg who compiled a model wine list for Gilberts (q.v.) and also bought the wine and controlled the noteable list at Downstairs at One Ninety. Beers and ciders are well chosen and there is an interesting list of non-alcoholic drinks. There is much to explore among the wines divided on the page by weight and style with a fairly generous number of bottles offered by the glass. It is customary to follow chefs from place to place but Wregg is a wine buff worth latching onto and he is also a sweet manager.

BLUE ELEPHANT

4–6 FULHAM BROADWAY SW6   385 6595

'A Thai village in Fulham Broadway'

£33

OPEN
LUNCH SUN–FRI
DINNER
MON–SUN

HOURS
12.00–2.30PM
7.00PM–12.30AM
SUN
7.00–10.30PM

To the cynical there is every signal that the Thai food here will be compromised: the tropical village decor complete with babbling brooks, lily ponds, koi carp swimming and thatched huts seating 240 among potted palms, the bevies of vacantly smiling staff in national costume, the frequent presence of tourists, big groups and hen parties, the long menu, but, in fact, standards of cooking are high. The consensus is that choosing the Royal Thai Banquet is the sensible approach to ordering. In terms of value for the range of dishes included it is demonstrably the canny move and it also obviates dithering and dissension at your table. From this menu which included a selection of starters – satay, fish cakes, spring rolls, vermicelli salad, paper prawns and dim sum all accompanied by their own sweet and spicy sauces – Thai beef salad, emerald chicken (wrapped in toey leaves), homok talay (lemon grass-flavoured fish stew with mussels, prawns, crabs and scallops), patani (stir-fried lamb with ginger and garlic), Bangkok fish (fried cod with ginger and garlic in a chilli sauce), massaman (a Muslim dish from the South of slow-cooked lamb), fried rice, noodles, mixed vegetables, plain steamed rice and dessert of vanilla ice cream with mixed fresh fruit, the highlights were patani, massaman and the fried rice. The only moment the meandering waiting staff showed any animation was when dessert was declined. Totally perplexed, they asked three times if this was really meant since dessert was included in the set price. Vegetarian menus are available and from time to time there are regional food festivals, such as the Laan Na festival focusing on cooking from the North. For anyone with short children it is worth knowing that on Sundays at the Royal Thai buffet, children up to 4ft tall are charged £2 per foot for their meal. Incidentally, Blue Elephant have now dropped their 15% service charge but to make themselves feel all right about it, increased the prices. In December 1995, Blue Elephant International, the parent company, are due to open a 300-seater Indian restaurant, La Porte des Indes, in Bryanston Street W1 which should be worth checking out.

CREDIT CARDS
AMEX DINER'S
MASTERCARD VISA

SERVICE
OPTIONAL

COVER CHARGE
£1.50

SET-PRICE LUNCH
£25

SET-PRICE DINNER
£28

SUNDAY BRUNCH

FACILITIES
SEATS 240
PRIVATE ROOM
SEATS 100
WHEELCHAIR
ACCESS (ALSO
WC)

NEAREST TUBE STATION
FULHAM
BROADWAY

MAP 2

BLUE PRINT CAFÉ

THE DESIGN MUSEUM SHAD THAMES SE1   378 7031

'Blueprint, white noise, hot tuna'

It is a good job that from most positions in this restaurant there is a fine view of the river and Tower Bridge because the acoustics are difficult. The ceiling is low and all the surfaces hard – no wonder the waiting staff can seem harried. Sensibly, they repeat food orders in firm voices. Chef Lucy Crabb, who made a brief sortie to Euphorium in Islington, is back in the kitchen with Jeremy Lee (ex-Alastair Little) in tow, and the menu carries on as before with favourite elements soups, salads,

£30

OPEN
LUNCH EVERY DAY
DINNER MON–SAT

HOURS
MON–SAT
12.00–3.00PM
6.00–11.00PM
SUN
12.00–3.30PM

CREDIT CARDS
DINER'S
MASTERCARD
SWITCH VISA

pasta and grills. A green minestrone and a salad of baby beetroot and hard-boiled eggs were both bright and carefully made. Main courses such as grilled tuna with black bean and ginger or rabbit with artichoke and olives have turned out to be agreeably austere. With the exception of the fish and chips, if you want starch and a profusion of vegetables these must be ordered in addition. Bear in mind that desserts, often based on seasonal fruit, are worth leaving space for. The Blue Print Café people manage to create a sense of separation from the Conran complex one minute upstream, and seem to offer better value too. 'One day,' said the companion of the evening, 'Conran's restaurants might stretch as far as Marlow.' What a prospect.

BODALI

78 HIGHBURY PARK N5   704 0741/359 3444

'A goal in Arsenal'

SERVICE
12½%

FACILITIES
SEATS 86
TABLES OUTSIDE
SEAT 40
WHEELCHAIR
ACCESS (ALSO
WC)

**NEAREST TUBE
STATION**
TOWER HILL/
LONDON BRIDGE

MAP 1

£16 BYO

OPEN
MON–SAT

HOURS
6.00–11.00PM

CREDIT CARDS
NONE

SERVICE
OPTIONAL

COVER CHARGE
£1.50

FACILITIES
SEATS 26
WHEELCHAIR
ACCESS

**NEAREST TUBE
STATION**
ARSENAL/
FINSBURY PARK/
HIGHBURY &
ISLINGTON

MAP 1

There were plans for 'reburbishment' when we visited in early August 1995 but it is hard to imagine dramatic changes possible in these simple, small, family-run premises. A new coat of paint will be welcome. The printed menu is long, too long to suggest more than various sauces being brought to meet various main ingredients at the moment of ordering but the interesting dishes at this basically Gujerati (but not vegetarian) restaurant are written on the blackboard. This is where the 'house sauce' comes into play, a mixture containing cashews, aubergines, coconut, dried apricots, red peppers, onions, tomatoes and cream, which is integrated with lamb, chicken tikka or king prawns. At least one of these should be chosen. Butter chicken, another blackboard offering, proved smooth and gentle in impact with noticeable flavour from the quantities of fenugreek included. Kingfish and sea trout curries are also a speciality. Vegetable dishes are above average. Try the Gujerati sambaro, a mix of cabbage, carrot, green pepper and peanuts; spinach and moong dal where fresh spinach is used; red kidney bean curry and the purposefully sweet courgette curry containing apple, sultanas and coconut. Rice assemblies, such as special fried rice with onion and egg, tend to be more impressive than the breads. Home-made chutneys should not be missed and nor should the exceptional cucumber raitha, a bowl of home-made yogurt topped with crunchy cucumber spears sprinkled with turmeric. The unlicensed Bodali (BYO) is a treasure in an arid area.

BOMBAY BRASSERIE

COURTFIELD CLOSE COURTFIELD ROAD SW7   370 4040

'Another world'

Any irritation at being obliged to sit in the bar and study a list of cocktails while 'your table is being made ready' slips away as you enter past a cocktail pianist at a white piano (in the evenings), the grand sweep of the dining room with its huge, 90-seater conservatory off to the right (the preferable place to sit). This decorative homage to the Raj is suitably majestic in scope and successfully transports you to another clime. Bombay being the city where all of India meets, the menu here gathers together various Indian regional dishes as well as some Bombay street snacks, such as sev batata puri and samosa chaat, which make diverting first courses. There are Parsi, Goan and Moghlai assemblies, house specialities such as lobster hara masala, vegetarian thalis and, of course, tandoor-cooked food from the North. Changes on the menu happen, but slowly. Of two new main courses, the Parsi margi ni curry and the Kashmiri (but very hot) mirchi korma, I can recommend the Parsi chicken dish and its subtle, silky sauce. The dense, slightly menacing, fiery Kashmiri lamb dish did not appeal. Vegetable dishes not to be missed are sabut aloo ki bhaji, baby potatoes in their skins dusted with spices; palak pakodi kadi, spinach and gram flour dumplings in yogurt sauce; paneer lababdar, cubes of curd cheese in a creamy sauce; and, when it is not overcooked, the bhindi Jaipuri, crisply fried okra and onions. Breads are excellent (try the laccha paratha) but the chutneys are a bit pedestrian. People complain of the price but I suspect would not do so eating comparably complex Western food in similarly agreeable surroundings. The trick here is to get known to the staff, not difficult since they seem to stay uncommonly loyal.

THE BRACKENBURY

129–131 BRACKENBURY ROAD W6   0181-748 0107

'Reason to move to Hammersmith'

Last year we remarked that success had not spoiled Rock Hunter (as personified by chef/proprietor Adam Robinson) and it is only pleasing to be able to say the same again. The menus, which change for every meal, remain compact, simple, strongly seasonal, low on waffle and always with some element of comfort within what is a boldly eclectic

---

£32

OPEN
EVERY DAY

HOURS
12.00–3.00PM
7.00PM–12.00AM

CREDIT CARDS
DINER'S
MASTERCARD VISA

SERVICE
OPTIONAL

SET-PRICE LUNCH
£14.95

SUNDAY BRUNCH

FACILITIES
SEATS 175
PRIVATE ROOM
SEATS 80

NEAREST TUBE STATION
GLOUCESTER ROAD

MAP 2

£24

OPEN
LUNCH
TUES–FRI & SUN
DINNER
MON–SAT

HOURS
12.30–2.45PM
7.00–10.45PM

DINER'S
MASTERCARD
SWITCH VISA

SERVICE
OPTIONAL

FACILITIES
SEATS 55
TABLES OUTSIDE
SEAT 20
WHEELCHAIR
ACCESS

**NEAREST TUBE
STATION**
GOLDHAWK ROAD/
HAMMERSMITH/
RAVENSCOURT
PARK

MAP 1

selection. Furthermore, they continue to offer some of the best value in London. A constant on the lists is the first course of a plate of savouries at £4.75, which as a correct definition of hors d'oeuvres is well worth ordering, but so much else beckons: for example, cullen skink (smoked haddock soup); warm salad of dandelion with rabbit, poached egg and bacon; crostini of lamb's brains with salsa verde; grilled anchovy and red pepper salad with deep-fried capers; purple sprouting broccoli with warm anchovy dressing. In the main course the policy of using undervalued – and therefore reasonably priced – ingredients delivers the sort of dishes that in an ideal world you might cook at home but in fact never get round to: ham and chicory gratin; crispy pork with spicy cabbage and black beans; lamb's sweet-bread and tongues with broad beans and mint; poached capon, salt beef and chorizo with butter beans and herb dressing. Sometimes the creative energy has run out by dessert time, as was proven by a sorry sherry trifle and a trio of rhubarb puddings – jelly, stewed fruit and mousse – which was a great idea but had no follow-through. Locals doubtless think that success has spoilt their bistro du coin as they discover they must book ahead, and the need to turn over tables can make a chap miffed when he's jostled through his dessert and coffee after having had to wait 20 minutes between first and main course. The Brackenbury remains a model of intelligent catering. The nous – there is no substitute – extends to the wine list on which mark-ups are reasonable and the offer of wines by the glass far greater than is usual. Good cider and ginger beer are also made available.

BRADY'S

696 FULHAM ROAD SW6   736 3938

'Fish and chips with bells on'

£15

OPEN
MON–SAT

HOURS
MON–SAT
7.00–10.30PM
TUES–THURS
7.00–10.45PM
FRI
7.00–11.00PM

CREDIT CARDS
NONE

SERVICE
10%

FACILITIES
SEATS 28

The success of Brady's in Wandsworth has spawned this new branch in Fulham. Not very far away, you might think, but London could sustain many such fish and chip restaurants if Amelia and Luke Brady had enough offspring to run them. Within seconds of stepping into the Fulham Road premises you feel you're at the seaside. There is a real whiff of West Wittering, beach huts and shrimping nets, an effect skilfully achieved with an understated colour scheme of bleached-out French grey woodwork and sandy coloured walls stencilled here and there with crabs and starfish. The black-

board menu lists starters such as rollmops, anchovies, smoked salmon, half a pint of prawns and potted shrimps, this last being infinitely superior to the mass-produced product. Main-course fish depends on the market and the season, but will probably include cod, plaice, haddock, lemon sole, skate, monkfish and tuna, glossily fresh, cooked either in a light-crisp batter or grilled. Chips are excellent and a bonus is the range of mayonnaise-based sauces with flavourings such as dill, tomato, spices and the making of sauce tartare. One diner reports being forgotten about after the delivery of the main courses and having to go to look for Mr Brady, who was found staring out to sea at the front of the restaurant. Her apple crumble when it came was a huge, untidy, delicious plateful served with a jug of cream and for only £1.05. Brady's is an example of English food at its best. No bookings but a quick turnaround of tables.
Also at: 513 Old York Road SW18 (0181-877 9599).

NEAREST TUBE STATION PARSONS GREEN

MAP 1

BRASSERIE DU MARCHÉ AUX PUCES

349 PORTOBELLO ROAD W10   0181-968 5828

'A flea-market find'

The flea market of the title is the northern end of Portobello Road, home to what would have to be a very wide definition of the word antiques. A finalist in the 1995 Most Sympathique Restaurant Award sponsored by Muscadet, this brasserie garners a loyal following through actually keeping brasserie hours – open all day – and conveying an easygoing approach towards ordering through a menu not divided into courses but – in small leaps and bounds – increasing in price from (in one example) £3 for soup of the day to £11 for goose magret with winter fruit compote, watercress and walnut salad. Along the way it takes in dishes such as steamed mussels with Thai broth; vegetable tart Tatin with beetroot butter sauce; cod fillet with pancetta, parsley mash and salsa verde. The list changes regularly but the dishes mentioned are indicative of the enterprising approach, the kind of approach that can – and here does – lead to unevenness in the quality of the cooking. But what you lose on the squid stew you might gain on the haunch of venison with celeriac purée. Tables are bare wood. Decor in the high-ceilinged room with windows on two sides is ad hoc but sparser than the name of the restaurant might imply. On winter nights it can seem comfortless.

£24

OPEN TUES–SAT

HOURS 10AM–11.00PM

CREDIT CARDS AMEX DELTA MASTERCARD SWITCH VISA

SERVICE OPTIONAL

SET–PRICE LUNCH £10.95

FACILITIES SEATS 40 TABLES OUTSIDE SEAT 16 PRIVATE ROOM SEATS 40

NEAREST TUBE STATION LADBROKE GROVE

MAP 1

BU SAN

'A good Korean move'

£26

OPEN
LUNCH MON–FRI
DINNER EVERY
DAY

HOURS
12.00–2.30PM
6.00–11.00PM

CREDIT CARDS
MASTERCARD VISA

SERVICE
10%

**SET-PRICE
LUNCH**
£4.20–£6.50

**SET-PRICE
DINNER**
(FOR TWO
PEOPLE) £27.50
& £34.50

FACILITIES
SEATS 46
WHEELCHAIR
ACCESS

**NEAREST TUBE
STATION**
HIGHBURY &
ISLINGTON

MAP 1

Most non-Koreans could probably go through life quite contentedly without ever trying Korean food, which possesses a garlicky belligerence absent from the sweet coquettishness of Thai cooking. However, the family-run Bu San sets out to woo a Western clientele and based on my latest customer survey, i.e. eating there again, succeeds almost worryingly well. Bu San (or Pusan) is a South Korean port from which on an exceptionally clear day you might see Japan. Chef/proprietor Y.H. Lee includes some Japanese dishes in his long menu even if the graphics (for example, Sa Shi Mi) do not make that immediately clear. These dishes, offered rather more cheaply than at most Japanese restaurants – £9.50 for the sashimi – provide useful contrast to the preponderance of assemblies with deeply savoury sauces. Deep-fried bean curd decked with flickering seaweed strands in a light soya stock sits well in the first course alongside scallops in a spicy sauce served in a shell perched on a mound of flaming salt. Most other 'appetizers' are in fact more like vegetable condiments to be picked at throughout the meal. A Korean would not contemplate eating without a bowl of kim chi – pickled Chinese cabbage – by his side to add high-octane chilli flavour when needed. Beef is another highly prized ingredient. Bul go gi, barbecued marinated steak (cooked at the table) served with fresh salad vegetables and bean paste sauce, is popular but I also like kalbi, grilled beef rib sticky from its sugary marinade. Add a fish dish – perhaps expressed as a robust soup – plus a vegetable choice more particular than fried mixed vegetables, a Korean omelette (pa jean) filled with oysters, shrimps and spring onions and steamed rice, and you would have a meal to divert most palates. Those stubbornly unconvinced could at least admire intricately carved vegetable garnishes. Service is sweet and helpful but can be painfully slow. The recently extended premises are simply decorated. On the outside, the façade is hung with framed press cuttings, of which there are many.

BUTLERS WHARF CHOP HOUSE

36E SHAD THAMES LONDON SE1   403 3403

'Englishness re-designed'

The Chop House enjoys the best relationship with the river of all the outlets in Conran's 'gastrodrome'. Proximity to the water and Tower Bridge and the wine list are definite lures; some aspects of the food, the haphazard, matey service and a colourless interior seemingly designed for maximum aural and physical discomfort beckon less brightly. Simple dishes, as befits a chop house, work best. Crab with saffron mayonnaise is fresh and clean, the white meat flecked with dill, the brown meat served as a scoop of mousse and the mayonnaise sunny with saffron, but smoked haddock baked with parsley and cheese, a dish in which unannounced chunks of tomato lurked, was simply salty in impact. Calf's liver with creamed watercress and shallots was a good steak-shaped piece of liver cooked rather less than well done as had been asked for, but this time my sympathies were with the chef. If Chop House sausages are home-made they should give up the bother and buy sausages at, say, Allen's in Mount Street. They come with a blanket of gravy in which slices of bacon fall asleep. Vegetables ignore the seasons to their detriment. Steak and kidney pudding, which is served for two, gets praise, as does roast veal kidney with bubble and squeak, black pudding and mustard sauce. Desserts are not a high point, something acknowledged by the staff. 'Don't have the cinnamon crunch,' one said, 'it's absolutely horrible.' At weekday lunch times chaps from the City usually predominate. Weekend brunch in the bar is a nice way to use the Chop House.

A QUAINTLY chatty list, much of it reading as though it has been badly translated from a foreign tongue. The index is quaint, too, divided as it is into Old World, New World, and Aquitaine – which you and I know as Bordeaux. There is nothing very interesting below £25 from either Burgundy or Bordeaux (sorry, Aquitaine), but California is ably served with Ridge, Saintsbury, Qupé and Peter Michael. Quite why Anselmi's brilliant Recioto di Soave is so much cheaper than the other dessert wines I've no idea – you can only buy it by the glass, though, so perhaps there are only a couple of fingers left in a long-since opened bottle.

£30

OPEN
EVERY DAY

HOURS
RESTAURANT
MON–FRI
12.00–3.00PM
6.00–11.00PM
SAT
6.00–11.00PM
SUN
12.00–3.00PM
BAR
MON–SAT
12.00–11.00PM
SUN
12.00–6.00PM

CREDIT CARDS
AMEX DINER'S
MASTERCARD VISA

SERVICE
12½%

**SET-PRICE
LUNCH**
£22.75

SUNDAY BRUNCH

FACILITIES
SEATS
RESTAURANT 115
BAR 40
TABLES OUTSIDE
SEAT 44
(RESTAURANT) &
29 (BAR)
WHEELCHAIR
ACCESS (ALSO
WC)

**NEAREST TUBE
STATION**
TOWER
HILL/LONDON
BRIDGE

MAP 1

CAFÉ DELL'UGO

56–58 TOOLEY STREET SE1   407 6001

'Arch without archness'

£23
OPEN
LUNCH MON–FRI
DINNER MON–SAT

HOURS
12.00–3.00PM
7.00–11.00PM

CREDIT CARDS
AMEX DELTA
DINER'S
MASTERCARD
SWITCH VISA

SERVICE
OPTIONAL

FACILITIES
SEATS 80
WHEELCHAIR
ACCESS (ALSO
WC)

NEAREST TUBE
STATION
LONDON BRIDGE

MAP 1

Antony Worrall-Thompson has successfully moved his Mediterranean Madness menu south of the river and demonstrably persuaded those who work around London Bridge of the wisdom of staying on to eat after office hours. The restaurant is located on the first floor of a converted railway arch – the ground floor has a bar and an arena for light meals – and the rumble of trains is a pleasing special effect, setting up escapist visions of journeys. Before you go, though, there is much to divert the palate, beginning with an impressive selection of breads to anoint with the eponymous olive oil ceremoniously poured from a risky height into a small bowl on the table. After that it is whatever grabs your appetite: could be linguine with grilled asparagus, Parmesan and walnut sauce; or pan-fried pork boudin with black pepper brioche and onion marmalade; or baked creamy brandade with parsley crust and herb leaf salad; or braised veal shank with bone marrow, borlotti beans and green tomato chutney. The world is your oyster – those come from Rossmore in Ireland. Test meals have revealed satisfaction with Jerusalem artichoke soup flavoured with ginger and coriander; pressed terrine of smoked haddock, soft herbs and tomato confit with rocket; pan-fried sea bass with polenta, creamed leeks and saffron; roast suckling pig with green beans and aubergine crisps but not with undercooked spring chicken with overpowering sesame oil and a citrus flavour which annihilated the accompanying nut pasta. Lemon tart with crème fraîche restored the balance in favour of the chef (Matthew Fanthorpe). Quantities served are generous, which tends to reinforce the notion that here a good time is had by all.

LE CAFÉ DU MARCHÉ

22 CHARTERHOUSE SQUARE EC1   608 1609

'More evidence of le franc fort'

£30
OPEN
LUNCH MON-FRI
DINNER MON-SAT

HOURS
12.00-2.30PM
6.00-12.00PM

CREDIT CARDS
MASTERCARD
SWITCH VISA

Le Café du Marché fulfils in almost every detail English expectations of a French bistro, right down to off-hand but efficient waiters and a picturesque location off an attractive *place*. In a converted warehouse, once used for the nearby Smithfield meat market, set-price menus at £19.75 for three courses are offered. Where dishes are not traditonally French they are Frenchified in description, for example, le bagel, gravad lax, crème fraîche or le fishcakes de crabe, sauce citron, unless they have their own foreign language in which case it is used, for example, sformata di verdura or szegediner goulash, confirming any English feelings of inferiority and inadequacy about their own cuisine. On the whole, the French dishes succeed best in every way since they conform to the expectations of the experience. This year there have been good reports on beef and mushroom consommé, chateaubriand garni, sauce Bearnaise for two (which attracts a £4 supplement), pot au feu and crème caramel. Wines are quite an interesting selection priced on the high side. Le Café du Marché, always busy, is often described as romantic, an effect more pronounced in the evenings with the pianist or jazz duo playing, but the bill including 15% suggested service can be a bit of a downer, as can the difficulty of finding a taxi at night in that part of town.

SERVICE
15%
SET-PRICE LUNCH AND DINNER
£19.75
FACILITIES
SEATS 100
PRIVATE ROOM
SEATS 50–60
WHEELCHAIR
ACCESS
NEAREST TUBE STATION
BARBICAN
MAP 1

CAFÉ FISH

39 PANTON STREET SW1   930 3999

'Best enjoyed as the same old kettle of'

Simple things seem best in this big and usually busy restaurant by Leicester Square. The plateau des fruits de mer is fine in price and freshness, though like several others in London it does contain the unwelcome whelk. Perhaps we should instigate our own version of the American steakhouse T-bone challenge, i.e. whoever can eat all their whelks eats for free? Grilled, meunière or battered fish with good chips and an OK salad is a sensible main course. The trouble with more complicated cooking (turbot with pink pepper and cognac sauce, prawn wontons with bean sprouts) is that, although there is a good chef in charge, with the numbers involved execution is not always exact. Smart service and reasonably priced wines are an attraction; the best place to sit in warm weather is towards the front where the windows open on to the street and the pianist's efforts to entertain are quietened by the din outside.

£28
OPEN
LUNCH MON–FRI
DINNER MON–SAT
HOURS
12.00–3.00PM
5.45–11.30PM
CREDIT CARDS
AMEX DELTA
DINER'S
MASTERCARD
SWITCH VISA
SERVICE
12½%
COVER CHARGE
£1.25
FACILITIES
SEATS 94
TABLES OUTSIDE
SEAT 6
WHEELCHAIR
ACCESS
NEAREST TUBE STATION
LEICESTER
SQUARE/
PICCADILLY
CIRCUS
MAP 4

CAFÉ MED

'Or Café Medium Rare, as steak-lovers say'

£28

OPEN
EVERY DAY

HOURS
11.30AM–12.00PM

CREDIT CARDS
AMEX DELTA
DINER'S
MASTERCARD
SWITCH VISA

SERVICE
OPTIONAL

SUNDAY BRUNCH

FACILITIES
SEATS 90
TABLES OUTSIDE
SEAT 8

**NEAREST TUBE
STATION**
NOTTING HILL
GATE/
LADBROKE GROVE

MAP 1

It is a little local mystery as to why the one restaurant offering good burgers and steaks should try to associate itself with the sunny south. To some extent the best sellers here are vastly improved versions of what the old Gate Diner once offered on the same spot. BLTs, Caesar salads, hamburgers, and, for Sundays, smoked salmon and scrambled eggs, make familiar reading. However, the quality of the ingredients and execution has been raised exponentially, so that the chips with everything are bootlace shaped and finely flavoured; salads are spruce; and the beef is from Scotland, well hung and accurately cooked on an open grill. Pasta has not impressed as much. New York cheesecake can floor two people in the nicest possible way. Nowadays the place looks Notting Hill trendy, with bright, differing colours on the walls and a mixture of furnishing styles. The main dining room is below street level, with a bar above serving correct cocktails, and then a balcony room for drinking or eating which seems the most attractive spot until a pall of grill fumes rises, as sometimes happens. A case for non-Mediterranean, powerful air conditioning, surely?

CAFÉ O

'Jackie O might have liked it'

£25

OPEN
LUNCH EVERY DAY
DINNER MON–SAT

HOURS
12.00–3.00PM
6.00–11.30PM
SUN
12.00–5.00PM

CREDIT CARDS
DELTA DINER'S
MASTERCARD
SWITCH VISA

SERVICE
12½%

FACILITIES
SEATS 50
TABLES OUTSIDE
SEAT 12

**NEAREST TUBE
STATION**
SOUTH
KENSINGTON

MAP 2

Café O opened in the early summer of 1995 promising modern Hellenic cuisine, one of those moves that makes you suddenly wonder why no one else in recent times has taken the taverna menu and applied to it some cooking finesse. Situated in Draycott Avenue more or less opposite Daphne's (q.v.) and Le Suquet (q.v.), the look of the restaurant is suitably cool, mercifully lacking any folklorique touches. A blue wavy wall on one side suggests sea and sunshine; the floor is tiled; the tables, some of which spread out on to the forecourt in warm weather, are zinc-covered. Waiting staff wear matelot T-shirts. The menu is familiar – Greek food is, after all, authentically hidebound in its composition – but fish soup, the various dips, savoury filo pies, salad horiatiki, souvlaki, stifado and so forth are prepared with uncommon care and, in some instances, refinement. Kakavia, fisherman's soup, is a smooth, dill-infused tomato broth in which pieces of fish and shellfish stand out like small, uninhabited islands. Veal stifado is long-cooked and properly vinegary – rather like a vindaloo without the hot spices – and perhaps in winter they might consider making it with hare. Roast chicken stuffed with feta cheese and spinach served with a butter and parsley sauce, and sea bass Spetsiota served with new potatoes and fennel are about as sophisticated as is sensible to get with this cuisine which most of us associate with ramshackle holidays. There are ten Greek wines included in the wine list and ouzo is there for the asking. A table of what seemed liked disapproving relatives in place the evening we visited was a particularly authoritative touch.

CAFÉ ROYAL GRILL ROOM

68 REGENT STREET W1   437 9090

'Should be the heart of London dining'

A ll the ingredients are in place: an historic rococco room with romantic and racy associations (Oscar Wilde, Aubrey Beardsley and Max Beerbohm all once draped themselves over the crimson plush banquettes here); an executive chef with a Michelin star; waiting staff who can carve a duck as quick as a cat can wink its eye or flame a crèpe as to the manner born; a maitre d' who has worked in the Hotel de Paris in Monaco, and yet, and yet, somehow London does not seem to take the Café Royal Grill to its heart. It should be one of the liveliest, most alluring venues in town but too often you find your fellow diners are groups of bemused tourists or businessmen cementing a deal about cement. Lunch time is perhaps more fun than dinner; the surroundings of a gilded, caryatid-supported windowless room more naughty then. Specialities among the mostly admirable dishes are feuilleté of smoked Finnan haddock and quail's eggs with English mustard sauce; nage of scallops, lobster and langoustines with Oriental spices; dishes prepared for two such as roast rack of lamb with truffled potatoes and roasted Bresse chicken and the worth-waiting-for dessert, hot almond and apple Pithivier with blackberry coulis and vanilla ice cream. Also worth consideration are the interesting first-course salads, such as the mix of artichokes, woodland mushrooms, and green beans dressed with pumpkin-seed oil and balsamic vinegar, and the 'modern' main courses such as médallions of veal with saffron risotto, spinach, vegetable confit and basil. The fact that it is Forté-owned and

£48

OPEN
LUNCH MON–SAT
DINNER MON–FRI

HOURS
12.00–2.30
6.00–10.45PM

CREDIT CARDS
AMEX DINER'S
MASTERCARD
SWITCH VISA

SERVICE CHARGE
OPTIONAL

SET-PRICE LUNCH
£24

SET-PRICE DINNER
£39

FACILITIES
SEATS 45
WHEELCHAIR
ACCESS (ALSO
WOMEN'S WC)

NEAREST TUBE STATION
PICCADILLY
CIRCUS

MAP 5

that Masonic meetings go in the basement rooms might militate against the renaissance of this treasure but if you hurry along in droves (bearing in mind set-price deals at £24 for lunch, £39 for dinner) perhaps you can bring it about .

A FAIRLY STANDARD grand hotel wine list, with heavy reliance on big names (which appear in very small print). There are a few good buys if you look hard enough – Torres' famous Black Label Cabernet 1985 at £36, for instance – and prices as a whole are less forceful than in many similar establishments: for what it's worth, you can save £405 by drinking Pétrus 1966 here rather than at the Dorchester. Forty bottles from the New World reveal some awareness of wine's wheel of change.

CALABASH

38 KING STREET WC2   836 1976

'Home cooking from The Heart of Darkness'

£17

OPEN
LUNCH MON–FRI
DINNER MON–SAT

HOURS
12.30–3.00PM
6.00–11.30PM

CREDIT CARDS
AMEX DINER'S
MASTERCARD VISA

SERVICE
OPTIONAL

COVER CHARGE
25P

FACILITIES
SEATS 70

**NEAREST TUBE
STATION**
CHARING CROSS/
COVENT GARDEN

MAP 4

This Covent Garden basement restaurant, owing nothing in style to the tourist-trash ethnic shop on the ground floor, is pleasantly Fifties in spirit, as 'moderne' as the Commonwealth Institute is and The Ceylon Tea Centre was. Foam-rubber cushioning pads the banquette seating, plastic keeps the plants evergreen and stainless steel divided serving dishes contribute an egalitarian canteen air to the proceedings. The menu is notably reasonably priced and gives just enough explanation to encourage the keen explorer. Among the starters, hot tomato salad is a dashingly simple mix of de-pipped tomato segments, slices of mild onion and green chilli. It can be accompanied by Ethiopian ingera – a bread cunningly fashioned to represent a face flannel, useful for wiping up sauces. The vegetarian sambusa (samosa) has a bland, anonymous green filling, making the minced meat version seem the better choice. Gizzard is available fried with onions, tomatoes, peppers and spices. The main courses come with geographical origin and range from the probably familiar North African couscous to the possibly less-known Nigerian egusi, a soup-stew of fish or meat and vegetables cooked in palm oil with melon seeds served with rice or pounded yam. Senegalese yassa is grilled chicken legs in a lemon and peppercorn sauce served with good rice. There is a wide range of vegetarian main courses, some with appeal to lovers of peanut butter. From the side dishes try the alluring caramelized fried plantain and black-eyed beans in a fresh-tasting tomato sauce. Puddings are disappointing. Chateau de Mascara – which, as you doubtless know, is an Algerian rosé – is on offer, but African beer is the wiser choice. Do not miss out on Abyssinian coffee served in a gourd-shaped pot with a spout purposively blocked with a piece of red plastic kitchen scourer resting on a native beadwork cushion.

LA CAPANNINA

24 ROMILLY STREET W1   437 2473

'Meals on wheels'

The little gingerbread house frontage is a landmark of old Soho, having stood since the days when bruschetta would have been dismissed as a cheap trick with toast. Inside, light gleams off polished copper utensils, varnished wood and the happy faces of advertising people released from business lunches to treat themselves to a second helping of Russian salad followed by wholesome, old-fashioned lasagne. The antipasti, catch of the day and desserts are all trolley-borne and as space is limited there can be tailbacks and near misses between reversing and advancing vehicles. A selection of antipasti and one of the plainer pastas can be recommended, main courses may be unreconstructed (cream, wine and brandy sauces in abundance), but the daily menu brings robust options the *Guide* favours such as ossobuco, bollito misto and stews made with Barolo. The word 'shop' in the damning sense is what springs to mind when spooning in either the crème caramel or tiramisu. If they are made in-house the recipe wants changing.

£26

OPEN
LUNCH MON–FRI
DINNER MON–SAT

HOURS
12.00–2.30PM
6.00–11.30PM

CREDIT CARDS
AMEX DINER'S
MASTERCARD VISA

SERVICE
OPTIONAL

COVER CHARGE
£1

FACILITIES
SEATS 90
PRIVATE ROOM
SEATS 25
WHEELCHAIR
ACCESS

**NEAREST TUBE
STATION**
LEICESTER
SQUARE/
PICCADILLY
CIRCUS

MAP 5

CAPITAL HOTEL

BASIL STREET SW3   589 5171

'Now with a more stylish setting for Britten's cooking'

Ruched, swagged and draped chintz curtains at the restaurant windows have been replaced by etched, glazed wooden screens made of English oak inlaid with burr walnut made by David Linley Designs. The windows themselves, part of the frontage of the (Levin) family-owned hotel, have been returned to a shape more appropriate to the architecture of this little street off Harrods. An altogether more delicate and flattering look (and lighting) in the Capital's small dining room – long the home of admirable food within an hotel – provides a

£50

OPEN
EVERY DAY

HOURS
12.30–2.30PM
7.30–11.15PM

CREDIT CARDS
AMEX DELTA
DINER'S
MASTERCARD
SWITCH VISA

SERVICE
INCLUDED

SET-PRICE
LUNCH
£25

SET-PRICE
DINNER
£40

FACILITIES
SEATS 40
PRIVATE ROOM
SEATS 22
WHEELCHAIR
ACCESS

NEAREST TUBE
STATION
KNIGHTSBRIDGE

MAP 2

newly alluring setting for the cooking of Philip Britten, chef since 1987. Britten is a craftsman chef, trained most formatively with Anton Mosimann and Nico Ladenis, whose nose-to-the-grindstone low profile contrasts sharply with that of Gary Rhodes, chef of The Greenhouse (q.v.), also owned by the Levins. Apart from devising a set-price six-course menu based on fish dishes, he strikes no attitude beyond providing a distillation of the progress that has been made in this country in both recipe inspiration and kitchen performance. The menus are expressed uncompromisingly in the mother tongue, but look to France and Italy for technique. Pasta dishes and risottos are uncommonly good, and there are imaginative hotel-funded flourishes such as using caviar for saltiness in a lasagne (loosely interpreted) of salmon and morilles with cucumber and chervil. Flavoured oils rather than butters tend to add emollience and there is a judicious use of wine in the saucing. One good example of the latter is honey-roasted long-cooked Barbary duckling in a claret sauce (prepared for two). Others are turbot gratin with Savoy cabbage and a Muscadet sabayon and pot-roasted saddle of rabbit with mushrooms and champagne. Desserts are usually faultless but those who say 'I'll just have coffee' can make up lost calories with the superior petits fours, including fruit jujubes and first-rate Florentines. Eating at the Capital is designed as an expensive affair for well-to-do folk and cutting corners either by opting for the set-price lunch menu or ordering house wines from the list of famous names in many vintages only robs you of getting the best out of the place. This is offered more in the spirit of an observation than a criticism, but there are fancy restaurants – Tante Claire (q.v.) for example – where taking the bargain lunch does not make you feel the poor relation. Service is polished, almost literally.

ONLY THE PRICES and the vintages (though not the port vintages, the youngest of which is 1966) tell you that this wine list has been put together in the 1990s rather than the 1960s. Champagne/claret/burgundy/port – that is what you get at the Capital: the previous 25 years of development within the wine trade may never have been. Now, this would not really matter if the wines were excellent, or had clearly been chosen for the right reasons, but virtually no selection looks to have taken place – throughout there is an almost total reliance upon the big names – names which were big 20 or 30 years ago.

LE CAPRICE

'A rare example of a place with genuine glamour'

Researching an article on fascistic tendencies exhibited by restaurants in the taking of bookings, I got an actor friend to ring Le Caprice and in particularly off-putting, naff tones ask for a table for four at 8.30pm for the following Friday evening. My ploy completely backfired as with – perhaps predictable – good grace the chap taking the details behaved impeccably and helpfully. Le Caprice is run by its owners Christopher Corbin and Jeremy King probably as well as a restaurant can be, and its name heads many people's lists of favourite eating places. Naturally, such popularity makes getting a table a problem and it escapes no-one that it will be easier if your name is Clive James (whose date may be the Princess of Wales), but once in, it would seem that practically anyone and everyone feels happy. Staff are briefed each day on who is coming and what their foibles are, as well as being expected to know what is being sung at Covent Garden or showing at The Royal Academy. So widely imitated is the menu that you have to cast your mind back to remember the days when a mix of dishes such as Caesar salad, sautéed foie gras, eggs Benedict, risotto nero, salmon fishcake, Lincolnshire sausage with bubble and squeak, grilled yellow-fin tuna steak with Provençal vegetables, grilled breast of chicken with Szechuan vegetables and deep-fried cod with minted pea purée and chips was anything but commonplace. It is not an exaggeration to say that much of the modern London menu originated here. It continues to be produced and delivered with unusual panache and habitués can look to the daily scribbled-in additions for novelty and short-seasonality where bargains may be found, such as fat English asparagus with Hollandaise for £3.50. Prices have crept up somewhat, but since the tables would still be filled if it were a good deal more expensive, you could say there is evidence of commendable restraint. Evidence of careful thought being given to what it is people want is everywhere; for those who want just a mouthful of sweetness after a meal but not dessert, there is the offer of Caprice chocolate truffles (2) or a plate of assorted cookies. Sunday brunch features bagels and cream cheese as well as kedgeree. The unreconstructed early Eighties black-and-chrome decor is becoming a period piece. At the time of writing there is talk of expansion.

£30

OPEN
EVERY DAY

HOURS
12.00–3.00PM
6.00PM–12.00AM

CREDIT CARDS
AMEX DELTA
DINER'S
MASTERCARD
SWITCH VISA

SERVICE
OPTIONAL

COVER CHARGE
£1.50

SUNDAY BRUNCH
12.00–3.30PM

FACILITIES
SEATS 70
WHEELCHAIR
ACCESS

**NEAREST TUBE
STATION**
GREEN PARK

MAP 3

A COMFORTING WINE LIST, serving both Le Caprice and The Ivy (q.v.), easy on the eye and on the pocket. There is perfect symmetry between the red and white selections in a tripartite division (France, Italy and Spain: Australia, New Zealand and California) and roughly half the 100 or so wines are under £20, many being offered by the glass or by the half-bottle. Just about everything is worth trying. Ten dessert wines from six different countries complete a very attractive package.

CARAFFINI

61-63 LOWER SLOANE STREET SW1   259 0235

'A Chelsea trattoria for grown-ups'

£26

OPEN
MON–SAT

HOURS
12.00–2.30PM
6.30–11.30PM

CREDIT CARDS
AMEX DELTA
DINER'S
MASTERCARD
SWITCH VISA

SERVICE
OPTIONAL

COVER CHARGE
£1

FACILITIES
SEATS 65
TABLES OUTSIDE
SEAT 16
WHEELCHAIR
ACCESS (ALSO
WC)

**NEAREST TUBE
STATION**
SLOANE SQUARE

MAP 2

Impervious as I am to the charms of Italian restaurants native to the Chelsea/Knightsbridge/South Kensington area whose names begin with S – Scalini, Sandrini, Sambuca, San Martini, San Lorenzo, Signor Sassi and Sale e Pepe are just some examples – I warm to Caraffini, opened in early 1995 on the site that was previously Gavvers and before that Le Gavroche (q.v.). Something of the gravitas of those incumbents seems to have impressed itself on the atmosphere and the cooking and prices are gentle, with several of the main courses under £7. Owner Paolo Caraffini, previously manager of Como Lario, knows how to work a room less egregiously than some of his compatriots, and dishes of the day provide liveliness and distraction in what could be termed a fairly formulaic menu. Two piatti del giorno which impressed were roasted quail wrapped in bacon and served with a grape sauce and fegato all'Ungherese, calf's liver sautéed with onions, mustard and paprika. The chef, who, oddly enough, is Spanish, seems less at home with pastas and risottos but can produce a frisky seafood salad. In general there is plenty for those who want to be sparing with their calories, for example chargrilled vegetables; fresh salmon carpaccio with arugula and mâche; brochette of fish with fresh mint and various grilled fish. The decor is subdued with a wooden strip floor giving rise to fewer decibels than would the traditional tiled variety. Some progress in the genre has definitely been made: there is, of course, a cover charge and customers are apt to set light to Amaretti wrappings to watch them float skywards but the wine list has some interesting Italian bottles and I don't recall being menaced with a pepper mill.

CAVIAR HOUSE – LA BRASSERIE

161 PICCADILLY W1   409 0445

'The place for a little eggy something on toast'

The Swiss company Caviar House Holdings, who with their seafood bars provide a touch of class at Heathrow and Gatwick, have opened the first UK restaurant outlet beside their Piccadilly shop. Given the price-induced elitist nature of the product and the decor which suggests a very thinly disguised bank, the atmosphere in the dining room is surprisingly relaxed and laid back. Waiters are kitted out in jeans and there seems no pressure to order more than one course if that is all you want. If it takes the form of caviar – served with blinis and boiled potatoes – prices, which have risen since last year, start at £16 for 30g of Sevruga or pressed caviar and climb to £216 for 125g of Beluga. Caviar House specials include fillet of seabass with tagliolini sprinkled with caviar; whole lobster dressed with a black truffle vinaigrette; Balik smoked salmon trilogy with Sevruga caviar. Something luxurious – perhaps just a slab of terrine of foie gras – seems the appropriate ordering response here, but there is the opportunity for the truly blasé to select, say, Caesar salad followed by rabbit casserole. The Italian chef is a dab hand at pasta, as you will discover if you start a meal with the spinach ricotta ravioli with sage butter and pine kernels. Desserts are simple and rich, probably the best way to be if you decide to dine out on caviar. The mark-up on wines is not grabby.

£36

OPEN
MON–SAT

HOURS
12.00–3.00PM
6.45–11.00PM

CREDIT CARDS
AMEX DINER'S
MASTERCARD
SWITCH VISA

SERVICE
OPTIONAL

**SET-PRICE
LUNCH & DINNER**
£19.50

FACILITIES
SEATS 38
PRIVATE ROOM
SEATS 10
WHEELCHAIR
ACCESS

**NEAREST TUBE
STATION**
GREEN PARK

MAP 3

CHADA THAI

208–210 BATTERSEA PARK ROAD SW11   622 2209

'Yum is the appropriate word here'

An eye-catching modern front does not prepare customers for the stateliness of the dining room, which has substantial furniture and starched tablecloths. The husband and wife who own Chada Thai remove any impression of stuffiness with their friendly attention. It would be foolish to miss the opportunity to discuss with them how to narrow down a selection from a menu that runs to 122 savoury dishes, taking into account a special list for vegetarians. Their advice against over-ordering may be wise too, for this is exemplary Thai cooking which deserves savouring rather than wolfing down to satisfy

£26

OPEN
LUNCH SUN–FRI
DINNER EVERY DAY

HOURS
MON–FRI
12.00–2.30PM
SUN
12.00–3.00PM
MON–THURS
6.30–11.00PM
FRI–SAT
6.30–11.30PM
SUN
7.00–10.30PM

CREDIT CARDS
AMEX DELTA
DINER'S
MASTERCARD
SWITCH VISA

SERVICE
10%

COVER CHARGE
70P

SUNDAY BRUNCH

FACILITIES
SEATS 50
WHEELCHAIR
ACCESS

NEAREST TUBE
STATION
SLOANE SQUARE/
VAUXHALL

MAP 1

chilli cravings. Familiar recipes like Thai dumplings or green and red curries are meticulously prepared and justify slightly higher than average prices. Straying off the beaten track is likely to bring excitingly flavoured rewards such as a piquant salad of pork, prawns and transparent noodles (yum sai roong); steamed cod with a Thai interpretation of Chinese flavourings including preserved plum, celery and ginger; or – a real surprise – a dish of moistly baked rice, sausage and peas (khao obb mod din) threaded with fine filaments of fried chicken. Here at last is a rice pudding that would be welcome at dinner again and again.

THE CHESTERFIELD – BUTLERS

35 CHARLES STREET W1   491 2622

'Where the supplier likes to eat his beef'

£38

OPEN
LUNCH SUN–FRI
DINNER EVERY
DAY

HOURS
12.00–2.00PM
6.00–10.00PM
(6.00–9.30PM
SAT)

CREDIT CARDS
AMEX DELTA
DINER'S
MASTERCARD
SWITCH VISA

SERVICE
OPTIONAL

SET-PRICE
LUNCH
£10

SET-PRICE
DINNER
£20.50

FACILITIES
SEATS 60
PRIVATE ROOM
SEATS 2–90
WHEELCHAIR
ACCESS (ALSO
WC)

NEAREST TUBE
STATION
GREEN PARK

MAP 3

Good restaurants use good suppliers so I listen carefully when Kevin, master butcher at Allen's of Mount Street, tells me where they deliver and where he eats. The restaurant of The Chesterfield, a Mayfair hotel occupying a site originally the eighteenth-century house of the third Earl of Chesterfield, was a discovery thanks to Kevin. Decor in the dining room is traditional, but within that description comfortable and generous with space between tables. The menu is modern and cooked by a chap who knows what he is doing when he ventures abroad with techniques, ingredients and spicing. Prices are astonishingly reasonable. Dishes from a spring menu that gave a good deal of pleasure were Colchester crab cake; lobster consommé with smoked chicken wontons; salad of quail eggs, asparagus and foie gras dressed with truffle oil; oak-seared Scotch salmon on truffled mash and leeks braised with balsamic vinegar; and calf's liver 'saltimbocca' with polenta and honey-roast onions. Scotch fillet 'Rossini' was, as you might expect, a great piece of beef. Sticky toffee pudding, dark and brooding, came with excellent vanilla bean ice cream. The wine list has not been left out of this (successful) attempt to bring discreet hotel eating into competition with reckonable independent restaurants in both price and culinary ambition. Beside the chintz-upholstered dining room is a leafy conservatory where lunch is served. Dishes from the à la carte feature as does a daily-changing speciality served from the trolley.

CHEZ BRUCE

2 BELLEVUE ROAD SW17   0181-672 0114

'Not so common in Wandsworth'

There was a series in a Sunday paper colour supplement where people in professions were asked to nominate the best within their peer groups. Thus would emerge the plastic surgeons' plastic surgeon, the literary agents' literary agent and so forth. Bruce Poole, chef of Chez Bruce, would seem to be the chefs' chef or, anyway, the English chefs' chef. Enthusiastic reports of Poole's robust cooking style honed at Bibendum, The Square and, most recently, Chez Max have poured in from his mentors and contemporaries. Perhaps they are in awe of his degree in medieval history from Exeter University. More likely they admire his home-made charcuterie – apparently he even makes his own version of Parma ham – a selection of which, entitled somewhat pretentiously Grande Assiette de Charcuterie Chez Bruce, comprises one of the first courses. Producing a Wandsworth ham is, however, a canny move when the chef most famously associated with this restaurant site which borders the common is Marco Pierre White. But new decor, as whimsical in its rustic way as the beauty-parlour look of Harveys which it replaces, much lower prices and a move back to French provincial basics have rapidly established Chez Bruce as a lure in its own right. Dishes that typify the style are soupe garbure; pissaladière; deep-fried brains with sauce gribiche; navarin of lamb; tête de veau sauce ravigote; côte de boeuf frites, sauce Bearnaise; poached turbot au beurre blanc; tarte fine aux pommes; praline parfait; chocolate and almond pudding. Sometimes brushstrokes can be clumsy or edges left ragged but it is good-hearted cooking at a price that encourages forgiveness, and just occasionally it is brilliant. A Cruvinet machine allows the entire list of 65 wines to be offered by the glass as well as the bottle.

£28

OPEN
LUNCH SUN–FRI
DINNER MON–SAT

HOURS
12.00–2.00PM
7.00–10.30PM
(12.30–3.00PM
SUN)

CREDIT CARDS
AMEX DELTA
DINER'S
MASTERCARD
SWITCH VISA

SERVICE
OPTIONAL

**SET-PRICE
LUNCH**
£12 & £15
TUES–FRI
£18 SUN

**SET-PRICE
DINNER**
£18.50 & £22
MON–SAT

FACILITIES
SEATS 70
PRIVATE ROOM
SEATS 18
WHEELCHAIR
ACCESS

**NEAREST TUBE
STATION**
BALHAM

MAP 1

CHEZ GERARD

8 CHARLOTTE STREET   636 4975

'Go for steak and chips'

If for some weird reason you decided to take your vegetarian date to Chez Gerard, he or she could choose from a menu entitled 'Vegetarien' which includes coucous aux legumes and boudin de pommes de terre et oignons. Although the offer of

£28

OPEN
EVERY DAY

HOURS
12.00–3.00PM
6.00–11.30PM

CREDIT CARDS
AMEX DINER'S
MASTERCARD
SWITCH VISA

SERVICE
12½%

COVER CHARGE
£1

**SET-PRICE
DINNER**
£15

FACILITIES
SEATS 100
TABLES OUTSIDE
SEAT 30
PRIVATE ROOM
SEATS 24
WHEELCHAIR
ACCESS

**NEAREST TUBE
STATION**
GOODGE STREET/
TOTTENHAM
COURT ROAD

MAP 4

such dishes is correct in every way, it conspicuously misses the point about Chez Gerard, which is beefsteak – chateaubriand, filet, côte de boeuf and onglet – of high quality, grilled by someone who understands that actually quite tricky process. With the steak, you have a breadcrumb-filled tomato, pommes frites and sauce Bearnaise. Recent testing suggests that the sensible first course is the assembly of crudités called Salade Chez Gerard, although you could maintain strict ethnicity in another way and start with a dozen snails baked with garlic butter. The waiting staff recommend, and with good reason, the petit pot au chocolat for dessert; it is rich, dark and high in cocoa solids. My preference is for cheese – reasonably priced – at £3.95 and perhaps another bottle of red, temptingly displayed at the rear of the Charlotte Street premises. The design by Virgile and Stone stylishly and without recourse to cliché reinforces the French theme, making the apparent desire to please all of the people all of the time seem the corporate decision it presumably is – ownership is by a quite large and getting steadily larger group. More board decisions are a cover charge of £1 per person for bread, anchovy butter, olives and nuts and a recommended 12½% service charge. Also at 31 Dover Street W1 (499 8171) and 119 Chancery Lane WC2 (405 0290), but my fave is Charlotte Street.

CHEZ MAX

£32

OPEN
LUNCH TUES–FRI
DINNER TUES–SAT

HOURS
12.30–2.30PM
7.00–11.15PM

CREDIT CARDS
AMEX DELTA
DINER'S
MASTERCARD
SWITCH VISA

SERVICE
OPTIONAL

**SET-PRICE
LUNCH**
£13.50, £15.50 &
£17.50

**SET-PRICE
DINNER**
£25.50

168 IFIELD ROAD SW10   835 0874

'Lyons corner house'

Take twins, in this case Max and Marc Renzland, with two restaurants, Chez Max and Le Petit Max (q.v.) and you would think with a little fast footwork they could convince you that they are always on hand. But sometimes the food betrays them, as it did one lunchtime at Chez Max when everything about the cooking was more than a little imprecise and it was made very clear to me by a waitress who appeared towards the end of the meal that the fault was entirely mine, since anyone with a bit more restaurant savvy would know not to come at such a quiet time. Also, in the unforgiving light of day, these Ifield Road premises can look and feel like a West London wine bar. There have been much better reports of evening meals when one or other twin is in situ, the light is softer and the framed menus from famed, mostly French, restaurants serve to inspire and set you wondering about French menu style devices:

the crinkle-edge paper effect, the Germanic olde-worlde typefaces, the usually completely irrelevant brown photographs of castles with crenellations. French cuisine bourgeoise, as perfected in Lyons, which the twins have espoused since their Richmond days, remains the backbone of the menu. Some dishes much liked have been terrine maison composed of duck, pork and foie gras studded with pistachios; English farmhouse chicken with a light peppercorn sauce, spinach and puréed potatoes; beautifully fried calf's liver with shallots and a potent red wine jus; pot au feu of guinea fowl which included bone marrow and petit salé; petit pot au chocolat riche; and poached peaches with mint granita, deemed an inspired dessert. Done well, as all this was, it is eminently satisfying; Frenchness comme il faut. The wine list has lengthened and improved since early days. You are still welcome to bring your own for a corkage charge of £7.50 a bottle, and even, it has been reported, a half-bottle. Note, there has been talk of a move to the West End.

THIRTY OR SO bottles, mainly French, and every one a winner, from the inky Collioure of Domaines des Paulilles to the elegant Billecart-Salmon 1982. Nothing is more than double its retail counterpart, which these days means good value, and the varied digestifs are also first class. Chez Max buy from Oddbins, whose dynamic range changes more frequently than most, so the current line-up may not last for long. But, so long as they keep this arrangement, substitutions should prove equally appealing.

FACILITIES
SEATS 75
TABLES OUTSIDE
SEAT 21
PRIVATE ROOM
SEATS 20

NEAREST TUBE
STATION
EARLS COURT

MAP 2

CHEZ MOI

1 ADDISON AVENUE W11   603 8267

'Nearly 30 years of t.l.c.'

True restaurant lovers – those who go to restaurants for all the right reasons – appreciate Chez Moi. Under the same ownership since it was started 1967 by chef Richard Walton and front-of-house Colin Smith it is a smoothly run, utterly professional operation but one that never loses a sense of invention or overlooks the pleasure inherent in hospitality. The surroundings are almost a cliché in restaurant romanticism. Raspberry-pink-striped walls, green banquettes, tables with

£32

OPEN
LUNCH MON–FRI
DINNER MON–SAT

HOURS
12.30–2.00PM
7.00–11.00PM

CREDIT CARDS
AMEX DINER'S
MASTERCARD VISA

SERVICE
OPTIONAL

SET-PRICE LUNCH
£14

FACILITIES
SEATS 45
WHEELCHAIR
ACCESS

NEAREST TUBE STATION
HOLLAND PARK

MAP 1

yellow cloths and little table lamps plus formally attired staff set you up for an old-fashioned experience, but the menu and the cooking deliver anything but. Walton keeps alive that fire of culinary discovery which writers and chefs such as Elizabeth David and Robert Carrier (for whom Walton and Smith once worked) ignited. Chez Moi has many regulars and has fostered many love affairs. The evening menu changes slowly but there is always something new to discover. At a recent visit it was a salad of spinach leaves topped with sautéed marinated pigeon breast with a hoi sin dressing followed by couscous d'agneau, where the casseroled lamb was the correct, quite humble cut, the grain a wonderful, separately served mound studded with dried fruit and nuts and the harissa (hot sauce) uncompromisingly fierce. The only criticism was too many peppers – a not very North African vegetable – in the stew. An old favourite enjoyed was coquilles St Jacques minute et sa ballotine Japonaise. Minute refers to cooking time and certainly not the scallops, which were large and matched in size by the chef's interesting version of a futo-maki roll using marinated salmon and avocado and not forgetting the wasabi (Japanese horseradish), an element that can give your glass of wine a kick in the teeth. Tournedos sauce Bearnaise is a fabulously thick chunk of meat perfectly, smokily grilled. Rack of lamb cooked either with mustard and Provençal breadcrumbs or with rosemary is a dish for which the restaurant is justly famous. The great-value set-price lunch is a beguiling mix of experimentation, for example, prawn and chicken dosa, and the classics time forgot, for example, chicken kromeski and beef fillet Diane. Enterprising canapés are included at lunch as well as at dinner and chocolates come with coffee. The wine list is sound and not over-priced.

CHIAROSCURO

24 COPTIC STREET WC1   636 2731

'Shades of light and dark, in pictures and in the owners'

£29

OPEN
EVERY DAY

HOURS
12.00–3.30PM
6.00–12.00PM

CREDIT CARDS
AMEX DELTA
DINER'S
MASTERCARD
SWITCH VISA

SERVICE
OPTIONAL

A terraced town house in Bloomsbury has been converted by Sally and Carl James into an enterprising modern restaurant on three floors, the second floor being dedicated to private parties. Of the other two levels the first-floor dining room of classic design and pleasing proportion is vastly preferable to the awkward, narrow ground floor decorated with a blue modern artwork, a Renaissance-style painting and the quite funny detail of a small picture window which frames the face of anyone studying the menu posted outside. There are menus for various mealtimes – Sunday brunch, lunch, pre-theatre, dinner, late supper – all offering up-to-the-minute, globe-trotting dishes, fizzing with bright ideas. At a test lunch it was noticed that a sort of mix and match approach to garnishes and accoutrements could backfire: if, for example, you started with the smoked haddock risotto – a delicious, superior kedgeree – topped with a deconstructed salsa verde and followed it with the chicken breast also topped with the same capery mixture you might suffer gustatory déjà vu. The presence of almost ubiquitous roasted tomatoes posed the same problem. However, some of the cooking is spot-on: a dolcelatte soufflé served with sautéed wild mushrooms, yogurt aïoli and, oh, a roasted tomato; Thai beef, lemongrass and noodle salad; game pie with green peppercorn jus; orange caramel with toffee clementine brioche. The antipasto, which can be ordered small or large, is a well-considered, well-differentiated assembly. Desserts finish the meal with a bang, not a whimper. Sally James was previously head chef at Café des Arts in Hampstead. She and her husband seem to be settling into this new area, attracting regulars among local businesspeople and late-night eaters (the supper at £10 for two courses with a choice of five dishes in each course is a bargain; think artichoke porcini risotto followed by gravadlax and rösti) and pleasing families at Sunday brunch by whole-heartedly welcoming children – the customers of the future.

SET-PRICE LUNCH
£14

SET-PRICE DINNER
£10 & £14
(SUPPER)

SUNDAY BRUNCH

FACILITIES
SEATS 70
TABLES OUTSIDE
SEAT 12
PRIVATE ROOM
SEATS 16
WHEELCHAIR
ACCESS

NEAREST TUBE STATION
TOTTENHAM
COURT ROAD/
HOLBORN

MAP 4

CHINA CITY

WHITE BEAR YARD 25A LISLE STREET WC2   734 3388

'Feeding the five hundred'

Although we are supposed to gasp with admiration when restaurants the size of Quaglino's (q.v.) and Belgo Centraal (q.v.) manage to function, the Chinese can feed the 500 – the number of seats at China City – without fanfare or fuss. Perhaps not serving the best dim sum nor the best Cantonese specialties in Chinatown, this three-storey restaurant at the back of White Bear Yard in which a fountain dribbles in a desultory way nevertheless has, in my view, the most agreeable premises in the Gerard Street/Wardour Street/Lisle Street axis. The look is unforced, resembling a Chinese interpretation of the word brasserie, and brasserie

£20

OPEN
EVERY DAY

HOURS
12.00–11.45PM

CREDIT CARDS
AMEX
MASTERCARD
SWITCH VISA

SERVICE
10%

SET-PRICE
LUNCH & DINNER
£8

FACILITIES
SEATS 500
PRIVATE ROOM
SEATS 30
WHEELCHAIR
ACCESS

NEAREST TUBE
STATION
LEICESTER
SQUARE/
PICCADILLY
CIRCUS

MAP 5

hours are kept – open daily from noon to 11.45pm. Staff are courteous and seem to have the notion of customers' enjoyment at the forefront of their minds. They will give two people a big table if a big table is available. The daytime dim sum list offered is long and nearly all of the items are translated into English. In the evenings some relatively interesting dishes can be found on the fairly banal list. However, if Chinese banal is what you like, the set menus, as always, provide it. Try eel fried in batter with chilli; king prawns in scrambled egg (more like an omelette); crispy belly pork; wide ho-fun noodles with beef and a hot-pot, preferably crab with glass noodles. Beer or tea is the best bet to drink, but if you want wine it is available.

CHINON

23 RICHMOND WAY W4   602 5968

'Doing his own thing'

£30

OPEN
MON–SAT

HOURS
12.30–2.00PM
6.30–10.30PM

CREDIT CARDS
AMEX DELTA
MASTERCARD
SWITCH VISA

SERVICE
OPTIONAL

FACILITIES
SEATS 50
TABLES OUTSIDE
SEAT 6
WHEELCHAIR
ACCESS

NEAREST TUBE
STATION
OLYMPIA/
SHEPHERD'S
BUSH

MAP 1

As increasing numbers of restaurants present modern menus written as if by-laws have been passed insisting that every licensed establishment must offer bruschetta, crostini, Caesar salad, grilled tuna, chicken corn-fed and duck confit, it is a relief to return to Jonathan Hayes' singular, complex, diverting cooking at this eccentrically run restaurant near Shepherd's Bush. You get the feeling that, as a child, Hayes must have enjoyed more than most the game of pass the parcel. Some first courses and many of the accompaniments to the main courses take the form of one lot of ingredients wrapped in another, as in a creamy stew of vegetables, or mashed potato contained in neatly folded leaves – dark green Savoy cabbage or light green Chinese leaf. This sort of playfulness only works if flavours are sound and true. They are. Ingredients are well-sourced, as is apparent in relatively simple assemblies such as the first-course salad of various leaves and shoots with a hazelnut oil dressing and what the menu calls shellfish manier (meunière?) which is served as a wicker steamer basket of mussels, prawns, clams and brown shrimp over a creamy fish soup/sauce. Ideas abound: a granita of spices spooned into a Charente melon half; leeks fried to a chewy sweetness contrasting with the flavours of smoked salmon and caviar as accompaniments to fillet of turbot; a Middle Eastern aubergine caviar (moutabal) served with new season's rack of lamb and fondant potatoes; orangewater used to scent a prune tart served with vanilla cream and rhubarb sorbet. Bread is excellent and good petits fours can be ordered with coffee. The bar and restaurant are now both in the sunny yellow-painted long narrow ground-floor room which has a glass wall at the back giving onto a jungly garden. Jazz tapes are well chosen. The name of the restaurant is not a particular inspiration for the wine list – for Loire wines go to RSJ (q.v.) – but there is an interesting, wide selection, with prices, as they say, to suit all pockets. My tip for dealing with the slightly bizarre service is unremitting cheerfulness on the part of you, the customer.

THE CHISWICK

131 CHISWICK HIGH ROAD   0181-994 6887

'Or as they say in the movies, Brackenbury II'

The Chiswick is son of The Brackenbury (q.v.), the highly esteemed restaurant owned by the Robinsons, Adam and Kate. The offspring was up to speed soon after opening with clever buying and cooking producing flavours of great clarity (chip off the old block) but ideas all of its own. Nettle soup; a risotto with chorizo; bream with lentils; squid with tomato; hand-cut ink pasta; plus his pot au chocolat and lychee and blood orange sorbets are all works of which the chef Ian Bates (ex-Bibendum, q.v.) can be proud, though you may not find them repeated because, like his boss, he changes the menu as often as the produce merits. The large lilac-coloured room does not have the character of the parent place; it seems to be either too noisy or too quiet. Chiswick has not quite woken up to the quality and value, both in food and in the intelligently eclectic selection of wines, it now has on its doorstep.

£25

OPEN
LUNCH SUN–FRI
DINNER MON–SAT

HOURS
12.30–2.45PM
7.00–11.30PM

CREDIT CARDS
AMEX DELTA
MASTERCARD
SWITCH VISA

SERVICE
OPTIONAL

SET-PRICE LUNCH
£8.50

FACILITIES
SEATS 70
TABLES OUTSIDE
SEAT 20
WHEELCHAIR
ACCESS (ALSO
WC)

NEAREST TUBE STATION
TURNHAM GREEN

CHRISTOPHER'S AMERICAN GRILL

18 WELLINGTON STREET WC2   240 4222

'UnAmerican activities'

In the entrance hall to this former nineteenth-century Covent Garden casino with its twirling stone staircase hang two posters for an anti-Thatcher book by Lord (Ian) Gilmour, the former cabinet minister; but the people mobilized by his son Christopher's enterprise look to be predominantly the late thirtysomethings who did well from Thatcherism. The chaps

£36

OPEN
LUNCH EVERY DAY
DINNER MON–SAT

HOURS
RESTAURANT
12.00–2.30PM
6.00–11.45PM
CAFÉ
11.30AM–11.00PM

CREDIT CARDS
AMEX DELTA
DINER'S
MASTERCARD
SWITCH VISA

SERVICE
12½%

**SET-PRICE
DINNER**
£15
(6.00–7.00PM)

SUNDAY BRUNCH

FACILITIES
SEATS 120
RESTAURANT
45 CAFÉ
PRIVATE ROOM
SEATS 32

**NEAREST TUBE
STATION**
COVENT GARDEN

MAP 4

tend towards short haircuts, garish ties and Benson & Hedges, the women black suits, blonde hair and important jewellery. The restaurant also attracts politicians from both sides of the House, media moguls, movie stars and, it must be noted, the Queen Mother, who took one of her bi-annual lunches out here. The restaurant is a success, into which you must read noisiness, a problem aggravated by the acoustics of the structure, hard surfaces and the sort of bad lighting that aggravates any problem. The menu sets out to be American, but unless you seize the day and order 8oz burger with fries or the 14oz New York strip steak or climb straight into the ring with a 3lb Maine lobster the object is not necessarily achieved. Some other dishes on the menu which seem more Chelsea than Chicago, for example, grilled goat's cheese with Provençal vegetables and salmon fish cakes with basil cream, have been only just all right. Clam chowder has tasted heavily of cream, which is not right at all. Steak tartare, a test of meat quality and the skill of whoever adds the flavourings, was a particular disappointment: a meat baseball of the wrong texture which tasted of nothing. Christopher's fries were (c.f. Thatcher's opinions of his father's politics) soggy. Separately priced vegetables such as creamed spinach, tobacco onions, celeriac mash and red cabbage with apples are good but add £2.50 each (plus 12½% service) to already stiff main-course prices. Things look up in the dessert course, where pecan pie and a date and pine nut pudding with pistachio sauce have come in for praise. For a cheaper and arguably more American meal, try the ground-floor café, also popular with families for Sunday brunch. American wine-making skills are, correctly, on offer.

CHUTNEY MARY

535 KING'S ROAD SW10   351 3113

'Time for the theming to stop'

£30

OPEN
EVERY DAY

HOURS
MON–SAT
12.30–2.30PM
7.00–11.30PM
SUN
12.30–3.00PM
7.00–10.30PM

CREDIT CARDS
AMEX DINER'S
MASTERCARD
SWITCH VISA

SERVICE
OPTIONAL

Now that the Anglo-Indian concept of Chutney Mary has been established it is perhaps time to ease up on the heavy-handedness in conveying the message and let the fact that there are some good chefs in the kitchen brought directly from India being encouraged to try new ideas be the USP (advertising jargon for unique selling point). Travellers to India will know from the grand hotel restaurants that large, colourfully decorated menus with whimsical pictures and fancy typefaces are just par for the course, but here in London they smack of restaurant chains and themed food. In puzzling over phrases like Dégustation of Mary's Specialities – in other words a thali – you might be sidetracked from realizing how truly excellent is, say, the highly spiced lamb korma served with utthapam, a pancake of lentil and rice flour resembling a thin crumpet, or how savvy is the idea of wrapping a dosa, a huge, thin, crisp pancake, around spiced chicken as a main course to be served with sambhar, a soupy lentil and vegetable curry, and coconut chutney. In fact, historical Anglo-Indian dishes are a very small part of the menu. Making kedgeree with scallops, cooking artichoke hearts and red peppers in the tandoor, topping a naan with smoked salmon, serving tandoori lamb chops on wilted greens is not what was happening during the Raj, but the product of someone thinking about how Indian culinary traditions can be adapted in a modern, healthy way. Having said that, I'm not so sure about the smoked salmon on naan. The dishes that evolved in the Christian communities in India – Goan green chicken curry, lamb lonvas, Mangalore prawn curry – are well worth trying, as are the side dishes of Sindhi lentils, Keralan spicy cashews and crisply fried okra. Among your first course include calamari chilli fry. Service is variable, sometimes hopeless, and markedly better when you are known to the staff. And when that is the case you are more likely to be given a table in the (preferable) conservatory.

COVER CHARGE
£1.50

SET-PRICE
LUNCH & DINNER
£10

FACILITIES
SEATS 110
PRIVATE ROOM
SEATS 60
WHEELCHAIR
ACCESS

NEAREST TUBE
STATION
FULHAM
BROADWAY

MAP 2

CHUTNEYS

124 DRUMMOND STREET NW1   388 0604

'It's the poori what gets the praise'

There is something about Drummond Street intriguingly out of step with the rest of London. With its many Indian restaurants punctuated by an assortment of eccentric shops selling army surplus gear, native American feathered apparel, outmoded cocktail dresses and mystic candles, it is as if the Sixties and Seventies were still waiting to happen. Chutneys, however, is up to date in appearance with a bold Habitat-style colour scheme of terracotta, canteloupe and mid-blue, complemented by colour-coordinated abstract paintings and overwrought iron light fittings. The staff, by comparison, seem rather low-key. Chutneys would be a good place to eat alone reading a book; you aren't going to be interrupted by people asking if everything is all right. The vegetarian menu has, in the words of one admirer, a noble austerity. Non-believers in

£16

OPEN
EVERY DAY

HOURS
MON–SAT
12.00–2.30PM
6.00–11.30PM
SUN
12.00–10.30PM

CREDIT CARDS
DELTA
MASTERCARD
SWITCH VISA

SERVICE
10% MON–SAT
EVENINGS

SET-PRICE
LUNCH
£3.95

SET-PRICE
DINNER
£5.95

FACILITIES
SEATS 120
PRIVATE ROOM
SEATS 60

NEAREST TUBE
STATION
EUSTON/EUSTON
SQUARE/WARREN
STREET

MAP 3

the meatless way are quickly won over by the tasty simplicity of the Western Indian snacks such as ragara pattice, potato patties with chick peas; the pooris, either crisp spheres or fan shapes garnished with sweet/sour and soft/crisp juxtapositions; the Southern Indian fermented batter dosas, dramatically large and friable, filled with vegetables and smoothed with coconut chutney; and the curries. Tarka dal flavoured with mustard seeds, fenugreek, garlic and fried onion is excellent, as is brinjal bhajee, aubergine beautifully textured and subtly spiced. The lunch-time buffet, self-styled on the menu as 'famous', is famously cheap: eat as much as you like from a selection of 12 dishes for £3.95.

CIBO

3 RUSSELL GARDENS W14   371 6271/2085

'A new-wave Italian prone to napkin waving'

£30

OPEN
LUNCH SUN–FRI
DINNER MON–SAT

HOURS
12.00–2.30PM
(12.30–3.30PM
SUN)
7.00–11.00PM
(7.00–11.30PM
SAT)

CREDIT CARDS
AMEX DINER'S
MASTERCARD
SWITCH VISA

SERVICE
12½% PARTIES OF
5 OR MORE

SET-PRICE
LUNCH
£12.50

FACILITIES
SEATS 50
TABLES OUTSIDE
SEAT 5
PRIVATE ROOM
SEATS 12–16
WHEELCHAIR
ACCESS

NEAREST TUBE
STATION
OLYMPIA/
SHEPHERD'S
BUSH

MAP 1

Since Gino Taddei relinquished the ownership of L'Altro to concentrate on his first restaurant, Cibo (opened in 1989 on the new wave of Italian cooking), culinary standards seem to have stabilized at a higher level. The chef's love affair with melted cheese has, mercifully, cooled down, although not quite petered out. The strengths of the kitchen remain interesting pasta assemblies, for example, ravioli of chestnut flour pasta filled with venison in a wild mushroom sauce, nettle-filled tortelli in a walnut sauce, spaghetti with bottarga (dried tuna roe) and wild rocket, and the reasonably priced, generously composed fish dishes. A test lunch chosen from the set-price menu at £12.50 for two courses delivered a dish of open ravioli with whole prawns and celery (substituted for the asparagus in the title) with an amount of crushed garlic and ginger that rendered the dish almost Chinese in feel, followed by beautifully cooked, flavourful roasted quails served with artichokes and polenta. Choice from the carte was squid grilled with chilli served with a pile of undressed rocket preceding a large, heaped plate of various precisely cooked fish and shellfish in a herb and tomato sauce. Colourful pottery plates hammer home the take on joie de vivre expressed by the splatter paintings of Martin Jones and the lubricious bas-reliefs by Frank Eidlitz hung on the custard-coloured walls. The address on the outer edge of Holland Park and Notting Hill attracts music biz types and a crowd of regulars. Sightings have been made of Bryan Ferry, Harold Pinter, John Cleese and, more than once, Michael

Winner. Late last orders for lunch and dinner, plus staff sometimes more notable for looks than efficiency, contribute to an agreeably languid atmosphere – as can the comprehensive list of Italian wines, some occasionally maddeningly unavailable.

CLARKE'S

124 KENSINGTON CHURCH STREET W8   221 9225

'Thou need not covet thy neighbour's evening meal'

I n the decade that Sally Clarke has been running her epony-mous restaurant (est. 1985) changes have taken place. Expansion next door into a bigger basement with an open-plan kitchen was followed by the creation of a shop on the ground floor selling baked goods, preserves, oils, wines, coffees, chocolates; the details of a meal to which Clarke attends so assiduously and successfully. What has not changed is the original concept: a small choice at lunch time and no choice in the four-course set-price (£37) evening meal. Sitting down to dinner at Clarke's you might feel a certain relief at not having to scrutinize a menu and make up your mind what you want but the solace only lasts as long as the food delights. If the main ingredient of the main course is dull – chargrilled guinea fowl breast is an example that springs to mind – then there is no place for the meal, as it were, to hide. You cannot covet your companion's luckier choice or, more charitably, take vicarious pleasure, both sensations usually part of the pleasure of eating out in restaurants. However, Clarke's Californian-inspired food, if not quite the revelation in style it once was, continues to delight many. It is perforce fundamentally conservative food – it would be marketing madness to try to oblige the whole room to eat, say, calf's sweetbreads or stuffed pig's trotters or even crayfish – so the strength is in the accoutrements, such as carefully chosen vegetables, herbs, leaves, berries, seeds, flavoured oils and so forth plus the healthy, delicate balance of the courses. Dessert for which you will find you 'have room' even after cheese (two pre-cut pieces) is often a particularly enticing, delectable confection. The wine list is also a significant lure. Wine writers and others in the trade are often to be found eating here along with the well heeled, well dressed of Kensington. If, like me, you have sometimes fantasized about producing a bill at the end of a dinner party, you could, in a sense, act that out here. Service in the attractive rooms decorated with modern art is well schooled. Miss Clarke's academy is a tight ship.

£40

OPEN
MON–FRI

HOURS
12.30–2.00PM
7.00–10.00PM

CREDIT CARDS
MASTERCARD
SWITCH VISA

SERVICE
INCLUDED

**SET-PRICE
LUNCH**
£22

**SET-PRICE
DINNER**
£37

FACILITIES
SEATS 90
WHEELCHAIR
ACCESS

**NEAREST TUBE
STATION**
NOTTING HILL
GATE

MAP 1

AN ENGAGINGLY different wine list. There is nothing from the Antipodes and virtually nothing from Bordeaux – Cabernet Sauvignon seems to be grape non grata here. Instead, California's more adventurous wineries are showcased. The late Geoffrey Roberts, whose private cellar has been used to swell the listings, would have approved. There's a strong hand of sweeties as well. Bonny Doon provides at least one attractive bottle for each course (try especially the Orange Muscat Vin de Glacière) as well as some unusual eaux de vie (Nectarine, Cherry, Poire and Prunus).

COAST

26B ALBEMARLE STREET   495 5999

'California dreaming'

O liver Peyton, the owner of The Atlantic Bar and Grill (q.v.), has turned his attention to the Pacific in the sense that the food at his second enterprise, Coast, is inspired by the cooking of the West coast of America. Chef Stephen Terry, previously working at The Canteen and before that for Marco Pierre White at Harvey's, has spent time travelling researching the subject. The result is a menu maddening in its vocabulary of silly kitchen Franglais but diverting and tempting in its content. There are interesting juxtapositions of ingredients – ravioli of duck and sweet potatoes; salmon with a sauce of oysters with caviar – Eastern incursions – salad of lobster and Chinese radish with sweet and sour vinaigrette; soup noodle of honey-roasted duck, Thai spices and choi sum – Middle-Eastern influences – roasted rump of lamb with harissa, aubergine tart and couscous – all underpinned by a training in a classical kitchen which can deliver dishes such as a pressed terrine (called for some reason a vinaigrette) of chicken confit, roasted sweetbreads and grilled asparagus; sauté of scallops with lettuce hearts and a creamed vanilla and lemon dressing; pear croustillants with spices. It is one of the most interesting menus to hit the streets in 1995 and it remains to be seen whether Terry can sustain the pace and trim some of the rough edges that were still apparent just after the opening in July. The conversion of a Volvo showroom in Albemarle Street has been done with a lot of self-conscious design to not a particularly alluring effect, but at least the lighting is something that can be fixed.

£40

OPEN
EVERY DAY

HOURS
12.00–3.00PM
6.00–1.00PM

CREDIT CARDS
AMEX
MASTERCARD
SWITCH VISA

SERVICE
OPTIONAL

FACILITIES
SEATS 150
PRIVATE ROOM
SEATS 20
WHEELCHAIR
ACCESS

**NEAREST TUBE
STATION**
GREEN PARK

MAP 3

THE CONNAUGHT HOTEL

CARLOS PLACE W1   499 7070

'Reassuringly static'

In a tumultuous world, The Connaught is a dignified fixed point. The menu, produced by a system which looks one up from a John Bull printing kit, retains its idiosyncratic mix of classic French and English dishes often with arcane titles such as oysters 'Christian Dior' – the only acknowledgement of any link between fashion and food – and if it is Thursday lunchtime then it is still boiled silverside with dumplings. The only relatively recent ripple on the surface has been the introduction of set-price menus at £25 for lunch (both rooms) and £35 for dinner (Grill Room only). The same daily-changing à la carte menu (and kitchen) serves the Restaurant and the Grill Room, and thus the choice is not style of food but between sitting in the spacious, glossily panelled Restaurant run by a full regiment of waiters or in the smaller, more feminine green and gilt Grill Room with its seemingly hand-picked crack troop of staff. American visitors described by a guest as 'women in pastel colours, their chins held up by clothes-pegs, their hairstyles like spun sugar in various hues ranging from blonde, to silver-blonde, to silver-grey, to grey, paid for by men in blazers carrying platinum credit cards' seem to favour, or perhaps are gently directed to, the Restaurant. Since classic French cooking is now something of a rarity, it would be good to be able to encourage orders such as lobster bisque followed by pintadeau en salmi aux morilles et champignons à la crème, but just such a meal proved indigestibly alcoholic (the bisque) and over-creamy (the guineau fowl sauces) and unredeemed by its main-course accompaniments of soggy white rice mixed with wild rice (billed as wild rice) and ungainly ratatouille. Conversely, an order of asparagus vinaigrette followed by grilled lobster with a politely garlicky butter and some beautifully cooked green beans proved well nigh perfect. In season, game is almost invariably a sound choice, and since it is possible to eat without spending thousands of calories – perhaps with oeuf en gelée Stendhal followed by oxtail braisé bourgeoise – there are many enjoyable ways of getting the perks: garnishes such as pommes soufflées that few kitchens can any more produce; the superb, professional, yet approachable service; the stateliness of surroundings; the feeling that nothing much – except prices – has changed since the last war.

£50

OPEN
RESTAURANT
LUNCH AND
DINNER EVERY
DAY
GRILL ROOM
LUNCH MON–FRI
DINNER EVERY
DAY

HOURS
RESTAURANT
12.30–2.30PM
6.30–10.30PM
GRILL ROOM
12.30–2.30PM
6.00–10.45PM

CREDIT CARDS
AMEX DINER'S
MASTERCARD VISA

SERVICE
15%

SET-PRICE LUNCH
£25 (SUN £30)

SET-PRICE DINNER
£35 (GRILL ROOM ONLY)

FACILITIES
SEATS
75 RESTAURANT
35 GRILL ROOM
PRIVATE ROOMS
SEAT 12 & 22
WHEELCHAIR
ACCESS (ALSO
MEN'S WC)

NEAREST TUBE STATION
GREEN PARK

MAP 3

THE COW

'Son of Conran'

£25

OPEN
LUNCH SAT–SUN
DINNER TUES–SAT

HOURS
12.30–2.30PM
7.30–11.00PM

CREDIT CARDS
MASTERCARD VISA

SERVICE
OPTIONAL

**SET-PRICE
LUNCH & DINNER**
£16.50

SUNDAY BRUNCH

FACILITIES
SEATS 30

**NEAREST TUBE
STATION**
ROYAL OAK/
WESTBOURNE
PARK

MAP 1

Pubs serving enterprising food are mushrooming. Tom Conran's The Cow is fortunate in having a sweet and stylish little dining room on the first floor where customers may book tables – some are large ones which couples would have to share – and thus remove themselves from the crush downstairs, where oysters, other shellfish and one or two hot dishes can be ordered. The menu in the Dining Room is a fixed-price more or less set meal (with a vegetarian option) which changes every evening. (Apart from weekends The Cow Dining Room is open only for dinner.) The style of cooking is positioned somewhere between French provincial, as in oeufs en meurette or lapin aux artichauts, and what you might call either Italian or simply fashionable, as in zampone lenticce or risotto primavera or vignole, a dish of spring vegetables which, with agreeable candour, the menu describes as having been pinched from The River Café (q.v.) A frequent cry these days is that the younger generation grow up without the benefit of good home cooking. This signally did not apply to Tom Conran (son of Caroline and Terence) and is, on the whole, proved by the attractive menus of The Cow. However, there are moments when the sort of sloppiness you might forgive in a domestic setting has to be swallowed in a public one. There are two sittings for dinner at 7.30pm and 9.30pm. As you might imagine, Notting Hillbillies cannot be relied upon to clear the decks at the moment they should.

CUCINA

'The restaurant Hampstead has been waiting for'

£24

OPEN
EVERY DAY

HOURS
12.00–2.30PM
7.00–10.30PM
(7.00–11.00PM
SAT)

CREDIT CARDS
AMEX
MASTERCARD
SWITCH VISA

SERVICE
10% PARTIES OF
10 OR MORE

North-west London, an area with plenty of restaurants but few of any note, was grateful for the arrival of Cucina in South End Green in the early spring of 1995. It is the joint venture of manager Vernon Mascarenhas and chefs Andy Poole and Stephen Baker, all of whom have been associated with another neighbourhood restaurant, Sonny's (q.v.) in Barnes, part-owned by Vernon's sister Rebecca. The site, part of a parade of shops, has a rather dramatic drawback in that the majority of the street frontage is occupied by an estate agent's office, but efforts have been made with artworks and chairs of high-definition design to render the spacious interior interesting. The menus, complete with Eastern incursions, are thoroughly modern with quite a lot of, presumably deliberate, appeal to vegetarians. Typically seductive meatless dishes are sweetcorn and chick pea fritters with cucumber and mint crème fraîche; twice-baked roasted garlic, Parmesan and herb soufflé; wild mushroom stroganoff with toasted sun-dried tomato bread. The pull of the Orient is evident in the plate of Japanese hors d'oeuvres, which misses a trick or two such as wasabi with the sushi; an excellent glass noodle salad with thin slices of seared, marinated beef; Thai green vegetable curry with jasmine rice and the dish we keen Hampstead cooks have been copying from Simon Hopkinson's and Alastair Little's books, five-spice braised belly pork with bok choy. The kitchen's competence also stretches to the more prosaic, for example cullen skink, penne alla puttanesca, chargrilled rib of beef and frites for two and roasted cornfed chicken with grilled vegetables and polenta mash. Where you might spot a weakness is in the dessert course, where some confections lack the necessary element of lusciousness. However, British and Irish cheeses are well chosen. The wine list is savvy. The menus extend their appeal with one-course café lunches and Sunday brunch.

SET-PRICE DINNER
£11.95

SUNDAY BRUNCH

FACILITIES
SEATS 90
WHEELCHAIR ACCESS

NEAREST TUBE STATION
BELSIZE PARK

MAP 1

DAPHNE'S

112 DRAYCOTT AVENUE SW3   584 6883

'In danger of losing its laurels?'

Chefs have become such nomads these days that the restaurateur deserves at least a degree of sympathy. Last year Daphne's was not only fashionable and full, but, with Edward Baines in charge of the kitchen, was serving modern Italian food of the highest quality. Now he has gone and the owner informs this guide that he judges the food 'at least as good if not better'. That does not tally with complaints about tiny portions, risotto that has gone wrong and insignificant side salads that cost £2.50. Pasta and rice make up a large part of the menu and should merit proper attention. The fact that a proportion of the population of SW3 is on a permanent diet does not justify serving everyone short. Those ladies who like to get out but don't really lunch take the contrived main-course salads that mix the likes of goat's cheese, peppers, tomato, radicchio, olives and pine nuts: the alternative is fairly simple

£30

OPEN
EVERY DAY

HOURS
12.00–3.00PM
7.00PM–12.00AM

CREDIT CARDS
AMEX DELTA
DINER'S
MASTERCARD
SWITCH VISA

SERVICE
OPTIONAL

SUNDAY BRUNCH

FACILITIES
SEATS 110
TABLES OUTSIDE SEAT 40
WHEELCHAIR ACCESS

NEAREST TUBE STATION
SOUTH KENSINGTON

MAP 2

meat and fish dishes such as grilled swordfish or calf's liver in the Venetian style. A lovely light room in which garden plants and furniture actually work is to Daphne's advantage, but young Italian staff who cannot take down orders in English subtract from enjoyment. Democrats may also dislike the way the degree of attention varies with customers' perceived status.

DEL BUONGUSTAIO

283 PUTNEY BRIDGE ROAD SW15   0181-780 9361

'Overheard as 'Del Bong-you-know''

£30

OPEN
LUNCH SUN–FRI
DINNER
EVERY DAY

HOURS
12.00–3.00PM
6.30–11.30PM
SUN
12.30–3.30PM
6.30–10.30PM

CREDIT CARDS
AMEX
MASTERCARD
SWITCH VISA

SERVICE
10% GROUPS OF 6
OR MORE

COVER CHARGE
90P

**SET-PRICE
LUNCH**
£9.50

**SET-PRICE
DINNER**
£19.50

FACILITIES
SEATS 50
WHEELCHAIR
ACCESS

**NEAREST TUBE
STATION**
EAST
PUTNEY/PUTNEY
BRIDGE

MAP 1

Putney people press into the putty-coloured room in the evenings towards the end of the week, making what might be interpreted as a glorious buzz of conviviality, or as too great a crowd for easy conversation and competent service depending on the mood of the diner. It is noticeable that they order good wine from a list that mixes Italy with Australia, but are conservative in the food they choose. Undaunted, the kitchen makes a point of offering one or two unusual recipes from the Italian regions – a 'pudding' of broccoli, egg and Parmesan; goat stuffed in the style of Venezia-Guilian on the carte – plus a few extras added in handwriting. The pies or rice tortas; large plates of antipasti; various pasta and risotto dishes; the stewed or roast game and ice cream in exciting flavours can normally be relied upon. However, there can be some loss of precision when the kitchen is under pressure. Evenings early in the week or weekday lunches may be more likely to make a favourable first impression.

EVEN THOUGH it merely reflects the joint ownership of the place, the combination of Italian and Australian wines here at Del Buongustaio is a winner. Wolf Blass, Brian Croser and Charles Melton are dependable representatives of the Australian contingent, and are well matched by their Italian counterparts such as Mascarello, Anselmi and Bergaglio. The organization of the list works better than it reads (wines are grouped under romantic-sounding headings such as 'What good memories are made of'), and only really special wines break the £20 barrier. The dessert wines are all Italian, and include Bartoli's famous Bukkuram: if I say that it tastes like a Muscat Beaumes de Venise blended with an oloroso sherry you probably won't want to try it, but you should.

DELL'UGO

'A food-fashion-victim's Paradise'

There is a dizzying range of dishes on offer on all three floors of this pulsating Soho restaurant masterminded by Antony Worrall-Thompson (cooked by head chef Mark Emberton). The menu reads like the apotheosis of early Nineties dining: every happening ingredient, combination, technique and culinary style crops up somewhere, if not among the tapas and meze in the ground-floor bar and café then in the menu for the first- and second-floor restaurants. It is a gastronomic tower of babel with Italian, Arabic, Spanish, French, Greek and English some of the languages utilized. Not all are spoken grammatically or pronounced clearly: ricotta and spinach dumplings have been dry and powdery and the roast tomato in their sauce a contrivance not borne out in the flavour; chargrilled tuna marred by overcooking; chicken hash-cake a bit big on potato, a bit light on chicken but with good spinach, poached egg and Hollandaise as accompaniments. However, other assemblies have been praised: the country breads for their wholesomeness and partners of tapenade and anchoiade; pappardelle with pan-fried chicken livers, raisins and wilted greens for its generosity and mix of colour, texture and flavour; a garnish of chargrilled vegetables for their colourfulness and willingness to be swamped with olive oil; lemon tart for its smooth filling delivering a zesty punch. Inevitable pressure on the kitchen can lead to edges being blurred and impact muted and the meal being less thrilling to eat than to read. However, the price is right, the energy is appealing and, as one customer has remarked, the youngish, sometimes raucous clientele do not seem the sort to dwell on the finer points of gastronomy and are probably happy with what they get. A constant complaint is of inefficient, harrassed service, some of it also suffering from a less than perfect command of our mother tongue. The wine list changes according to the supplier.

£26

OPEN
MON–SAT

HOURS
11.00AM–12.15AM

CREDIT CARDS
AMEX DELTA
DINER'S
MASTERCARD
SWITCH VISA

SERVICE
OPTIONAL

FACILITIES
SEATS 180
TABLES OUTSIDE
SEAT 16
PRIVATE ROOM
SEATS 14

NEAREST TUBE STATION
LEICESTER
SQUARE/
TOTTENHAM
COURT ROAD

MAP 5

THE DORCHESTER HOTEL

£45 (GRILL)
£35 (BAR)

OPEN
EVERY DAY

HOURS
BAR
11.00AM–12.00AM
GRILL ROOM
MON–SAT
12.30–2.30PM
6.00–11.00PM
SUN
12.30–2.30PM
7.00–10.30PM

CREDIT CARDS
AMEX DINER'S
MASTERCARD
SWITCH VISA

SERVICE
OPTIONAL

SET-PRICE
LUNCH
£24.50 (GRILL
ROOM)

SET-PRICE
DINNER
£32 (GRILL ROOM)

FACILITIES
SEATS
70 (BAR)
81 (GRILL ROOM)
WHEELCHAIR
ACCESS (ALSO
WC)

NEAREST TUBE
STATION
HYDE PARK
CORNER/GREEN
PARK/MARBLE
ARCH

MAP 3

PARK LANE W1   629 8888

'A hotel with much to offer'

A source of British cooking which doesn't always leap first to mind is **The Dorchester Grill**, a restaurant decorated illogically enough in Spanish baronial style, which has changed little since the hotel opened in 1931. In scarlet splendour you sit at widely spaced tables, the preferable ones having sofa seating backed against the walls. There, as if in some magnificent supermarket in Brigadoon, ornate silver trolleys are pushed to and fro carrying roasts, smoked salmon, salads, cheeses and also an impressive selection of breads. As at any grand hotel, prices are high but here are fully inclusive (card slips closed) and also main courses come fully garnished. Some of the less expensive dishes in the first course such as Morecambe Bay potted shrimps and cock-a-leekie soup instil a patriotic glow. The shrimps are not embalmed in waxy butter but are succulent and full of flavour. At lunch time there are specialities according to the day of the week: boiled silverside and caraway dumplings on Mondays, roast saddle of lamb on Tuesdays, steak and kidney pudding on Wednesdays and so forth. Some of these dishes appear on the à la carte where roast Angus beef with Yorkshire pudding and roast potatoes also beckons. There are good fish dishes and, true to the restaurant's name, also straightforward grills. The dessert trolley is picturesque, but the most fitting finale is crêpes Suzette or peppered peaches flamed at the table. The service is formally attired but friendly and interested.

Hotel bars have a louche charm of their own and **The Dorchester Bar** with its mirrored ceiling, Delft tiles and mustard-yellow bucket chairs is no exception. However, here you do not have to content yourself with cashew nuts or crisps, there is an interesting Italian menu prepared by Paolo Sari who comes from Treviso in the Veneto with, at lunchtime, a display of antipasti that serves as an imaginative buffet (at £13 per person inclusive). Sari's pasta assemblies are noteable: for example, cannette al pesto di Levante, fresh spinach pasta with pesto, French beans and new potatoes; raviolone con asparagi e crema di porcini, open ravioli with asparagus and a porcini sauce; tagliatelle di grano saraceno al cavaiale Beluga, buckwheat noodles with Beluga caviar. These dishes make an ideal one-course meal with which you can try glasses of Italian wine from the well-chosen range nearly all offered by the glass.

There are also fish and meat main courses, and desserts. In the evenings, when the jazz trio plays, you can have the quite beguiling out-of-body experience of being a tourist in your own city.

A COMFORTABLY SIZED and clearly presented wine list, with reassuring rather than exciting names throughout. Of course, one expects drinking at the Dorchester to be a wallet-thinning experience, but there has been genuine effort to provide choice under £25, and the dozen cheapish 'sommelier's selection' wines form a sensible, painless introduction to the unreachable grandeur beyond. Australia receives a mean allocation which in no way reflects modern tastes, while a trio of rarely seen Swiss wines is a reminder of a famous ex-chef. The maturity of the clarets is not matched in Burgundy, which is bereft of reds from the great 1985 vintage, and of whites from the correspondingly great 1986.

LA DORDOGNE

5 DEVONSHIRE ROAD W4   0181-747 1836

*'Forget the Channel tunnel, take
the tube to Turnham Green'*

Just off Chiswick High Road, this very French, French restaurant is situated in one of those streets that has, in the past few years, developed a character all its own – within yards of the restaurant you can buy a live parrot, a second-hand typewriter, a haunch of venison, a hand-thrown tea pot, a fresh lobster, a set of carpet bowls, or a trip to a little-known part of Latin America. And you can get your palm read and your clothes made to measure. La Dordogne has an enclosed pavement area for meals on a sunny day, but, once within, with the pink curtains drawn, walls of British Racing Green, darkly polished woodwork and staff standing sentry, discreet but ever watchful, it is easy to forget the time of day or the city outside. The menu is un-deconstructed French with the fish section – Nos Poissons – embellished with the offer of oysters and lobsters. You might start with foie gras de la maison and the 'recommended' glass of sweet Jurançon – interesting fact, French royalty swore by this wine and invariably used it to baptise their infants – or terrine of vegetables with tomato coulis, cunningly constructed and glamorous to look at, or salade Dordogne featuring both cured and cooked duck breast.

£30

OPEN
LUNCH MON–FRI
DINNER EVERY
DAY

HOURS
12.00–2.30PM
7.00–11.00PM

CREDIT CARDS
AMEX DINER'S
MASTERCARD
SWITCH VISA

SERVICE
10%

COVER CHARGE
£1

FACILITIES
SEATS 80
TABLES OUTSIDE
SEAT 20
PRIVATE ROOMS
SEAT 20 & 30
WHEELCHAIR
ACCESS (ALSO
WC)

**NEAREST TUBE
STATION**
TURNHAM GREEN

Duck breast as a main course is upstaged by its raspberry sauce; sea bass with crab sauce has been described as excellent. Desserts come in for great praise, particularly the hand-crafted, French apple tart with a vanilla-flavoured pastry the colour of toasted parchment served with a large blob of home-made ice cream. There is an Assiette Gourmande for dessert ditherers. The wine list is long and, naturally, French. Welcome is cordial from an appropriately soignée manageress whose eagle-eyed supervision keeps both staff and customers on their mettle.

THE EAGLE

159 FARRINGDON ROAD EC1   837 1353

'Having landed, it took off'

£20

OPEN
MON–FRI

HOURS
12.30–2.30PM
6.30–10.30PM

CREDIT CARDS
NONE

SERVICE
OPTIONAL

FACILITIES
SEATS 55
TABLES OUTSIDE
SEAT 20
WHEELCHAIR
ACCESS

**NEAREST TUBE
STATION**
FARRINGDON

MAP 1

When I first reviewed this pub converted by Michael Belben and David Eyre in 1991, I said how I wished other pubs would follow suit. Well, I got my wish: many more individuals have seen the potential in large, informal sites, often well situated – see reviews this year of The Peasant, The Lansdowne, The Engineer, The Cow, Prince Bonaparte and The Blenheim. The Eagle bashes on, turning out well-made and imaginatively conceived Mediterranean dishes for the hordes who pack the place. Getting a table or even a chair is a common problem. Dishes from a typical menu are roast green tomatoes, grilled sweet green chillies, olives, coriander and goat's cheese salad; fettucine with ricotta, peas, bacon and basil; grilled swordfish steak with 'salmoriglio' (a Sicilian herb and olive oil dressing) and Egyptian potato salad; 'arista', Tuscan pork loin roast with garlic, fennel and parsley with roast potatoes. The only constant on a menu that changes twice daily is 'bife Ana', a Portuguese-style steak sandwich using marinated rump steak. All wines – a cosmopolitan selection – are offered by the glass as well as the bottle. Keen to maintain the pubbiness of The Eagle, the management exerts no pressure on customers to eat, takes no credit cards and does not extend the facility of running up a tab.

ELENA'S L'ÉTOILE

30 CHARLOTTE STREET W1   636 7189

'The conjunction of two stars'

The Restaurant Partnership of which Roy Ackerman is chairman would seem to specialize in acquiring historic restaurants; first The Gay Hussar (q.v.), then L'Étoile (established 1904), following that the nearby White Tower (q.v.). Rumours are circulating that L'Epicure will complete this unbeatable hand in the game of nostalgia noshing. Canny enough to, on the whole, leave a good thing alone – and God knows these places could have all become Pizza Huts – Ackerman played a masterstroke in uniting Elena Salvoni, one of life's (few) natural caterers who started working in Soho restaurants at the age of 14, with the fading star that was L'Étoile in its last years. Changes have been made to the interior – Ackerman seems unable to resist the urge to bistro things up – but enough remains, for example, the etched glass screens and the burgundy Anaglypta wallpaper, to comfort those who loved the place in its heyday. The menu sensibly settles for a middlebrow interpretation of French cooking rather than emulating the Escoffier-rich dishes of yore or, worse, introducing modern eclecticism. Chef is Kevin Hopgood who worked with Elena when she was at L'Escargot (q.v.) in the days of Nick Lander's ownership. Dishes he is proud of, and does well, are parfait de foies de volaille a l'armagnac; timbale de chevre aux tomates et olives; gnocchi Elena; foie de veau au lard et pommes purées a l'ail. Some dishes such as demi-poulet poché and canard aux choux rouges braisés are served in casseroles, allowing you to cut and come again, an activity that suits the style of the place and Elena's motherly nurturing. Signed photographs of stars of stage and screen on the restaurant's walls attest to those who kiss and have kissed her cheek, but Elena's talent lies in making everyone feel, for the duration of the meal, a famous customer. On the first floor there is a large table which single diners can share, a boon at lunchtime when there is a reasonable set-price menu.

£30

OPEN
LUNCH MON–FRI
DINNER MON–SAT

HOURS
12.00–2.30PM
6.00–11.30PM
(6.00–12.00PM
SAT)

CREDIT CARDS
AMEX DELTA
DINER'S
MASTERCARD
SWITCH VISA

SERVICE
OPTIONAL

COVER CHARGE
£1.50

**SET-PRICE
LUNCH**
£12 & £14

FACILITIES
SEATS 80
TABLES OUTSIDE
SEAT 6
PRIVATE ROOM
SEATS 20–25
WHEELCHAIR
ACCESS

**NEAREST TUBE
STATION**
TOTTENHAM
COURT ROAD/
GOODGE STREET

MAP 4

THE ENGINEER

£22

OPEN
LUNCH WED–MON
DINNER EVERY
DAY

HOURS
12.00–3.00PM
6.00–11.00PM

CREDIT CARDS
MASTERCARD
SWITCH VISA

SERVICE
OPTIONAL

SUNDAY BRUNCH

FACILITIES
SEATS 70
TABLES OUTSIDE
SEAT 40
PRIVATE ROOM
SEATS 32
WHEELCHAIR
ACCESS

**NEAREST TUBE
STATION**
CAMDEN TOWN/
CHALK FARM

MAP 1

65 GLOUCESTER AVENUE NW1   722 0950

'A pub converted comfortably'

The fact that in London there is a pub on practically every corner will soon mean that there will be a restaurant on practically every corner. Abigail Osborne and Tamsin Olivier are the partners responsible for this new NW1 pub conversion just yards away from an earlier example, The Lansdowne (q.v.). To make an invidious comparison between the two, what you might lose on excitement about food at The Engineer you gain from the fact that tables can be booked and there is waiter service. Also, in the right sort of weather there is a secluded yard at the back for outdoor eating. The menu, presented without a break into courses, is the now familiar Mediterranean mix plus a few other incursions such as potato cakes, smoked salmon, crème fraîche and chives (good) or free-range chicken curry with yogurt and poppy seed naan (less triumphant). There is a soup, pasta and fish of the day plus grills of both vegetables and meat. The Engineer has been a huge hit with the locals and if you do not know the locale, it is one I can recommend for its attractiveness, particularly as you wander towards Primrose Hill.

ENOTECA

£25

OPEN
LUNCH MON–FRI
DINNER MON–SAT

HOURS
12.30–2.30PM
7.00–11.00PM

CREDIT CARDS
AMEX DELTA
DINER'S
MASTERCARD
SWITCH VISA

SERVICE
OPTIONAL

**SET-PRICE
LUNCH**
£6.50 & £9.50

FACILITIES
SEATS 35
PRIVATE ROOM
SEATS 40
WHEELCHAIR
ACCESS

28 PUTNEY HIGH STREET SW15   0181-785 4449

'Enough to bring on penne envy?'

Lucky Putney has two good Italian restaurants of its own, and the option of Riva (q.v.) or the River Café (q.v.) not far away. Enoteca seems the most homely operation, with Pamela Turi taking the orders and her husband Guiseppe in charge of the kitchen. He is from Apulia, an area famous for pasta and also unique in Italy in that it sanctions the same as a main course. Signor Turi prices his excellent pasta (for example, black tagliolini with a buttery fish sauce and an assortment of shell-fish, or orecchiette with vegetables) as a main course, and knocks £1 off to those who want it earlier in the meal. His style is a mix of tradition and inspiration: scallops with a purée of smoked aubergine and pesto, and lamb with ginger and balsamic vinegar seem modern and turn out to be thrillingly flavoured, whereas kid stewed in milk is real down-home Southern cooking. There is much of interest on the menu and wine list, and if I Dolci – tiramisu, ices, zuppa Inglese – seemed staid on last inspection, that might be down to enthusiastic overindulgence in savoury things.

AN EFFICIENT and user-friendly introduction to Italy's diverse winemaking traditions. Both reds and whites are split into three weight divisions, and patient, informative notes help you decide between the wines you had never heard of, such as Schiopettino di Gramagliano and I Sodi di San Niccolo. Not many halves (a problem with all Italian lists, as the producers rarely bottle halves) but the cheaper items are all worth a go.

L'ESCARGOT BRASSERIE

48 GREEK STREET W1   437 2679

'Post-modern irony?'

The feature of having two Michelin-starred chefs brought together into one kitchen has rather collapsed with the departure of David Cavalier. Garry Hollihead – winner of The Soho Festival waiter's race 1995 – remains in place. The management describe the aims of the place as 'hearty provincial French dishes' in the ground-floor brasserie, whilst 'the first-floor dining room serves gastronomy'. It seems a rather odd distinction to make. Test meals were taken in the brasserie, where the menu is presented at a fixed price for each course: starters £6.50, main courses £12.50 (lunch time £10.50), desserts £4.50. Coffee and chocolate (snail-shaped) is £2. There is a 12½% service charge. As well as being inflexible, which brasseries are not supposed to be, the pricing is not cheap, nearly £30 a head before you drink anything. In the description of the dishes quotation marks are used in a peculiar way, highlighting certain French words but not others: salad of trotters, fried potatoes 'sauce gribiche'; sole 'Veronique'; 'daube' of beef, red wine jus, parsnip purée; but chicken boudin; salade de pommes de terre à l'huile de truffe. In trying to find out whether the chef was affecting post-modern irony we could only discover that 'confit' of rabbit Niçoise, lemon vinaigrette seemed to mean nothing of the sort; the meat came across as poached. Sauce gribiche was a fairly classical rendering – hard-boiled egg yolks, gherkins, capers in a thick vinaigrette – and generally the trotter dish is excellent. Gazpacho contained cream which seems all wrong and did not appeal. Tuna carpaccio warmed with horseradish and soya dressing; roast duck

£36

OPEN
MON–SAT

HOURS
12.00–2.15PM
6.00–11.15PM

CREDIT CARDS
AMEX DELTA
DINER'S
MASTERCARD
SWITCH VISA

SERVICE
12½%

SET-PRICE
LUNCH
£21.50

SET-PRICE
DINNER
£23.50

FACILITIES
SEATS 90
PRIVATE ROOMS
SEAT 25 & 60

NEAREST TUBE
STATION
LEICESTER
SQUARE

MAP 5

breast with a gratin of turnips; the daube of beef were all sound dishes, especially the daube where Hollihead's considerable abilities really came into play. Desserts are a high point. Compote de rhubarb (sic) avec crème à la vanille and torte glace à la framboise were raved about. The wine list is, appropriately enough, strong on France. Mediocre paintings for sale only serve to reinforce the feeling that these days this old Soho restaurant has no settled sense of itself.

L'ESTAMINET

14 GARRICK STREET WC2   379 1432

'That rarity – bourgeois French food'

£28

OPEN
MON–SAT

HOURS
12.00–2.30PM
6.00–11.30PM

CREDIT CARDS
AMEX
MASTERCARD
SWITCH VISA

SERVICE
OPTIONAL

COVER CHARGE
£1.50

**SET-PRICE
DINNER**
£9.99 (PRE-
THEATRE)
£14.99 (SAT
ONLY)

FACILITIES
SEATS 70
PRIVATE ROOM
SEATS 30
WHEELCHAIR
ACCESS

**NEAREST TUBE
STATION**
LEICESTER
SQUARE/
COVENT GARDEN

MAP 4

The word restaurant is, after all, a French one, but bourgeois French food, the mainstay of the menu at this Covent Garden tavern, is now relatively rarely offered in this city in thrall to culinary fashions. Good-value set menus and reasonable prices à la carte, allied with the rare sightings of une douzaine d'escargots en cassolette, vol-au-vent financière, omelette au choix, escalope de veau panée and poulet Basquaise, ensure popularity, as does, I am sure, the smiling competence of the manageress who runs the rooms – decorated comme il faut with pictures interspersed with shiny copper pans – with a firm hand. A cover charge of £1.50 brings saucisson on slices of baguette. Trolleys, or, as they put it, chariots, display an excellent array of cheeses in fine condition – another scarce sight these days – and a fairly predictable display of dessert tarts and mousses. The sensible move in the main course is the section entitled Les Grillades. Sharing côte de boeuf or chateaubriand – good, although not great meat – cooked to your dictate, brings with it a well-made sauce Bearnaise, proper pommes frites, firm green beans and a grilled tomato crowned with breadcrumbs (à la Provençale). There are departures from the style, for example poisson à la Chinoise and bangers and mash, but ordering those would seem to me to be missing the point of the place, which is the straightforward seriousness a French businessman would bring to the proposition of lunch or dinner and a decent bottle or two. His British equivalent makes up a good proportion of the clientele. In the basement, a wine bar, La Tartine, offers the eponymous open sandwiches plus salads and dishes such as croque monsieur, merguez frites and assiette de fromage; useful before or after the opera at the other end of the street, or, indeed, a play or movie.

LA FAMIGLIA

7 LANGTON STREET SW10   351 0761

'A rare restaurant in that it promises to serve up a fiasco'

Familiar faces at La Famiglia include Chelsea's no-good boyos (Taki, Alan de Cadenet and others), brought out by the merest hint of good weather to lunch in their shirt sleeves under the canopies in the garden. Of course this restaurant is a senior example of a whole London SW species, but it is included while most others are not because Alvaro Maccioni runs a tight ship – indeed the naval image suits the dazzling white and azure paintwork and smart staff uniform. All-comers get a courteous greeting and their fair share of attention. Seats outdoors are allocated to those arriving earliest. The menu mixes the sort of Italian food every chef is now having a go at (crostini – in this case a true Tuscan one with chicken liver – panzanella, carpaccio and so forth) with recipes whose Italian provenance might surprise: costatine Monteverde described as 'teenage loin of lamb in breadcrumbs and fresh chopped mint leaves' or the pollo al mattone which is cooked in a brick and, quoting from the menu, 'rather burnt on the outside'. Tuscan cooking is a speciality, as in the delicate white beans cooked in a flask al Fiasco (neither the waiters nor the Oxford English Dictionary can explain this leap of meaning) or an excellent roast pigeon with sage and wine selected from the weekly menu. Pasta is a good choice too, and if sized-up as a main course comes in an overwhelming serving, whereas salads seem a poor option compared with some of the antipasti at the same price. As a final torment to the social X-ray, up trundles a trolley covered in fruit and sweet things. Go on, be a devil: if you visit in the evening you are committed to spending £18.50 each anyhow.

£30

OPEN
EVERY DAY

HOURS
12.00–3.00PM
7.00–11.45PM

CREDIT CARDS
AMEX DELTA
DINER'S
MASTERCARD
SWITCH VISA

SERVICE
OPTIONAL

FACILITIES
SEATS 120
TABLES OUTSIDE
SEAT 80
PRIVATE ROOM
SEATS 30
WHEELCHAIR
ACCESS

**NEAREST TUBE
STATION**
SLOANE SQUARE

MAP 2

FENG SHANG
FLOATING RESTAURANT

CUMBERLAND BASIN PRINCE ALBERT ROAD NW1 485 8137

'Chinese on the canal'

There is something to be said for eating vegetarian duck – a Buddhist Zhai dish fashioned rather unconvincingly from wheat gluten – while gazing at the real thing paddling in the static waters of the canal in Regent's Park. The setting, a gaudy boat looking like the poor relation of the Jumbo in Hong Kong,

£30

OPEN
EVERY DAY

HOURS
12.00PM–12.00AM

CREDIT CARDS
AMEX
MASTERCARD VISA

SERVICE
10%

SET-PRICE
DINNER
£25

SUNDAY BRUNCH

FACILITIES
SEATS 130
WHEELCHAIR
ACCESS

NEAREST TUBE
STATION
CAMDEN TOWN

MAP 1

is without doubt a large part of the allure of a Chinese meal here, but the menu is not without its high points and the staff are unusually gracious and also loyal to their boss Mr. Wong; the same faces stick around. There is a tendency on the part of the kitchen to see the pairing of poultry or meat with fruit as being le dernier cri but such dishes are avoidable if, like me, you don't share that point of view. From the hot appetizers try Phoenix prawns; steamed mussels with ginger, chilli and spring onions; salt and pepper frog's legs and moushou pork – a dish to wrap in pancakes – with its sinewy content of black Chinese mushrooms. Interesting among the cold hors d'oeuvres are braised beef and shredded jellyfish with salad. In the main course bass or Dover sole are usually commendably sparklingly fresh. Szechuan roast duck with Chinese bread makes a subtle change from Peking duck with pancakes. Shredded chicken fried noodles are good, as are the grilled Peking dumplings. Prices are relatively high – you pay for the experience of floating. It would be nice if there was a bit more razzmatazz – or even movement – to justify it.

FIFTH FLOOR

HARVEY NICHOLS KNIGHTSBRIDGE SW1   235 5250

'Carrying a Harrods bag you'll be given the worst table'

£35

OPEN
MON–SAT

HOURS
12.00–3.00PM
(12.00–3.30PM
SAT)
6.30–11.30PM

CREDIT CARDS
AMEX DELTA
DINER'S
MASTERCARD
SWITCH VISA

SERVICE
OPTIONAL

SET-PRICE
LUNCH & DINNER
£17.50 & £21.50

FACILITIES
SEATS 110
WHEELCHAIR
ACCESS (ALSO
WC)

NEAREST TUBE
STATION
KNIGHTSBRIDGE

MAP 2

On the top floor of Harvey Nichols' department store well-heeled food shoppers come and go or pause for a cappuccino. Those who wish to grab a snack in style are referred to the café, those who might wish to pick up something else, the bar – without doubt the only department store bar with a bouncer. In the part of the complex overlooking Knightsbridge and its mansion blocks like iced cakes is the Fifth Floor restaurant. Denied that view you will actually be more entertained at the window giving on to the food counters and café where sights like an elderly gentleman in MCC tie wrestling into submission a trendy sandwich are commonplace. The pace of the restaurant is more sedate. Talk is in murmurs or sometimes not at all from a species of rich female luncher. She merely looks about and makes minute adjustments to her apparel. What do such women make of chef Henry Harris's humorous touches, such as sending out excellent tandoori chicken and chutney sheltering under a poppadom? Or his enthusiasm for items like garlic and chilli taken to reckless extremes? Here is a conundrum: Bibendum-trained Harris – his brother is head chef at Bibendum (q.v.) – is energetically doing what more obviously Bohemian restaurants manage less and less; that is constantly changing, playing around, making things up off the top of his head, mixing and matching. The lunch menu changes each day, as does the fixed-price dinner, and elements in the long dinner carte alter frequently too – the chap has a huge repertory. With his expertise and the backing of a good brigade, Henry Harris does not go far wrong, but inevitably with such an (admirably) volatile menu there can be the odd hiccup in finesse. Self-styled specialities are Henry's black bean soup; native oysters with grilled spicy sausages; panfried scallops, Bordelaise sauce and shredded duck confit; lobster with coriander, ginger and noodles; rump of lamb au poivre, flageolet beans and roast garlic. Dishes that call out to me are Oriental-style tripe; stir-fried bok choy; scrambled eggs with shaved botarga (salted, dried mullet roe); morels on toast with Comté cheese; grilled veal kidneys; aubergine and couscous salad, harissa dressing and minted yogurt; crepinette de museau sauce moutarde; pear Pithivier, Poire William chantilly. There is also an enterprising vegetarian menu and nice veg to order separately. Properly ripened cheeses and the restaurant's own superb sorbets and ices are tasteful full stops. Or not quite, because the coffee here should not be missed. Fifth Floor is a triumphant in-store restaurant but you can't help feeling that Harris would benefit from a clientele that was a bit broader – in the beam, as a section of society and in its tastes. The wine list is admirable (see below) and on Monday evenings wines are sold at shop, not restaurant, prices.

EVEN THOUGH many will happily stick to the Little List with its pleasing range of sub-£20 bottles, the Big List offers a truly marvellous selection of the globe's wines, and if you ask for it a 20-minute time out is essential. One of its many virtues is a bracing indifference to fashion – hence the dozen or so exquisite Mosels from Egon Müller, J.J. Prüm and Carl Von Schubert. There are also good wines from Israel (Yarden) and the Lebanon (Ch Musar), a decent smattering of California's hottest names, and just about every champagne that you care to think of. The claret and burgundy selections are top heavy in the way that many big lists are, but elsewhere prices range from fair to good. Best of all is the news that dessert wines 'are offered at our wine shop prices', which allows you to drink Ch Climens 1976 and Ch Gilette 1956 for less than £50 a bottle.

FINA ESTAMPA

'Peruvian pub'

£24

OPEN
LUNCH
TUES–SUN
DINNER
TUES–SAT

HOURS
12.00–3.00PM
(12.00–4.30PM
SUN)
6.00–10.00PM

CREDIT CARDS
AMEX DINER'S
MASTERCARD VISA

SERVICE
OPTIONAL

COVER CHARGE
10%

**SET-PRICE
LUNCH & DINNER**
£13.95, £15.95 &
£18

SUNDAY BRUNCH

FACILITIES
SEATS 40

**NEAREST TUBE
STATION**
TOWER
HILL/LONDON
BRIDGE

MAP 1

Word got out, doubtless helped by *Time Out* which voted Fina Estampa its Best South American in the *Time Out* Eating & Drinking Awards 1995, and now you do not have to book ahead for Peruvian specialities at Bianca and Richard Jones' pub conversion. Bianca, who does the cooking, comes from Lima. Richard, who runs the front of house and makes a mean pisco sour, is English. There is more to a meal here than just satisfying curiosity about what might be an unfamiliar cuisine. The surroundings are engaging, with a piano taking pride of place in the front room and fancy gilt-framed mirrors and ornate lanterns fleshing out notions about Peruvian interior decor. Salsa tapes are played (too loudly in my view) and the staff are anxious for your enjoyment. The food is presented as menus at various prices, from £13.95 to £15.95, or as 'Piqueo' consisting of an array of four dishes at £18 per person. Dishes I would recommend seeking out in whatever format are ocopa, new potatoes covered with a piquant peanut and walnut sauce garnished with garlic-imbued king prawns; choritos à la chalaca, deep-fried mussels served beside their shells filled with a salsa criolla; carapulera which features Inca-style dried potatoes – resulting in something resembling plantain – incorporated in a sauce served with pork or chicken alongside fried cassava and parsley rice; seco of lamb, the meat served in masses of green coriander sauce with basmati rice, Peruvian-style beans and salsa criolla. Unless you love salmon, I would give the main-course fish dishes a miss. South American wines are on the list but you might not want too much after a couple of pisco sours. If you know something about the cuisine, it is probably still worth ringing up ahead to discuss your menu.

FLORIANS

'Carissimi Amici'

£28

OPEN
EVERY DAY

HOURS
RESTAURANT
12.00–3.00PM
7.00–11.00PM
BAR
12.00–11.00PM

As far as I'm concerned, since the rumour circulated that Bob Dylan was going to buy a house in Crouch End and that he could often be found in one of the local Indian restaurants, N8 has been the postal district for me. Fortunately among its many restaurants, brasseries, bars and bistros there is

Florians, a comparatively long-running (est. 1989) Italian restaurant where, despite familiarity having bred a definite nonchalance about items such as bruschette, crostone, carpaccio, salcicce al rosmarino, coniglio in agrodolce, salata di rucola, pancetta e olive and the vegetali e polenta grigliati which seemed so groundbreaking only six or seven years ago, there is still good enough cooking to keep me – and many others – coming. The wine list, including interesting dessert wines, and the long list of grappe are not inconsiderable lures either. Florians is divided into three areas: a bar with its own short menu and Bar Special deal of two courses and coffee for £5.95, a small, bright mezzanine, and a larger painted-brick rear dining room. In summer a garden is also pressed into use. There is generosity in the cooking and affability in the serving of it – ideal neighbourhood virtues. The sense of community is further enhanced by the monthly newsletter starting 'Carissimi Amici' and going on to introduce special events such as the festival of mattanza (the annual tuna catch), wine tastings, regional festivals, recipes and the availability of Florians polo shirts complete with logo.

SHORT, WELL CHOSEN, well annotated, neatly laid out and affordable, this all-Italian wine list contains nothing over £25 and yet includes an Amarone, a Brunello di Montalcino, a 1985 Barolo Riserva, and a white from Silvio Jermann. Contratto have contributed a 100% Pinot Noir sparkler labelled 'Reserve for England' – the house tipple of footballer Matt Le Tissier, perhaps.

CREDIT CARDS
MASTERCARD
SWITCH VISA

SERVICE
OPTIONAL

SET-PRICE
DINNER
£5.95

SUNDAY BRUNCH

FACILITIES
SEATS 70
TABLES OUTSIDE
SEAT 16
PRIVATE ROOM
SEATS 24
WHEELCHAIR
ACCESS (ALSO
WC)

NEAREST TUBE
STATION
HIGHGATE

FORMULA VENETA

14 HOLLYWOOD ROAD SW10   352 7612

'In pole position in Hollywood Road'

Formula does not apply to the menu, as you might well infer from an Italian establishment located in the raucous restaurant strip that is Hoorays for Hollywood Road, but to the sport of motor racing. 'I think he has been in a car,' said a friend and a regular at Formula Veneta about owner Gianni Pauro, but whether or not Gianni was once a racing driver, he has pals who are (or were) and photographs on the walls to prove it. Able to do 0 to 60 in a couple of seconds is a useful talent Gianni possesses when attempting to seat the customers who crowd in. They are the sort I would drive a long way to avoid, but the

£30

OPEN
LUNCH EVERY DAY
DINNER MON–SAT

HOURS
12.30–2.30PM
7.00–11.15PM

CREDIT CARDS
AMEX DELTA
DINER'S
MASTERCARD
SWITCH VISA

SERVICE
OPTIONAL

COVER CHARGE
£1

SET-PRICE
LUNCH
£9.95

SUNDAY BRUNCH

FACILITIES
SEATS 68
TABLES OUTSIDE
SEAT 35
PRIVATE ROOM
SEATS 32
WHEELCHAIR
ACCESS (ALSO WC)

NEAREST TUBE
STATION
SOUTH
KENSINGTON/
GLOUCESTER
ROAD

MAP 2

Northern Italian food and the wines from the grander part of the Italian wine list (entitled Cantina) are reasons enough to try to turn a deaf ear to their braying. The interesting cooking is on the list headed Specials or it is for those who would rather eat eel, sturgeon, wood pigeon and pig's trotter than scampi, poussin or veal scaloppine. A good first course from this list is salad of scallops, chick peas and ribbons of courgette bathed in a savoury broth which you can slick with olive oil. Risotti are a feature and, encouragingly, you are warned of a 20-minute wait and obliged to order for a minimum of two people. There are interesting pasta assemblies but tomatoes can creep into sauces unheralded. Desserts are accorded an authentically Italian lack of interest. A pretty garden at the rear seating 35 is an important attraction in the appropriate weather.

FOUR SEASONS

84 QUEENSWAY W2   229 4320

'A perennial among Bayswater's Chinese blooms'

£23

OPEN
EVERY DAY

HOURS
12.00–11.15PM

CREDIT CARDS
AMEX
MASTERCARD
SWITCH VISA

SERVICE
OPTIONAL

SET-PRICE
DINNER
£10.50–£16

FACILITIES
SEATS 70

NEAREST TUBE
STATION
BAYSWATER

MAP 1

The evenings until 9pm are not the time to have a really relaxed meal in the Four Seasons, as a queue clogs up the door and the staff move with such momentum that customers leaving their chairs risk being mown down. Bookings are possible, but only if you keep your side of the bargain and arrive on time. What makes an interesting cross section of West Londoners and tourists take the trouble to eat here is the quality of the Cantonese cooking at this family-run restaurant. Chef Wong's char-siu, special Cantonese roast duck, and soy chicken are made so that the flesh is moist and the skin delectably flavoured. Our inside informant thinks that the char-siu is best at lunch time and that every meal should begin with a request for the house soup, which does not appear on the menu but materializes on request, incorporating whatever ingredients suit the kitchen in potent, earthy broth. A vegetable dish of Chinese broccoli with ginger juice and the slow-cooked pork belly called muichoi moulded pork were two other tips that were spot-on. Stir-fried dishes seem more run-of-the-mill. The special menu brings such textural thrills as fried intestine or melon with sea cucumber and fish lips. Although the list is only partly translated, the staff are able and willing to help. A young woman called Carol gave us good advice.

FOUR SEASONS RESTAURANT

HAMILTON PLACE PARK LANE W1   499 0888

'Hotel dining with an offal lot of difference'

The labourers employed in heavy manual work who could truly do justice to the richness and complexity of a meal here are, sadly, highly unlikely to be a part of the clientele. This being the restaurant of an expensive modern hotel, the customers tend towards the international businessperson, a species not known to confer glamour or excitement on a room. You wonder how they view the long menu, made twice as long by everything being translated from French, and the intricacy of nearly all of the dishes. But who cares what they think; the keen eater will be there to see what chef Jean-Christophe Novelli can do. Novelli is an inventive, youngish, rather driven chef, keen to display his mastery of techniques and his willingness to learn and evolve – his cooking now features the flavoured oils pioneered by New York-based Jean-Georges Vongerichten who was a guest chef here. An appreciation of offal is one of his trademarks. Indeed the meat section on the menu is headed Viandes et Abats. In his enthusiasm he has been known wildly to over-reduce the sauce that covers the over-munificent display of innards – ox cheek, pig's tail, sweetbread, brain, lamb's tongue, kidney – thus rendering the dish so heavyweight and oppressive as to make you question whether the chef tastes his food. But there are many lighter options, some even starred to indicate low levels of calories, cholesterol, sodium and fat, and, logically enough, menus are slanted to reflect the different seasons. In Spring, a first course of ravioli of goat's cheese and artichoke surrounded by an immense variety of tiny diced vegetables and a Provençal infusion proved delicate and true to its tastes. Salmon poached in chicken velouté with quail's egg, truffle essence and Parmesan shavings slicked by olive oil (like a Tuscan bean soup) was hearty haute cuisine. From the main-course fish dishes a light and delectable choice would have been turbot poached in coconut milk on almond and cauliflower purée with green leaves slightly sweetened with honey – evidence of highly creative input with respect to toning flavours. Novelli likes Eastern intrusions, cunningly employing stalks of lemon grass as skewers with built-in piquancy for brochettes of either shellfish or poulet de Bresse. Desserts are dramatic, and if you have avoided overload you can enjoy items such as banana tarte Tatin with rum and raisin ice cream and caramel sauce fashioned to resemble the Sydney Opera House.

£50

OPEN
EVERY DAY

HOURS
12.30–3.00PM
7.00–10.30PM

CREDIT CARDS
AMEX DINER'S
MASTERCARD VISA

SERVICE
INCLUDED

SET-PRICE LUNCH
£19.50 & £25

SET-PRICE DINNER
£45

FACILITIES
SEATS 55
PRIVATE ROOM
SEATS 16
WHEELCHAIR
ACCESS (ALSO
WC)

NEAREST TUBE STATION
HYDE PARK
CORNER/GREEN
PARK

MAP 3

Start with lunch, usually a merrier meal at The Four Seasons, when set-price menus are a lot cheaper than eating dinner à la carte. The formally attired brigade of waiters support the kitchen (not always the case) and they are not prone to lording it over the inexperienced customer. The sommelier is adept in extracting affordable vinous interest from the long, expensive, wide-ranging but unexciting list.

THE FRENCH HOUSE DINING ROOM

49 DEAN STREET W1   437 2477

'Come in Daniel Farson, your time is up'

£25

OPEN
MON–SAT

HOURS
12.30–4.30PM
7.00PM–1.00AM

CREDIT CARDS
AMEX DELTA
DINER'S
MASTERCARD
SWITCH VISA

SERVICE
OPTIONAL

FACILITIES
SEATS 30

**NEAREST TUBE
STATION**
PICCADILLY
CIRCUS

MAP 5

Presumably to the chagrin of the Soho nostalgia bores who might well buttonhole you in the ground-floor bar of this legendary pub (aka The York Minster) to tell you 'I knew Soho when it was really Soho', the restaurant upstairs has done nothing but improve. People loved the first-floor dining room during the Second World War because you could get a very basic French meal for about 2s 6d. It is conceivable that the look is not much different: theatrical-red tortoiseshell-pattern wallpaper and a large mirror which fools no-one into thinking the room is larger than it is. Each small table is rickety in a different way and a good amount of ill-afforded time is spent by the waiter sticking bits of paper under different legs. The menu, devised by the same team who operate the Eros-award-winning St John (q.v.), is a short list which changes twice daily, capitalizing on what is seasonal, vigorous and sometimes scorned, meaning – fortunately – cheap to buy and challenging to present. First courses might be grilled lamb's tongues served with green sauce or herring and cream with beetroot made delectable even to a beetrootphobe. There is always an interesting soup, for example borlotti bean, sweet potato and carrot. A vegetarian main course is a constant but the kitchen's heart is in the preparation of dishes such as 'sumptuous' chump lamb chops basted in the cooking with their unfashionably robust layer of fat, served with a stew of chick peas, onions and tomatoes; and thick-cut calf's liver, milky in its tenderness, accompanied by bacon and a 'brilliant' grilled tomato. This is home cooking with the extra depth of flavour professionals can achieve. There is a savoury such as Welsh rarebit, sometimes cheese and Eccles cakes, and stout-hearted puddings or refined patisserie. Good coffee, a reasonable wine list, a great place.

FROCKS

95 LAURISTON ROAD E9   0181-986 3161

'If they hadn't removed the sewing machines you might run one up yourself'

Frocks looks lovely. In the summer there are tables out front and in a small paved garden at the back. The dining-room tables are old sewing machine bases covered in Liberty print plastic, the walls are wood panelled, the telephone Bakelite. Flowers, candles and a quaint blackboard on which beverages are chalked add to the charm. Although the chefs describe their food as modern British, disseminated Californian influences seem to be at work. Whence a fine piece of wild salmon in a sea of olive oil, the two elements not on speaking terms? More cooking of any nationality would have helped a salad of under-done chick peas and untoasted pine nuts dressed with a vinaigrette which contained a regrettable dose of raw garlic. The salad was ordered, thinking it would be a kinder choice than a risotto including ginger and pineapple – just the kind of thing a kitchen is likely to come a cropper on. Good business indicates a following for the likes of black pudding with trout fillet, or courgette, carrot, walnut and almond in a filo parcel with orange on a citrus sauce, or the rich, un-modern British puddings. Portions are good and the pricing is fair. An 11am–4pm breakfast menu on Saturday and Sunday also draws many local fans, some en famille.

£22

OPEN
LUNCH EVERY DAY
DINNER MON–SAT

HOURS
11.00AM–2.30PM
6.30–11.00PM
SAT
11.00AM–4.00PM
6.30–11.00PM
SUN
11.00AM–4.00PM

CREDIT CARDS
AMEX DELTA
DINER'S
MASTERCARD
SWITCH VISA

SERVICE
OPTIONAL

**SET-PRICE
LUNCH**
£9.50

SUNDAY BRUNCH

FACILITIES
SEATS 55
TABLES OUTSIDE
SEAT 22
PRIVATE ROOM
SEATS 30
WHEELCHAIR
ACCESS

**NEAREST TUBE
STATION**
MILE END/
BETHNAL GREEN

MAP 1

FULHAM ROAD

257–259 FULHAM ROAD SW3   351 7823

'A change of chef to be checked out'

At the time the guide is published (October 1995) Richard Corrigan will have left the kitchen of this stylish restaurant owned by Stephen Bull (see eponymous entries) to go, quite literally, to the dogs. He is masterminding the kitchens at London Stadium, Hackney. He is being replaced by Roux-trained Adam Newell who has made something of a name for himself at The Heights, on the top floor of the Forté-owned St George's Hotel. Newell has an elaborate approach to the creation of dishes, the exaggerations of which, I suspect Bull – himself a reckonable chef – will be able to curb. I do believe Fulham Road with its new kitchen brigade will be worth checking out.

£35

OPEN
LUNCH SUN–FRI
DINNER EVERY
DAY

HOURS
12.00–2.30PM
7.00–11.00PM

CREDIT CARDS
AMEX
MASTERCARD VISA

SERVICE
OPTIONAL

**SET-PRICE
LUNCH**
£22

FACILITIES
SEATS 80
PRIVATE ROOM
SEATS 12
WHEELCHAIR
ACCESS (ALSO
WC)

**NEAREST TUBE
STATION**
GLOUCESTER
ROAD

MAP 2

THE FULHAM ROAD wine list is a touch more showy and certainly more expensive than those of Stephen Bull's (q.v.) eponymous establishments. A list of this ambition should really find room for some of the grander Rhônes (there is no Hermitage and no Côte Rôtie), an omission aggravated by the correspondingly overlong line-up of clarets (18 in all). But there is something for everyone, both in price and style, and the variety within the half-bottle rack is especially commendable.

FUNG SHING

15 LISLE STREET WC2   437 1539

'A phoenix, by the time you get there'

£28

OPEN
EVERY DAY

HOURS
12.00–11.30PM

CREDIT CARDS
AMEX DELTA
DINER'S
MASTERCARD
SWITCH VISA

SERVICE
OPTIONAL

**SET-PRICE
LUNCH & DINNER**
£12

FACILITIES
SEATS 85
PRIVATE ROOM
SEATS 28

**NEAREST TUBE
STATION**
LEICESTER
SQUARE

MAP 5

Protracted renovations after a particularly destructive fire have made timely testing of this favourite Chinatown Cantonese restaurant (recipient of an Eros award for the last two years) impossible. However, when the team is back in place, Kwan Fu as chef, Jimmy Jim (as he is known) as manager, I dare say it will be business as usual but in a new environment. Fung Shing has been rightly praised for consistency – a rare virtue in Chinatown – which to some extent must be a function of the chef being one of the partners (as at nearby Mr Kong, q.v.). Within the characteristically long menu of 146 dishes, there is a section entitled Chef Special where many of the most interesting assemblies can be found. There are extravagant ones based on abalone, shark's fin and lobster and more homely ones such as grilled minced pork with salted fish; eel with coriander; stewed duck with yam in pot – one hot pot dish should be part of any order – and venison with yellow bean sauce. Steamed boneless chicken with ham and vegetable or boneless chicken stuffed with prawn meat and crabmeat sauce, which can be ordered half or whole, make a good centrepiece dish in a meal. Under Vegetable & Miscellaneous do not miss stir-fried milk with scrambled egg white, a difficult dish to make, here done very well. Fung Shing values its regular customers, both Oriental and Occidental, sometimes organizing banquets where some exceptional dishes are served. To some extent it is possible to do this for yourself by ringing in advance to discuss a menu, agreeing on how much you want to spend and conveying your preferences and no-go areas. Obviously this is more worthwhile for quite a large group. The restaurant's printed set menus really only become interesting if you are prepared to spend about £30 a head.

THE GATE

51 QUEEN CAROLINE STREET W6   0181-748 6932

'Opens up vegetarian food'

In what was Brangwyn's studio added on to a church behind the Hammersmith Odeon is The Gate restaurant. On evenings towards the end of the week it goes pell-mell, full of noisy diners and rich, garlicky smells. Those who do not book are likely to be turned away – tactfully – by the young waiting staff. The simple room with a huge window and midnight-blue walls looks rather like a refectory. The cooking hops about the world, listing Japanese soba noodles and vegetarian sushi, Caribbean stews, pasta and polenta, tortilla turned into tostada; a selection that changes once or twice a month. On a quick reckoning, only about a third of the menu would do for vegans. A more apposite observation might be that closer attention should be paid to seasonal vegetables. Why no baby broad beans, peas, courgettes or new potatoes on a May menu? This is said with no wish to dampen the cooks' exuberance – no doubt vegetarians have their conventions about what is posh nosh when eating out just like the rest of us; perhaps mushrooms (much in evidence) are as compulsory here as is steak when writing a carte to appeal to carnivores. The puddings certainly live up to the notion that those who renounce flesh do themselves proud with sweet things. For imaginative vegetarian cooking, fair prices, decent cheap wine, choice of music, conviviality and slightly unorthodox surroundings The Gate scores highly.

£20

OPEN
LUNCH TUES–FRI
DINNER MON–SAT

HOURS
12.00–2.50PM
6.00–11.00PM

CREDIT CARDS
AMEX DELTA
DINER'S
MASTERCARD
SWITCH VISA

SERVICE
OPTIONAL

FACILITIES
SEATS 50
TABLES OUTSIDE
SEAT 25

**NEAREST TUBE
STATION**
HAMMERSMITH

MAP 1

THE GAUCHO GRILL

19 SWALLOW STREET W1   734 4040

'Rolling, rolling, rollling, keep them dogies rolling'

There is common ownership (Dutch South-African) to this Argentinian restaurant and Down Mexico Way, located in the adjacent building. The juxtaposition of what are in fact very different cuisines – as different as North and South – has little logic and points up a themed approach to the ventures. The look of the basement dining room of The Gaucho Grill with its rather dogged and dispiriting decorator touches re-inforces the suspicion. However, if you are keen on beef, the Argentinian beef, sent over unfrozen – 'held and stored at precisely 1°C' – and cunningly aged without shrinkage in vacuum packs, deliv-

£30

OPEN
EVERY DAY

HOURS
12.00PM–12.00AM
(12.00–10.30PM
SUN)

CREDIT CARDS
AMEX DELTA
DINER'S
MASTERCARD
SWITCH VISA

SERVICE
OPTIONAL

**SET-PRICE
LUNCH & DINNER**
£19.25

FACILITIES
SEATS 126

NEAREST TUBE
STATION
PICCADILLY
CIRCUS

MAP 3

ers great steaks. Rump, sirloin, fillet and rib-eye are offered at weights of either 9oz or 12oz and are cooked on the assado (grill) which sits at one end of the restaurant in view of the customers. Pepper sauce, garlic sauce, Hollandaise and Bearnaise can be ordered separately, as can baked potato, hand-cut fries or rice. Assuming carnivorous tendencies, start with mollejas – grilled calf's sweetbreads, or chorizos – spiced sausages. There are other options; you could come here and eat corn on the cob followed by grilled salmon steak and a mixed salad but that would be completely and utterly missing the point and it is conceivable that your sensitivities would be offended by the pinto-pony skin upholstery. Flan con dulce de leche is a better choice of dessert than the seemingly bought-in chocolate tart. Drink Argentinian wine.

LE GAVROCHE

£75

OPEN
MON–FRI

HOURS
12.00–2.00PM
7.00–11.00PM

CREDIT CARDS
AMEX DINER'S
MASTERCARD
SWITCH VISA

SERVICE
INCLUDED

SET-PRICE
LUNCH
£38 & £55

SET-PRICE
DINNER
£55

FACILITIES
SEATS 60
PRIVATE ROOM
SEATS 8–20

NEAREST TUBE
STATION
MARBLE ARCH

MAP 3

43 UPPER BROOK STREET W1   408 0881

'The Rolls Royce of restaurants'

There have been changes to the format of the menu at London's long-established shrine to gastronomy which solemnify the handing over of responsibility from father to son. Dishes which are identified with Le Gavroche and which were perfected by Albert Roux – for example soufflé Suissesse, l'assiette du boucher, omelette Rothschild – appear framed and entitled Hommage à Mon Père. Beneath there is a set-price three-course menu at £55, Le Menu Choisi par Michel, and the à la carte follows on. If this seems a trifle grandiloquent – cher Albert is, after all, still full of beans and full of projects – then it is entirely in keeping with the style of the restaurant. Formality is an important part of the formula here and it has its appeal in the unobtrusive, perfectly choreographed service and the luxurious amount of space on the tables and between tables in the expensively but totally conventionally furnished rooms, but it leaves to the cooking a lot to deliver in the way of diversion and delight. Often a dish can accomplish it, as did pavé de grosse sole au jambon et legumes frits, an astonishingly thick cut of beautifully cooked fish seasoned by the ham and given textural contrast by the tempura vegetables, but when there is a slip, as happened with an escalope de foie gras au pain d'épices being over-fiercely cooked, the sense of disappointment is perhaps exaggerated. Râble de lapin et galette au Parmesan (from Michel's menu) was terrific-tasting meat sandwiched between crisp discs of melted Parmesan with an exquisite sauce but, although I am not one for masses of vegetables, the dish needed something to counter the pure protein attack. Reports of the set lunches this year have expressed disappointment in their 'ordinariness', despite the relative good value when compared to eating à la carte. The accoutrements of a meal – the canapés and petits fours – are excellent, as is the coffee.

THE LE GAVROCHE CELLAR houses over 800 wines, all wonderfully grand and wince-makingly expensive. Two-thirds hail from Bordeaux and Burgundy, and although Bordeaux is the more extensive, it is Burgundy that takes the eye, fielding as it does many rarely seen 1978s and 1985s. Alsace, Rhône and Loire are more compact, but not, alas, their prices, and if you want to kick off with a bottle of bubbly you must bear in mind that the cheapest (House of Albert Roux, £42) will cost you more than the all-in set-price lunch. So, where do thirsty non-millionaires look? Not, as might have been expected, to the token assortment of non-Gallic wines: the Italians average £72 a bottle, the Spanish nearly £50, and the Californians £80. Indeed, the task of tracking down worthwhile bottles under £30 is a more time-consuming exercise than it should be (try Jaffelin's white St Romain and Alain Graillot's red Crozes, both £26). Everything is crammed, in chunky 12-point, on to 16 stout pages: some may find this wearing on the eye, but I personally prefer it to the book-length documents one usually has to handle in such restaurants.

THE GAY HUSSAR

2 GREEK STREET W1   437 0973

'Soured cream and schmaltz'

Pre-war Budapest must have been like this: red plush, dark wood, white tablecloths, thick red-and-white china and a Central European atmosphere redolent of pickled cabbage, Bulls Blood and hot air. Leftwingers from the political and journalistic world traditionally love this restaurant with its Labour poster and trophies, cartoons, signed copies of forgotten books and general air of being as resistant to change as the Tribune Group. As at an old-fashioned club you know you will be safe here; unlikely to be threatened by stylishness in food or anything else. The long menu and the good value of the set lunch do not change. The soups, including the famous and very

£30

OPEN
MON–SAT

HOURS
12.30–2.30PM
5.30–10.45PM

CREDIT CARDS
AMEX DELTA
DINER'S
MASTERCARD
SWITCH VISA

SERVICE
OPTIONAL

SET-PRICE LUNCH
£16

Facilities
SEATS 70
WHEELCHAIR
ACCESS
PRIVATE ROOMS
SEAT 12 & 22
WHEELCHAIR
ACCESS

NEAREST TUBE
STATION
TOTTENHAM
COURT ROAD

MAP 5

pink wild cherry, are more alluring than the rather dull plate of mixed hors d'oeuvres. Cold pike with beetroot sauce and cucumber salad is an agreeable assembly, the slices of cucumber properly wearied through salting. Main courses are huge plate-fuls of home cooking; the stuffed cabbage is like your granny would make were she Hungarian, and features dumplings, sausage and a fat slice of bacon as well. Chicken paprika comes with generous spoonfuls of soured cream; Hungarian style as applied to calf's liver seems to mean thick but tender. Smoked breast of goose is an item seldom found elsewhere. It goes well with red cabbage and tarhonya (egg barley) or galuska (thimble egg dumplings). Desserts validate the Hungarian claim to being great patissiers. Poppy seed strudel is a favourite; somloi delice is a cake resembling a very special trifle made with rum, cream and walnuts. Prices seem to have crept up a little, but given the worth of consistency and generosity it would be uncomradely to quibble. Service is old-fashioned and assiduous.

GEALES FISH AND CHIP RESTAURANT

2 FARMER STREET W8   727 7969

'Put on weight in W8'

The old-fashioned appearance of this family-owned fish and chip specialist makes it popular with a canny class of tourist, as well as with those who live in its catchment area. Eating there, an American visitor remarked that he found it hard to believe that the British ever had the willpower to conquer the world after putting away a 12-ounce piece of battered haddock and at least half a pound of chips. It would have been pedantic to explain that the average Briton of the Empire days was malnourished and that deep frying fish in batter was developed as a way of making it last longer – it was mostly sold cold and old. Besides, ancient fish should scarcely be mentioned in Geales where freshness is a fetish and the fish comes straight from Grimsby or the South Coast. The fish soup, salmon fishcakes and catch of the day in batter are very good indeed, as is the choice of drinks and the set-lunch deal, but the chips are not of the same calibre. Sad to say, this may be because the tradition of frying chips (not fish) in beef fat is upheld here.

£17

OPEN
TUES–SAT

HOURS
12.00–3.00PM
6.00–11.00PM

CREDIT CARDS
DELTA
MASTERCARD
SWITCH VISA

SERVICE
OPTIONAL

COVER CHARGE
15P

SET-PRICE
LUNCH
£7.50

FACILITIES
SEATS 100
TABLES OUTSIDE
SEAT 14
PRIVATE ROOM
SEATS 30
WHEELCHAIR
ACCESS (ALSO
WC)

NEAREST TUBE
STATION
NOTTING HILL
GATE

MAP 1

GILBERT'S

2 EXHIBITION ROAD SW7   589 8947

'A wine lover's retreat in South Kensington'

The lovely old shop front with its arched windows is Gilbert's prettiest feature. The room behind is painted a rich orange and, on a sunny lunch time, seems serene: couples lunch quietly and a single waiter smiles and moves back and forth between the tables and the serving hatch. What he brings has a pared-down quality. A small breast of duck fan-cut into a pool of a very gentle ginger and lemon grass sauce or a lean little rack of lamb with thyme-scented gravy and a shared helping (again quite small) of perfectly cooked vegetables are fairly typical excerpts from the short, set-price menu. Nothing in the way of large portions of starch seems to be served, so the hungry may find themselves calling several times for the nutty/sweet, freshly baked bread. Some braver flavours from the new, half-Belgian, half-Malay chef would be welcome, perhaps also freedom from the confines of a set-price policy which anyway breaks up under the imposition of supplements.

GILBERT'S has fully exploited the marvellous range of wines available to the UK drinker, even though many of the bottles have clearly been bought 'on the wine route', after vineyard and winery visits. The layout (by grape variety) is easy to follow, and the knowledge, curiosity and enthusiasm of the buying can be inferred from the intelligent and unusually informative notes. Excellent halves include Gerard Chavy's Puligny Folatières 1993 and Ch de Beaucastel 1990 (both young, true, but impressively adventurous choices in this format). The Everest among the peaks is the dessert wine selection which contains Cauhapé's Jurançon, Bonny Doon's Muscat Canelli, Klein Constantia's Vin de Constance, and a red 1959 Vieux Rivesaltes, which at £4.75 a glass just has to be tried.

£26

OPEN
LUNCH MON–FRI
DINNER MON–SAT

HOURS
12.00–2.00PM
5.30–10.00PM
HOURS EXTENDED
DURING PROMS

CREDIT CARDS
AMEX DINER'S
MASTERCARD
SWITCH VISA

SERVICE
OPTIONAL

**SET-PRICE
LUNCH**
£12.50

**SET-PRICE
DINNER**
£17

FACILITIES
SEATS 30
TABLES OUTSIDE
SEAT 6
WHEELCHAIR
ACCESS

**NEAREST TUBE
STATION**
SOUTH
KENSINGTON

MAP 2

IL GOLOSO

204 FULHAM ROAD SW10   352 9827

'100% Italian, friendly, amusing and good value'

Competing with a large number of restaurants on Fulham Road, the family-run Il Goloso looks and smells inviting and has the additional allure of offering good value, particularly in the set-price meals at lunch and dinner at £5.95 and £9.95

£18

OPEN
MON–SAT

HOURS
12.00–3.00PM
6.30–12.00AM

CREDIT CARDS
AMEX DELTA
DINER'S
MASTERCARD
SWITCH VISA

SERVICE
12½%

COVER CHARGE
85p (DINNER
ONLY)

**SET-PRICE
LUNCH**
£5.95

**SET-PRICE
DINNER**
£9.95

FACILITIES
SEATS 48
TABLES OUTSIDE
SEAT 6
WHEELCHAIR
ACCESS

**NEAREST TUBE
STATION**
EARLS
COURT/FULHAM
BROADWAY/
GLOUCESTER
ROAD

MAP 2

respectively for two courses and coffee. Its popularity can create long waits – one customer said that despite the waiters appearing to dance attendance and putting on a brilliant display of urgent Italian behaviour, the restaurant should be called Il Go Slo. The menu is pretty much the standard Italian list, but some presumably customized dishes come described al Goloso (the word means glutton). Melanzane al Goloso is a delicious, large, baked, stuffed aubergine. Vitello Goloso comes with the rather surprising garnish of crab and 'olandese' sauce. Cuttlefish in black sauce with polenta has been admired for its bouncy flesh and the inky swamp of rich black sauce, and full marks were given to half a crispy duck in Grand Marnier sauce. Vegetables can be disappointing and some desserts suffer a sort of jet-lag from too long a trip on the trolley. The style is Sixties trat but with the improvement in cooking that time passing has brought.

GONBEI

151 KING'S CROSS ROAD WC1`   278 0619

'A pearl in a swinish area'

£22

OPEN
MON–SAT

HOURS
6.00–11.00PM

CREDIT CARDS
DELTA DINER'S
MASTERCARD
SWITCH VISA

SERVICE
10%

**SET-PRICE
DINNER**
£16–£19.80

FACILITIES
SEATS 31
PRIVATE ROOM
SEATS 16

**NEAREST TUBE
STATION**
KING'S CROSS

MAP 1

King's Cross is an area that has little to commend it outside of St Pancras station. Elsewhere everything is lowest common denominator. Except Gonbei. This off-limits gem is the kind of after-work 'drink and eat' that I imagine abounds in Tokyo and other Japanese cities but is still not commonplace here. The sushi bar is not just a display but a real working area turning out immaculate sushi based on a wide range of fish, shellfish and roe. Set dinners (Gonbei is open only in the evenings) start at £16 which represents good value, but the à la carte is by no means difficult to decipher and can deliver items like grilled salted mackerel so fresh it almost jumps out of its dish. Ebi tempura – cooked from raw prawns – is exemplary with no overtones of fried scampi or tired oil. Suki-yaki and yose-nabe cooked for two at the table are also offered. The tempura and noodle assemblies in soup make an ideal one-dish quick meal. Prices generally are fair. Service is fluent, friendly and swift. Drink sake, Kirin or Chivas Regal. Salarymen who work nearby have discovered the merits of Gonbei.

GOURMET GARDEN

59 WATFORD WAY NW4   0181-202 9639

'Where Malaysian and Singaporean dishes bloom'

Gourmet Garden in Hendon is a Chinese restaurant most interesting for its Malaysian and Singaporean dishes, plus those on the laminated list entitled Chef's Recommendation. As with most Chinese restaurants it is least interesting for its set menus. Even if the whole business of ordering an Oriental meal spells confusion rather than Confucius, avoid these banal round-ups. Try as first courses poh pia, a prawn and pork spring roll which has grown up and shrugged off the too facile appeal of deep-frying, the robust Thai fish cakes and perhaps some satay. A centrepiece dish might be their speciality of crab or lobster with belecan sauce. After this agreeable hammering to your tastebuds one of the hot-pot dishes follows well: eel and belly pork or ikan bilis (dried, salted anchovy), chicken and aubergine or braised vegetarian glass noodles. The dish of pig's trotter you will like if you are the sort of person who can appreciate gelatinous skin and tendons genuflecting to the superior power of soy and vinegar. This is satisfyingly offset by hor fun noodles with their slices of fish cake and a slightly cornfloury sheen to the fish stock. The staff are notably civil as if the presence of a woman chef has had a profound socializing influence. Even if Hendon is not your stamping ground (such people must exist), if you are interested in Straits Chinese cooking, it is worth making the journey to dig in at Gourmet Garden.

£20

OPEN
EVERY DAY

HOURS
12.00–2.30
6.00–11.30PM
(12.00–3.00PM
6.00–11.00PM
SUN)

CREDIT CARDS
AMEX DELTA
MASTERCARD
SWITCH VISA

SERVICE
OPTIONAL

**SET-PRICE
LUNCH**
£3.50 & £4.50

**SET-PRICE
DINNER**
£10.80 & £14.80

FACILITIES
SEATS 75
WHEELCHAIR
ACCESS

**NEAREST TUBE
STATION**
HENDON CENTRAL

GRANITA

127 UPPER STREET N1   226 3222

'Paintings only on the plate'

As a description of the decor, minimalist would be an understatement. It comes as no surprise to find that architect John Pawson has played an advisory role here. Apparently he advised on the tabletops – bare beechwood – and on the wooden bench at the back of the room. Those who use the word Islington to describe a state of mind or a political attitude would doubtless claim not to be surprised by the lack of creature comforts in this spare space with not even a picture to draw your eye. However, the ethos of austerity is not applied to the food. Chef and co-owner (with Vicky Leffman) Ahmed

£25

OPEN
LUNCH WED–SUN
DINNER
TUES–SUN

HOURS
12.30–2.30PM
6.30–12.00AM

CREDIT CARDS
MASTERCARD VISA

SERVICE
OPTIONAL

**SET-PRICE
LUNCH**
£11.50

FACILITIES
SEATS 62
WHEELCHAIR
ACCESS
**NEAREST TUBE
STATION**
HIGHBURY &
ISLINGTON/ANGEL
MAP 1

Kharshoum produces a weekly-changing, lively, modern menu where what you read is what you get. Thus, salad of red oak leaves, butter lettuce, avocado, Gruyère, garlic croûtons, Dijon vinaigrette is exactly that, but assembled with a good sense of balance and a skilful hand in the dressing. Roasted cornfed guinea fowl, crispy roast potatoes, roasted parsnips and onions, jus, perhaps fails to convey the innate deliciousness, particularly in the roasted vegetables. In spiedino of lamb, marinated and chargrilled, with eggplant, plum tomato, courgettes, thyme and olive oil torta and new potatoes, the meat was succulent, perfectly cooked. Not everything is perfect: a spring roll had stagnant bean shoots inside and a greasy skin, and providing poor bread even on a Sunday evening is these days inexcusable. Desserts chosen randomly include upside-down apple pudding with cinnamon ice cream; city chocolate, espresso custard (an uncharacteristically silly name masking chocolate mousse); macaroon crème brûlée. There are always British cheeses served with home-made oatcakes. Despite or perhaps because of the lack of fripperies, great attention is paid to details like the teas, coffees, dessert wines and digestifs and, usually, the bread. Granita is ideally placed for lunch if you have been at the Business Design Centre or dinner if you have been at the Almeida Theatre.

MANY BOTTLES on this slimline list are cheaper than the anonymous house plonks of grander restaurants – only one (Stag's Leap Chardonnay) breaks £20, and then only just. In other words, you can drink pretty well here without trebling the bill, which is what so often happens elsewhere. The New World is its strong point – France is treated with a perfunctoriness which some may find reassuring.

GREAT NEPALESE

48 EVERSHOLT STREET NW1   388 6737/5935

'Much better than a balti'

£18
OPEN
EVERY DAY
HOURS
12.00–2.45PM
6.00–11.45PM
CREDIT CARDS
AMEX DELTA
DINER'S
MASTERCARD
SWITCH VISA
SERVICE
10%

It is best to forget the tall tales about the ancient art of balti cooking, brought down from an obscure hill province of Asia to Birmingham in a special cookery pot that looks suspiciously like a wok. The finest Himalayan food in London is to be found behind Euston Station and is the work of Nepalese cooks. If you choose from the Nepalese section of the menu the regional distinction will be apparent. A liking for a sharpness is evident in the main meat dishes and the several, exciting pickles. Herbs and spices are used stridently rather than to a curried effect. There is proper mutton for those who appreciate that and, or perhaps or, a variety of Nepalese and Tibetan vegetarian dishes. Excellent recent choices included the ginger and green herb-flavoured Bhutuwa chicken; a dry pickle of chard or spinach stem (gundruko achar); the cold potato salad dressed with ground sesame; the black lentil dal and the coriander pickle (the latter is runny and intended for rice). Bargain-hunters should order the set meal, a Nepalese full monty for £10.95, but in fact many customers stick to the part of the menu that has the familiar names from the Subcontinent, the likes of tandoori, korma or phall ('very, very hot curry' they say, the culinary equivalent of showing the yellow card). This is not a flashy restaurant (note the location) but the room is neat and the staff are a joy. It is also worth noting the location and keeping The Great Nepalese in mind when planning rail travel – you may not fare so well farther up the line.

SET-PRICE LUNCH & DINNER £10.95

FACILITIES SEATS 48 WHEELCHAIR ACCESS

NEAREST TUBE STATION EUSTON

MAP 1

THE GREENHOUSE

27A HAY'S MEWS W1   499 3331

'Mayfair's dining hall'

When The Greenhouse opened about 18 years ago, it seemed a thrillingly large restaurant (seating nearly 100). Now we are used to establishments seating two and three and four times that, its impact does not reside in size. Nor does it any more quite lie with British cuisine, dragged into the late twentieth century by celebrity chef Gary Rhodes, who arguably began making his name here with his espousal of faggots and braised oxtail. As each year passes, the roots of the cooking spread more widely, so much so that the menu is quite difficult to choose from; your meal tends to have no coherent theme. That said, it is also difficult in the sense that there is much that is appealing. Dishes that have been praised include sautéed foie gras with caramelized red onions on toast, accurately cooked and perfectly balanced; open leek tart with red wine vinaigrette and a warm poached egg, the leeks soft and emerald green, the egg enriching, the vinaigrette adding edge; red wine risotto with 'crispy' black pudding, a meeting of Mediterranean and British which seemed positively Europhile; spiced belly of pork with rice, a homely Chinese-style dish of soft slices of meat

£35

OPEN LUNCH SUN–FRI DINNER EVERY DAY

HOURS 12.00–2.30PM 7.00–11.00PM SUN 12.30–3.00PM 7.00–10.00PM

CREDIT CARDS AMEX DINER'S MASTERCARD SWITCH VISA

SERVICE OPTIONAL

COVER CHARGE £1

SUNDAY BRUNCH

SET-PRICE LUNCH £19.50 (SUNDAY ONLY)

FACILITIES SEATS 96 WHEELCHAIR ACCESS

NEAREST TUBE
STATION
GREEN
PARK/HYDE PARK
CORNER

MAP 3

with a spicy crust served over lots of spring onions and rice; hot apple fritters with vanilla ice cream which were faultless. Vegetables, which are priced separately, can disappoint and seem hardly worth ordering. The Greenhouse appeals to middle England and in particular to the male of the species. Some lunch times there is scarcely a skirt to be seen. The massed bands of Britain's bourgeoisie seem persuaded that it is good value, but cover charge, vegetable charges, expensive coffee and mineral water and wines at very much West End prices can disabuse you of that notion. Staff are friendly and efficient. By the way, the location is not a greenhouse, but an air-conditioned apartment-block ground floor decorated with some petrified topiary reached from a mews courtyard. There is a separate menu for the set-price Sunday lunch.

THE GREEN STREET RESTAURANT

3 GREEN STREET W1   409 0453

'Once I had a secret lunch (Doris Day)'

£26

OPEN
MON–FRI

HOURS
12.30–6.00PM

CREDIT CARDS
AMEX DELTA
MASTERCARD
SWITCH VISA

SERVICE
OPTIONAL

SET-PRICE
LUNCH
£11

FACILITIES
SEATS 50

NEAREST TUBE
STATION
MARBLE
ARCH/BOND
STREET

MAP 3

This is a place which gives no clue to the fact that it is a restaurant (open to non-members of what is in fact a club only for weekday lunch). You enter a rather dingy-looking hall and proceed into a dark-green drawing room/bar containing a large number of chairs draped in linen shrouds. On the mantelpiece sits a strange stuffed animal, a leathery, dusty thing with a wan expression and a receding chin. It crossed the mind of my companion that she had fetched up in the waiting room of some discreetly unspecified clinic. She was cheered by the basement dining room/conservatory which she likened to a nursery newly decorated by enlightened parents for a wacky new baby. The tempting, daily-changing menu seems to reflect the bold appoach of the interior. Chef Simon Browne has successfully seized the baton from Peter Gordon now cooking at The Sugar Club (q.v.). Gaspacho, sweet and tangy, had good colour and consistency and extended an invitation to slices of bread so crammed full of olives they looked like chocolate chip cookies. Salmon and tuna sashimi were thick translucent slices with a soy and wasabi sauce which had the kick of a mule. Sweet potato, tomato and goat's cheese bruschetta on rocket salad glowed like a traffic light with the canteloupe orange of the sweet potato contrasting with green leaves and red tomato. Grilled baby squid on mixed salad with dill aïoli had a smoky taste, a sensuous texture. Thai fish cakes; lamb's brains with lemon, ginger and almonds on salad; and poached chicken breast with watercress cream look promising and even sausages and bacon on mash begins to sound interesting on these terms. Two representative desserts are chocolate walnut cake with cream and strawberries and raspberry crème brûlée. Service is good looking. The guiding spirit of the wine list is 'something decent that people have heard of'.

GREEN'S RESTAURANT & OYSTER BAR

36 Duke Street SW1   930 4566

'Old and new England'

What is England coming to when Green's, that bastion of clubman's nursery food, lists as a first course on one of the menus chervil soup with frothy cappuccino milk? It is to the mahogany-panelled, pin-striped, padded-headband Green's that we retreat in order to avoid the questionable manifestations of food fashion such as the one for whipping up a layer of foam on soups and sauces. Sadly, reports on the other menu offered, entitled Traditional British, do not enable me to say 'just stick to that list'. The fishcakes, famed in song and story, have been described as bland, oddly squared-off in shape and aggressively deep-fried; dressed crab as unappetizingly served with the meat spread over a plate and a boring mixed salad on the side; and the onion gravy accompanying bangers and mash as viscous yet tasteless. Despite this, the restaurant remains hugely popular, a fact that might be the clincher in Green's bid for Englishness. However, oysters, smoked salmon, potted shrimps, fish and chips, grilled Dover sole and cold roast sirloin of beef are there as reliable bets, as are the daily dishes which include shepherd's pie, Irish stew and faggots with pease pudding. The atmosphere is seductively smart with an appealing raffish charm not unconnected to the well-connected owner Simon Parker-Bowles. Green's is where you could take your uncle from Gloucestershire who thinks London has gone to the dogs, well-heeled visiting Americans keen to see a slice of English life, an actress who will appreciate the flattering lighting and a chap who has promised you a dead cert for the 3.30 at Aintree. They will all feel at home. It is expensive; worth the outlay for the atmosphere and service rather than – at time of writing – the cooking. There is a good wine list.

£40

OPEN
Lunch Every Day
Dinner Mon–Sat

HOURS
12.30–3.00PM
6.00–10.45PM

CREDIT CARDS
Amex Diner's
Mastercard Visa

SERVICE
Optional

COVER CHARGE
£1

SET-PRICE
LUNCH
£35

SET-PRICE
DINNER
£38.50

SUNDAY BRUNCH

FACILITIES
Seats 80
Private room
seats 26–44
Wheelchair
access

NEAREST TUBE
STATION
Green Park/
Piccadilly
Circus

MAP 3

GRILL ST QUENTIN

£27

OPEN
EVERY DAY

HOURS
12.00–3.00PM
6.30–11.30PM

CREDIT CARDS
AMEX DELTA
DINER'S
MASTERCARD
SWITCH VISA

SERVICE
OPTIONAL

SET-PRICE
LUNCH & DINNER
£9 (DINNER
BEFORE 7.30PM)

FACILITIES
SEATS 140

NEAREST TUBE
STATION
SOUTH
KENSINGTON/
KNIGHTSBRIDGE

MAP 2

3 YEOMAN'S ROW SW3   581 8377

'Nothing exciting but it's the vrai chose'

This surprisingly large Knightsbridge basement is owned by The Savoy Group plc, and would seem to be used by them as a training ground for young French staff who are given to a certain amount of aimless wandering. To train the English clientele in the ways of ordering meat, there is a guide printed on the bilingual menu giving definitions of bleu, saignant, à point etc. Beefsteak and other cuts of meat such as lamb cutlets, veal chop and calf's liver are in fact sage (French for wise, sound, sensible) choices here. The quality of ingredient is good and it is usually precisely cooked. You can also add to your vocabulary cru because steak tartare is expertly mixed. Chips, however, are stringy and dull. To start you could have oysters, crab mayonnaise or plateau de fruits de mer. There are soups, rillettes and various salads. Entrées include fish dishes, roast, spiced duck breast and kidneys in mustard sauce. It is a formulaic French menu, satisfying when properly done. The grand sweep of well-spaced tables in the pillared room, vaguely reminiscent of La Coupole, is suited to group outings, business meals or spur-of-the-moment filling up rather than the *intime* event. The value of the set-price lunch and early-evening menu is not traduced by wine prices; they are reasonable.

HALCYON HOTEL – THE ROOM

£34

OPEN
LUNCH SUN–FRI
DINNER EVERY
DAY

HOURS
MON–FRI
12.00–2.30PM
SUN
12.00–3.00PM
MON–THURS
7.00–10.30PM
FRI–SAT
7.00–11.00PM
SUN
7.00–10.00PM
BAR
OPEN ALL DAY

CREDIT CARDS
AMEX DELTA
DINER'S
MASTERCARD
SWITCH VISA

129 HOLLAND PARK AVENUE W12   221 5411

'A Los Angelenos' idea of London at its best'

The Room as in dining room here benefits from the hotel's reputation as a rock and roll haunt, so it is rather a comedown to find, once again, only a mixture of Beverly Hills and Notting Hill occupying its tables. Chef Martin Hadden's cooking has evolved from classical French cuisine. He lists grilled scallops with noodles and cep sauce, and squab with a morel boudin blanc, as his specialities, and has worked under that hard taskmaster Nico Ladenis. Despite such drilling his kitchen can have longueurs, sending out a Hollandaise sauce that is almost scrambled or a Sunday roast of dull sirloin and tough Yorkshire pudding. Delicate fish dishes, on the other hand, win praise, as do the puddings. There is a choice between set menus or ordering à la carte except on Sunday, when the brunch (black pudding, crab cakes, salads, pasta and risotto) is the most eclectic meal of the week. Sweet-natured, swift service is all to the good, but be warned that drinks are pricey (including £3.50 for bottled water) and the wine list goes quickly into the realms of Hollywood agent affordability, without pausing for many refreshing little wines at lesser sums.

THE HALKIN HOTEL RESTAURANT

HALKIN STREET SW1   333 1234

'Wear Armani, eat risotto'

The restaurant at this small hotel off Belgrave Square is the antithesis of most London hotel restaurants. Sleek, mercifully uncluttered modern design makes the fact of an Italian menu no surprise. Chef Stefano Cavallini worked here when Gualtiero Marchesi, the three-star Michelin Milanese chef, was, for a while, consultant. The Michelin, who like to back up their own, sometimes bizarre, judgements, have given one star to The Halkin with Cavallini as head chef. This award is a clue to the cooking style in the sense that one suspects that The River Café (q.v.), with its more rustic and therefore more authentic Italian approach, will never get a Michelin star. When dishes are good, as the riso mantacato allo zafferano e midollo (fundametally risotto Milanese) is good, the marble floors, live guitarist, designer-dressed staff and even the tables being set with the flatware diagonal to the place setting seem highly desirable. When lapses occur, as they did with Grosseto pigeon with green peas, mushroom mille-feuille and garlic, where the meat taken off the bone was lacking in depth of flavour, the mille-feuille mistakenly conceived and the garlic nowhere to be savoured, then it all seems a bit pretentious and far too expensive. A way round the last problem is to go to The Halkin at lunch time when the set-price deal is £18 with tax and service included for two courses (interestingly, £1.50 cheaper than last year).

SERVICE
OPTIONAL

SET-PRICE LUNCH
£21 & £32

SET-PRICE DINNER
£26 & £32

SUNDAY BRUNCH

FACILITIES
SEATS 55
TABLES OUTSIDE SEAT 22
PRIVATE ROOM SEATS 12

NEAREST TUBE STATION
HOLLAND PARK

MAP 1

£40

OPEN
LUNCH MON–FRI
DINNER EVERY DAY

HOURS
12.30–2.30PM
7.30–11.00PM
SUN
7.00–10.00PM

CREDIT CARDS
AMEX DELTA
DINER'S
MASTERCARD
SWITCH VISA

SERVICE
OPTIONAL

SET-PRICE LUNCH
£18

FACILITIES
SEATS 50
PRIVATE ROOM SEATS 26
WHEELCHAIR ACCESS (ALSO WC)

NEAREST TUBE STATION
HYDE PARK
CORNER/VICTORIA

NEAREST BR STATION
VICTORIA

MAP 2

HILAIRE

'Sunny side up'

OPEN
LUNCH MON–FRI
DINNER MON–SAT

HOURS
12.15–2.30PM
6.30–11.30PM

CREDIT CARDS
AMEX DELTA
DINER'S
MASTERCARD
SWITCH VISA

SERVICE
OPTIONAL

**SET-PRICE
LUNCH**
£16.50 & £20.50

**SET-PRICE
DINNER**
£16.50 & £32.50

FACILITIES
SEATS 60
PRIVATE ROOMS
SEAT 30 & 50
WHEELCHAIR
ACCESS

**NEAREST TUBE
STATION**
SOUTH
KENSINGTON

MAP 2

You wonder why it took so long: the sludge-green paintwork on the tongue-and-groove panelled walls at this South Kensington restaurant (opposite Christie's), in place since its opening nearly 12 years ago, has been repainted a sunny yellow. Curtains at the front window pick up the colour in their cottage garden pattern and the net result is a livelier, more welcoming interior. Chef Bryan Webb has streamlined his menus in the sense of banishing supplements from the set-price deal, but adding £4 since last year, making it £16.50 for two courses at lunchtime, early evening and after 10pm. In the mid-evening there is also a set-price menu at £32.50 for four courses in addition to the carte. His eclectic cooking style stays in place, allowing travel during one lunch around Spanish gaspacho, Italian foccacia with buffalo mozzarella, avocado and sweet and sour peppers – a simple but beautifully composed dish – Thai dipping sauce accompanying crisp goujons of sole and French beurre blanc napping sautéed scallops. Spaghetti with girolles and sweetbreads failed to strike any relationship between the three participants. Choosing à la carte, stalwarts on a daily-changing menu are oysters au gratin with laverbread, reflecting Webb's Welsh heritage (in case you were wondering where he was coming from); fillet of brill with pea-mashed potato and mustard sauce; leg of rabbit in Serrano ham with braised cabbage and mustard; braised shin of veal in Madeira with carrots; apricot and almond tart with crème fraîche. For a clientele which is predominantly middle aged, middle class but slightly higher than middle management, this is culinary excitement enough. Service is professional.

A NEAT, mid-length list, presented with admirable clarity, and featuring good producers from Old World and New. The wines are arranged by style rather than by country, which I always think is an opportunity (missed here) to smuggle in a couple of Germany's wonderfully delicate aperitif wines. Descriptions are crisp, though you may quibble with the claim that drinking a bottle of Meursault constitutes 'the finest sensual experience'. What are arguably the New World's finest Pinot Noir and Chardonnay – Williams Selyem and Kistler respectively – are both on offer for around £50. Beyond the house selections prices are stiff.

HYDE PARK HOTEL – THE RESTAURANT

66 Knightsbridge SW1 259 5380

'Nobody does it better – Carly Simon'

As the *Guide* goes to press, Marco Pierre White is having his barely two-year-old restaurant within the Hyde Park Hotel redecorated, changing the flooring (currently very Crucial Trading) to parquet and, if I understand correctly, trimming the curtains in silver. If you think that the wherewithal for this is contained in his prices – £70 for three courses à la carte, with some supplements of as much as £12, plus £6 for coffee with chocolates – it is, according to Marco, not so. His food costs, he says, are sometimes 51% of the prices (good business sense dictates no more than 33% to be appropriate). Is it worth the outlay? It depends how interested you are in food. Marco is passionate about it. I know no other chef who talks about food with the same intensity, love and understanding and who has the ability in the kitchen to bully, probably literally, the very best out of ingredients. Salmon is a fish that left me cold until I ate his first course of ballotine of salmon with crayfish, herbs and fromage blanc where somehow the flavour had been intensified into something quite new. Other remarkable fish dishes are panaché of grilled sea scallops with caramelized calamari and sauce nero (based on squid ink); tranchonette of turbot with grilled sea scallops, creamed parsley, young garlic and girolles, jus Sauternes where the elusive flavours dusting the fish can be traced to Indian spices; escalope of brill with a soft herb crust, young spinach and a sabayon of chives, an incredibly delicate assembly. Dishes on the menu, which will have changed, mainly in detail, with the autumn reopening, are no longer listed according to the year of their birth, which is an improvement in both psychology and style. Longtime favourites such as braised pig's trotter 'Pierre Koffmann' and pot-roast pork with spices and ginger (using pig's head) have not been abandoned, and new discoveries – to me anyway – such as bressoles of squab pigeon Mouginoise, confit of garlic, pomme fondante and fumet of truffles are joined by seasonal dishes such as roast grey-leg partridge with choucroute Alsace and a juniper berry sauce. Desserts are masterly, and since you have paid for three courses you will probably have one, perhaps tarte Tatin of pears to share, lemon tart, or soufflé of bitter chocolate with chocolate sauce. Some people have remarked that there is a price to pay for Marco Pierre White's food and

£85

Open
Lunch Mon–Fri
Dinner Mon–Sat

Hours
12.30–2.30pm
7.00–11.00pm

Credit Cards
Amex Diner's
Mastercard Visa

Service
Optional

Set-Price
Lunch £25

Set-Price
Dinner £70

Facilities
Seats 50
Wheelchair
access (also
WC)

**Nearest Tube
Station**
Knightsbridge

Map 2

they are not talking only about the damage to their bank balance. He is capable of petulant behaviour, but I write as I find and I found the food wonderful. Marco's new venture is The Criterion in Piccadilly, where he will do what every grand chef not so deep down wants to do: serve brasserie-style food.

IT WAS ACUTE of Marco Pierre White to have his cellar stocked by Anthony Byrne, who must distribute the wines of more top-notch estates than any other wine merchant, and who has especially good selections of the restaurant-friendly regions of Alsace and the Rhône. The resulting list is huge – 61 pages long – and showy, especially in the 23-pages-worth of burgundies, but tricked out with the domaines which are really delivering. Mark-ups range from surprisingly reasonable at the top end (Ch Pétrus is no more unaffordable here than anywhere else) to unacceptable at the bottom (Ch Musar is £36, a weighting of 500%). Many will view this as a snub to the more careful customer. And a much greater snub is delivered to one of the world's great wine-making nations – Germany – which boasts a single bottle amongst the 1000 or so on the list.

IMPERIAL CITY

ROYAL EXCHANGE, CORNHILL EC3   626 3437

'Homilies'

£32

OPEN
MON–FRI

HOURS
11.30–8.30PM

CREDIT CARDS
AMEX DELTA
DINER'S
MASTERCARD
SWITCH VISA

SERVICE
12½%

**SET-PRICE
LUNCH & DINNER**
£14.90–£24.90

FACILITIES
SEATS 180
PRIVATE ROOM
SEATS 16
WHEELCHAIR
ACCESS (ALSO
WC)

MAP 1

This stylishly designed Chinese restaurant in an extensive brick-vaulted basement below the Royal Exchange keeps City hours and habits. Opening weekdays at 11.30am, the first sitting is over by 1pm and sometimes the clientele seems like a sea of suits. That Ken Hom remains consultant is indicated by the display of his cookery books near the entrance. His menu, or anyway the menu, seems to have changed little since last year. It stays eminently handleable, listing only 60 dishes including desserts, and the fact that there is no uninteresting 'padding' is apparent in the uncommonly alluring set-price menus which also feature some dishes not offered à la carte. Doubtless businesspeople find these menus an efficient way of ordering, minimizing dialogue with the impassive Thai waitresses who are not exactly ready with jokes, descriptions or suggestions. From the appetizers, salt and pepper prawns have this year come in for particular praise. They are cooked in their shells, made fiery with chilli but are tender, sweet and plump inside. Northern-style dumplings are crescent moons filled with pork and prawns. If you decide you are able to forego duck with pancakes, either Peking (classically prepared) or Szechuan style, as a second course, then try instead mu shu pork with lettuce at £9.50 for two which is noteably well made. In the main course, classic Cantonese steamed bass; crackling Northern-style chicken with garlic; Cantonese pressed duck; and braised red pork casserole Shanghai are some of the interesting choices. If you want red cooked oxtail stew, which sounds promising, it is reached via set menu three at £24.90 per person (plus 12½% service charge). Szechuan dan dan noodles pack a nice mustardy punch. Unusually for a Chinese meal the high point at one test run was a dessert – firecracker sweet wontons (crisp, cigarette slim, filled with a raisin, coconut, butter and brown sugar mix, accompanied by ice cream). The wine list is well composed but beer and mineral water seem the usual orders.

INAHO

4 HEREFORD ROAD W2   221 8495

'A slightly cuckoo place'

Unusually for a Japanese restaurant, Inaho has become a hang-out for the non-Japanese locals who have taken a liking to the owner, Mr Nakamura, a man rarely seen without a Hawaiian shirt. His tiny dining room only holds 20, plus a cuckoo clock, and is usually full in the evenings. Despite such popularity it was a puzzle when the Gault Millau guide decided to rate Inaho as one of the best restaurants of any type in the capital. The quality of the food does vary with the degree of pressure the kitchen is under. It does not fall below an acceptable standard but, for example, the starter of deep-fried tofu with ginger sauce can be beautifully presented and of perfect texture on one occasion, then rather ordinary the next, ditto the fried noodles yaki udon. Sashimi and sushi (the latter only available during the evenings from Wednesday to Saturday) are competent and an asset in the area, but cookery is the restaurant's forte. It therefore makes sense to select a hot starter from the list inscribed on a special little wooden stand, such as aubergine baked until it melts or a rich soup of salmon and saki, following with the simple-sounding meat dishes which the kitchen handles very well: even pork tonkasu, essentially a version of Wiener Schnitzel, is perfectly coated and succulent. The friendliness of Inaho is faultless, and perhaps that was what won over the Gault Millau inspectors.

£28

OPEN
LUNCH MON–FRI
DINNER MON–SAT

HOURS
12.30–3.00PM
7.00–11.30PM

CREDIT CARDS
DELTA
MASTERCARD VISA

SERVICE
OPTIONAL

SET-PRICE LUNCH
£8 & £10

SET-PRICE DINNER
£20 & £22

FACILITIES
SEATS 20
WHEELCHAIR
ACCESS (ALSO
WC)

NEAREST TUBE STATION
NOTTING HILL
GATE/BAYSWATER

MAP 1

L'INCONTRO

87 PIMLICO ROAD SW1   730 6327

'You need to be rich and you're probably thin'

£38

OPEN
LUNCH MON–FRI
DINNER EVERY
DAY

HOURS
12.30–2.30PM
7.00–11.30PM
SAT
7.00–11.30PM
SUN
7.00–10.30PM

CREDIT CARDS
AMEX DINER'S
MASTERCARD VISA

SERVICE
OPTIONAL

COVER CHARGE
£1.50 (DINNER
ONLY)

**SET-PRICE
LUNCH**
£13.50 & £16.50

**SET-PRICE
DINNER**
£45

FACILITIES
SEATS 80
PRIVATE ROOM
SEATS 35
WHEELCHAIR
ACCESS

**NEAREST TUBE
STATION**
SLOANE SQUARE

MAP 2

Incontrovertibly smart, this Pimlico Italian restaurant appeals to a clientele who set a great deal of store by appearance and perhaps are less fussed about content. In order not to have to spend what will almost inevitably seem too much for what you get, go at lunchtime when a set-price two- or three-course deal is on offer, as is something called the one-dish lunch. Pastas, which are home-made, and risotto tend to be quite inventive and well prepared, and should make up one of the courses of the set lunch. Grilled fish might be another. Eating à la carte, it might make sense to pick up on owner Gino Santin's Venetian background and order the dishes of that region, such as capasante (scallops) alla Veneta; baccala mantecato (purée of salt cod served with polenta); seppie (cuttlefish) con nero (ink). A test meal revealed a lack of seasoning and acidity in the dressing for warm salad of canellini beans with scampi and king prawns. Spaghetti with lobster (£20.50) comprised a mound of spaghetti, a dice of tomato as 'sauce' and some lobster flesh which, when marshalled on the plate, did not prove sufficient to have come from the half lobster shell used as decoration but obviously not derivation. Galletto inferocito, spatchcocked, breadcrumbed baby chicken in hot sauce, was well performed, the chilli enough to give life but not so much as to kill. A minute slice of torta di mandorla was dry and stale but coffee excellent. The wine list has plenty of the famous names and some of the new-wave makers. Mark-ups are no less enthusiastic than those for the food. I asked a friend about her visit to L'Incontro and she was more concerned to tell me that she had sat between Iman with David Bowie and Lord Linley with his wife than about the food. There you have it.

INTER-CONTINENTAL HOTEL – LE SOUFFLÉ

1 HAMILTON PLACE W1   409 3131

'Still rising to the occasion'

£44

OPEN
LUNCH SUN–FRI
DINNER
TUES–SAT

The main restaurant of the Inter-Continental Hotel is pretty in yellow and turquoise, but nothing quite compensates for the absence of windows. As a consolation come all the accoutrements of hotel dining: the breads; the complimentary appetizers; the costly utensils; the petit fours and ranks of serious staff dressed in a rather fetching blue. The man behind the menu is Peter Kromberg, Executive Chef here for over 20 years. He has a reputation as a considerate man, not a thing that can be said of all chefs, and this seems to be borne out by the way his selections cater to different appetites. Picky eaters can look for the heart sign to find food low in calories and cholesterol; ostentatious eaters will find foie gras and also lobster several ways (jellied with tarragon and caviar, or fricasséed with asparagus, or in a steamed mousse circumnavigated with sole all on one carte). The blasé can have superior smoked salmon and steak, or call for the savoury soufflé of their fancy, whereas those with an appetite for adventure will also find things of interest: shellfish gazpacho with crab pizzas; 'rillettes' of trout or salmon 'ossobuco' with pasta. Pastry- and sorbet-making are excellent, but, as the name indicates, soufflés are the speciality. A little test of a special order brought a lovely lemon soufflé into the crust of which thick cream was carefully spooned. No heart symbol for that.

HOURS
12.30–3.00PM
7.00–10.30PM
SAT
7.00–11.15PM
SUN
12.00–4.00PM

CREDIT CARDS
AMEX DELTA
DINER'S
MASTERCARD
SWITCH VISA

SERVICE
OPTIONAL

SET-PRICE LUNCH
£27.50

SET-PRICE DINNER
£43

SUNDAY BRUNCH

FACILITIES
SEATS 80
WHEELCHAIR
ACCESS (ALSO
WC)

NEAREST TUBE STATION
HYDE PARK
CORNER

MAP 3

INTERLUDE DE CHAVOT

5 CHARLOTTE STREET W1   637 0222

'Michelin-star food at almost bistro prices'

The Chavot of the title – a title that suggests ringing to check that he is still there – is chef Eric Crouillère-Chavot, a protegé of Marco Pierre White and a graduate of some of the glittering, star-struck kitchens in Britain: those of Pierre Koffmann, Raymond Blanc and Nico Ladenis. White has installed Chavot in what was previously the fish restaurant Walsh's, entering into a partnership with the Emmanuel family, whose daughter Elaine stays as manager. (The Emmanuels own The French Horn at Sonning by a piece of the Thames where White likes to fish.) The look of the various rooms of this Fitzrovia house which runs through to Rathbone Street is now in keeping with serious eating, but this is expressed more in napery and glassware than in fancy decorative flourishes and finishes. There is an agreeable air of simplicity in keeping with reasonable, nay cheap, prices for the style and integrity of the cooking – at time of writing £24.50 for three courses. Chavot seems at the moment a brilliant draughtsman rather than a

£35

OPEN
LUNCH MON–FRI
DINNER MON–SAT

HOURS
12.00–2.30PM
7.00–11.00PM

CREDIT CARDS
AMEX DINER'S
MASTERCARD
SWITCH VISA

SERVICE
OPTIONAL

FACILITIES
SEATS 50
PRIVATE ROOM
SEATS 16
WHEELCHAIR
ACCESS

NEAREST TUBE STATION
TOTTENHAM
COURT ROAD

MAP 4

creative artist, but it would be hard to tell the copies of some of his masters' dishes from the originals. Particularly impressive in the first course are foie gras and chicken liver parfait with toasted brioche; scallops on warm tomato and shallot vinaigrette; and a quail Pithivier with a port and sherry reduction which is masterly and utterly delicious. Main courses to try are the resonant daube de boeuf and roasted poulet noir – chicken with exceptional flavour – served with salsifis, a luscious fondant potato and tarragon-flavoured jus. If you skip desserts, which hold few surprises, there are tempting petits fours to make good the calories. The relatively short wine list – larded with a fine wine selection of famous names – is not rapaciously marked-up. The Meursault Hospices de Beaune Cuvée Loppin '92 at £27.50 is a treat.

ISOHAMA

312 VAUXHALL BRIDGE ROAD SW1   834 2145

'Victoria in the raw'

In a plain little room directly opposite the theatre still showing *Starlight Express*, a high standard of Japanese food is prepared by chef-proprietor Yukio Saito. Raw fish is a particularly strong suit of his, and to avoid the annoyance of arriving after the rice for sushi has run out, a request in advance may be wise for evenings towards the end of the week when the restaurant is busy. Rice as delicately flavoured and correctly cooked as that sampled here on other occasions can't be made to appear in minutes as if by magic and it is a shame to miss out. Ditto on the Japanese family outings, which in central London are an unusual and rather riveting sight – not all junior Japanese are angels or adept with chopsticks. The evening also brings an intriguing list of little dishes, to be ordered as appetizers – something from among the likes of deep fried stingfish, various dumplings and grilled salmon head should be attempted. The saki list looks serious too. Beautifully cut sashimi and the various forms of sushi are obviously recommended (a chirashi lunch box of salmon and roe was splendid), the grilled dishes are done with care and the rice dishes described as 'in hot tea soup' are based on rice and broth in big bowlfuls which are both delicate and satisfying. Tempura seems not to be quite so praiseworthy. As the sighting of families might have already suggested to you, this is a reasonably priced restaurant by the standards of a particularly expensive cuisine.

£28

OPEN
LUNCH MON–FRI
DINNER
MON–SUN

HOURS
12.00–2.30PM
6.00–10.30PM
SAT–SUN
5.00–9.30PM

CREDIT CARDS
AMEX DINER'S
MASTERCARD VISA

SERVICE
OPTIONAL

**SET-PRICE
LUNCH**
£6.50

**SET-PRICE
DINNER**
£25

FACILITIES
SEATS 38

**NEAREST TUBE
STATION**
VICTORIA

MAP 1

ISTANBUL ISKEMBECISI

9 STOKE NEWINGTON ROAD N16   254 7291

'Talking tripe'

£18

OPEN
LUNCH SUN
DINNER EVERY
DAY

HOURS
5.00PM–5.00AM
SUN
2.00PM–5.00AM

CREDIT CARDS
AMEX DINER'S
MASTERCARD
SWITCH VISA

SERVICE
OPTIONAL

FACILITIES
SEATS 80

**NEAREST BR
STATION**
DALSTON
KINGSLAND

MAP 1

If you like Middle Eastern and in particular Turkish food, you should go along sometime to this friendly Stoke Newington restaurant considerably open until 5am, but if you appreciate offal get your skates on. Iskembecisi means tripe restaurant. The first dish on the menu is tripe soup, a garlic-scented broth with chopped lamb's tripe to which you add condiments – salt, vinegar, lemon juice and chilli flakes – to suit your tastebuds. As an introduction to the delicacy it is far more beguiling than the English approach via milk and onions. Another soup made from boiled head of lamb is served in similar fashion. There is a long list of hot and cold mezeler from which you might select the definitive version of imam bayildi, aubergine stuffed with tomato, green pepper and onions, cooked to an intense flavour and not swimming in oil; a superior hummus – chick pea purée; and grilled and blistered hellim cheese. There are many more of these first-course offerings, the majority vegetarian. If you liked the tripe soup, you'll love kokarec, charcoal-grilled lamb's intestines served as a pile of unattributable crisp golden shreds with salads and spices to mix in. From the same section – Iskembe Cesitleri – kelle sogus, roasted head of lamb, comes in three parts: tongue, crisp and chewy; brain, melting and soft; and meat from the head itself – mostly cheek – unctuous and rich. Eat with chilli-pickled vegetables and Turkish bread. There are plenty of more familiar assemblies including manti, the delicious Turkish take on ravioli, served with a topping of yogurt and garlic. The manager also recommends hunkar begendi, a lamb stew which is a classic of Ottoman Palace cuisine. Desserts are soothing. Drink arak or beer. Staff here are benign and family-loving. The value is terrific.

THE IVY

1 WEST STREET WC2   836 4751

'A role-model of a restaurant'

£34

OPEN
EVERY DAY

HOURS
12.00–3.00PM
5.30PM–12.00AM

CREDIT CARDS
AMEX DINER'S
MASTERCARD
SWITCH VISA

Booking is not easy at London's showbiz restaurant par excellence, but if you say you are coming after a particular performance, the person taking details will know exactly when it ends. When you arrive and are seated, the offer of a drink is immediate. Later, when you request the bill, it is brought

SERVICE
OPTIONAL

COVER CHARGE
£1.50

**SET-PRICE
LUNCH**
£14.50
(SAT–SUN ONLY)

FACILITIES
SEATS 100
PRIVATE ROOM
SEATS 60

**NEAREST TUBE
STATION**
LEICESTER
SQUARE

MAP 5

quickly. None of these things sounds difficult to achieve but it is extraordinary how few establishments manage it. Christopher Corbin and Jeremy King who also own and run Le Caprice (q.v.) are the wit and organization behind this production now running into its seventh uproarious year, and one of them is usually on hand. He will also usually already have seen the play or movie you thought you were so clever in getting to early on. The menu, divided like the classic lists of old, is long and varied. A regular says that it reminds him of Stevie Smith's line: 'She saw the variety of nature/ the ant, the mole, the sky.' Without translating too precisely, this might be expressed by dishes as different as mixed Oriental seafood hors d'oeuvres; pousse spinach and Roquefort salad; seared Orkney scallops with spinach, sorrel and crispy bacon; sautéed foie gras with onion galette and Sauternes jus; chicken masala with cardamom rice; confit of goose with mashed parsnips, apples and Calvados jus; chocolate pudding soufflé, all, incidentally, approved of and recommended. Given the wide-ranging scope of the menu there are, perhaps inevitably, disappointments. A playwright I know orders only fish and chips to be on the safe side, but on the whole standards are high and the greatest pleasure is often to be found in the dishes of the day scribbled on to the menu, such as risotto of new season morels and wild garlic, or boiled bacon, or a vegetable dish of broad beans and peas. Pommes allumettes get everyone's vote. The look is updated clubbiness, but all thought out afresh. Lighting is low after 8pm but noise levels can get high. The air is conditioned. You will usually see a familiar face, but more importantly, after only a visit or two you are made to feel that you are one too.

JADE GARDEN

£24

OPEN
EVERY DAY

HOURS
12.00–11.45PM

CREDIT CARDS
AMEX DELTA
MASTERCARD
SWITCH VISA

SERVICE
OPTIONAL

15 WARDOUR STREET W1   437 5065

'Cantonese hideaway'

So thronged of an evening is the part of Wardour Street which leads from Leicester Square towards Chinatown (Gerrard Street and Lisle Street) that the rather dim and dowdy recesses of Jade Garden, with its themed green furnishings and theatrical sweep of a staircase to the balcony level, come across as a civilized safe haven. Renowned for its dim sum (served until 4.45pm), Jade Garden's main menu also offers some of the best Cantonese food in the area. The waiting staff tend to pull the usual long faces if round-eyes try to order the more 'interesting' dishes but if the prospect of duck's feet with fish lips and the like does not make you come over all queer, persevere with your wishes, as the chef seems not to know the word compromise. Insisting that we would like chicken still on the bone resulted in discovering that baked chicken with salt is a delicious, subtle dish, the flavourful, juicy meat being served with a dipping sauce resembling a tofu-based vinaigrette. Seafood seems extra fresh, and a crab prepared either with ginger and spring onion or chilli and black bean sauce makes a great start to a meal. Fried fillet of eel with garlic comes in a profoundly savoury gravy. Crabmeat makes a slippery sauce for various vegetables, including asparagus and prawn balls. From the noodle list try ho fun with dried beef for its seductive smoky flavours. I have earmarked stewed mutton with dried beancurd in oyster sauce for my next visit.

SET-PRICE
LUNCH & DINNER
£9.50–£17

FACILITIES
SEATS 140

NEAREST TUBE
STATION
LEICESTER
SQUARE/
PICCADILLY
CIRCUS

MAP 5

JASON'S

OPPOSITE 60 BLOMFIELD ROAD W9   286 6752

'Go fishing by the canal'

This is not a boathouse turned restaurant, but a restaurant built to look like a boathouse on a bank of the Grand Union Canal at Little Venice. Chef is Sylvain Ho Wing Cheong, who has been associated with various Mauritian fish restaurants in London, including the short-lived Bateau Gourmand on the Thames. Here he has the best of both worlds of terra firma and water: a proper kitchen (on view to the dining room) and a picturesque, if slightly murky, aqueous outlook where houseboats and narrow boats provide a sense of community. His menu varies according to supplies, which range from conventional fish and shellfish to more exotic, colourful warmwater species. He prepares them with spicy sauces such as black bean, Creole or ginger and lemon grass or with French sauces where ingredients such as cream, brandy and green peppercorns, which have all but vanished from fashionable kitchens, are brought back into play. The fricassées or grillades of mixed fish are a good way to sample a range of what is on offer. The long, hot summer of 1995 got Jason's off to a lively start, but I can imagine the premises seeming a romantic, cosy hideaway in winter too.

£30

OPEN
LUNCH EVERY DAY
DINNER MON–SAT

HOURS
MON–FRI
12.30–3.00PM
6.30–10.00PM
SAT
12.30–10.30PM
SUN
12.30–5.00PM

CREDIT CARDS
AMEX
MASTERCARD VISA

SERVICE
OPTIONAL

SET-PRICE
LUNCH
£12.95

SET-PRICE
DINNER
£16.95

FACILITIES
SEATS 40
TABLES OUTSIDE
SEAT 16
PRIVATE BOAT
SEATS 28
WHEELCHAIR
ACCESS (ALSO
WC)

NEAREST TUBE
STATION
WARWICK AVENUE

MAP 1

JIMMY BEEZ

303 PORTOBELLO ROAD W10   0181-964 9100

'Oh, for a bee's experience
Of clovers and of noon! (Emily Dickinson)'

£24

OPEN
EVERY DAY

HOURS
11.00AM–11.00PM

CREDIT CARDS
AMEX
MASTERCARD VISA

SERVICE
12% PARTIES OF
6 OR MORE

**SET-PRICE
DINNER**
£20

SUNDAY BRUNCH

FACILITIES
SEATS 75
TABLES OUTSIDE
SEAT 16
PRIVATE ROOM
SEATS 20
WHEELCHAIR
ACCESS

**NEAREST TUBE
STATION**
LADBROKE GROVE

MAP 1

Evidence of success takes different forms. I dare say the fact that in May 1995 Jimmy Beez briefly closed in order to extend the premises and increase covers from 48 to 75 is somewhat more significant than its triumph in being given the award Tabasco 'Hot New Chef of the Year' by Egon Ronay's Britvic Guide 1995 Just a Bite, particularly as the hot chef referred to left, to be replaced by William Panton who joined as sous-chef when the restaurant and bar opened. Panton was evidently influential in developing the fashionable menus which are served non-stop every day from 11am until 11pm. Until 6pm a lunch menu is in operation, offering a good mix in 'weight' of salads, pastas, grills, South-East Asian noodle assemblies, open sandwiches, egg dishes and a burger, as well as what is unfelicitously called 'brekkie': either a British fry-up or a vegetarian 'brekkie'. Dinner is more grown-up and inventive. Dishes such as Confucius chicken salad with Chinese leaves and sesame oil vinaigrette; grilled fresh figs wrapped in Parma ham with rocket and mascarpone; shredded sea bass with soy vegetables; chargrilled 10oz entrecôte with fries and Hollandaise; crispy spinach; Kumera potatoes (a Jamaican recipe); lemon tart with a fragile, crunchy glaze have been described as being cooked and served with panache. Staff cope cheerfully – the restaurant has been known to turn over 250 covers at the weekend brunch. They are led by a cool, sophisti-cated girl, 'like a scale model of Sigourney Weaver'. Noise levels can get high, exacerbated by live music every other Friday evening and at weekend brunch.

JONES RESTAURANT AND BAR

25 EARLHAM STREET WC2   240 2662

'Paying attention to the insides'

£28

OPEN
LUNCH MON–FRI
DINNER MON–SAT

HOURS
12.00–3.00PM
6.00–11.30PM

CREDIT CARDS
AMEX DELTA
DINER'S
MASTERCARD
SWITCH VISA

As fashions in food come and go as frequently as hemlines plunge or soar, redefining proportion anew, it is perhaps only expected that frock shops should start to think about feeding the inner child/woman. Jones is a fashion emporium apparently known for dramatic backdrops for its product. At the Covent Garden outlet architects and designers were hired to transform the basement into a restaurant and bar. If the look is groovy, that fashion has passed me by, but at no turn are you left unreminded that some tormented soul has deliberated over light fittings, flooring, wall surfaces, chair shapes, cruet sets. It is bearable and almost dismissable because chef Daniel McDowell and his predominantly female brigade send out of the kitchen-on-view (de rigueur, my dears) such very good dishes. McDowell has worked at The River Café (q.v.) and Alastair Little (q.v.) and also travelled extensively. His menu is the mongrel sort where, for example, spinach soup with Cashel Blue croûtons shares the page with spring vegetable tempura with seaweed salad; chicken livers grilled on rosemary branches with garlic sourdough; grilled lamb's liver with lamb and mint sausages, bacon and sweet potato bubble and squeak; chargrilled guinea fowl with pumpkin salad and pumpkin seed sauce (a gifted plundering of one vegetable). In a short space it roams the world, but dishes are prepared with great care and in accordance with a finely tuned palate. Accessories to a main ingredient are as carefully considered as the hat and shoes and earrings and hairstyle a fashion designer might deliberate over before sending his latest creation out on the catwalk. The patissier is accomplished, as has been understood from coffee panna cotta with warm chocolate sauce and pear and ginger tarte Tatin with crème fraîche. Owner and manager Caroline Stirling is an enthusiast and her zeal stretches to the wine list. Jones has space in its serpentine layout for privacy, but bear in mind it is a bar as well as a restaurant. And it is in Covent Garden.

SERVICE
12½% PARTIES OF 7 OR MORE

SET-PRICE LUNCH
£9.50 & £12.50

SET-PRICE DINNER
£10.50 & £13.50

FACILITIES
SEATS 70

NEAREST TUBE STATION
COVENT GARDEN/ LEICESTER SQUARE

MAP 4

JOY LUCK

545 BATTERSEA PARK ROAD SW11   738 2228

'Not a club but a Chinese restaurant plus'

Nonya cooking – the food of the Straits Chinese in Malaysia – Szechuan and Hunan dishes, freshly made Peking 'ravioli', pork dumplings, and South-East Asian noodle assemblies lift the menu of this serene little family-run Battersea Chinese restaurant out of the ordinary. Among the hors d'oeuvres chicken 'soong', chopped chicken and vegetables spiced with Szechuan pickle and served with lettuce as a wrap; three delicious salads of shredded pork, cucumber and celery in a ma-la sauce; Vietnamese spring rolls with a pungent dip; and Peking spring onion pancakes – quite fiddly to prepare and thus

£22

OPEN
LUNCH SUN DINNER EVERY DAY

HOURS
6.00–12.00PM SUN
12.00–3.00PM
7.00–11.00PM

CREDIT CARDS
AMEX DELTA MASTERCARD SWITCH VISA

SERVICE
OPTIONAL

not often offered – make a good introductory spread. For soup try the Singaporean laksa with its coconut milk broth. Duck is offered three ways; lacquered, Cantonese style, makes a change from the crispy (i.e. deep-fried) aromatic duck. A Malaysian sambal sauce accompanies several of the seafood dishes. Singaporean chicken joints in spiced soy sauce are almost gritty with freshly ground spices. Perhaps in deference to the neighbourhood they seem to pull their punches with the chilli in the Hunan lemon and garlic lamb, which is a pity. Fried hokkien mee, soft noodles with shrimps, pork, chicken shreds and bean sprouts, is a highly satisfying noodle dish. Staff here are exceptionally gentle and considerate.

KALAMARAS, MEGA & MICRO

| 76–78 INVERNESS MEWS W2 | 727 9122 |
| 66 INVERNESS MEWS W2 | 727 5082 |

'The bouzouki goes on'

Stelios Platanos, who has been synonymous with these two Greek, as opposed to Greek/Cypriot, tavernas – big and small, licensed and un-licensed – since the Sixties, has, sadly, but reasonably enough, retired. The new management has pledged to carry on in much the same way which, given the popularity of this mini plaka in a mews off Queensway, shows sound business sense. At a test lunch under the new management (Kalamaras was previously only open for dinner), melitzanosalata (aubergine purée flavoured with garlic, lemon juice and olive oil); yogourtoslata (home-made yogurt with garlic, olive oil and mint); salata horiatiki (country salad); saganaki kefalotiri (grilled cheese with lemon juice); kalamarakia (tender deep-fried squid) and garidoptes (filo parcels of scampi and shrimp) were all enjoyed as a first-course spread, all the more so thanks to freshly made little filo-wrapped spinach and cheese pies being brought warm from the oven by the manager who was keen they should be tried. The chosen main course, arknaki souvla horiatiki, a new addition to the original menu, was a large platter of oven-cooked lamb flavoured with garlic and lemon juice sliced thinly and served with sliced new potatoes drizzled with olive oil and sliced fresh tomatoes: excellent value at £7.90. In the evenings liveliness is promised with Greek and flamenco music. The new manager, who is from Gibraltar, has been playing the guitar at the nearby Las Estrellas for the past 20 years.

KASTOORI

188 UPPER TOOTING ROAD SW17   0181-767 7027

'Discussing some Ugandan delicacies'

Tooting is fortunate in its regional Indian restaurants with Shree Krishna (q.v.) in Tooting High Street offering South Indian food and Kastoori the vegetarian and vegan cooking of Gujerat, with particular reference to the region of Katia Wahd where the climate, unusually, favours the cultivation of the New World fruit, the tomato. The Gujerati Thanki family who own and run Kastoori lived for some years in Uganda where, experimenting with the local vegetables, they evolved various family recipes which are also on offer here; different dishes according to the day of the week. Neither the façade – a bright shopfront among many similar – nor the functional interior gives much of a clue to the creativity with grains, pulses, vegetables and spices on offer, or the kindliness of service. Vegetarians will claim such virtues as naturally theirs; non-vegetarians might concede that a restricted palette of ingredients can be a force for originality and subtlety. Bhajias, samosas and crisp and intricate bhel puris make up most of the list of first courses. A simple dal soup has been described as limpid in texture, beautifully spiced, alluring enough to be ordered three times over. Masala kachori, mashed lentils, is sharper in impact, mined with vibrant spices including a pronounced taste of cinnamon. The tomato legacy comes into its own in special tomato curry made with whole chunks of tomato, beguilingly soft and sweet and also unusual. Palak panir, spinach with Indian cottage cheese, is rich and creamy, with the spinach taking on a completely different aspect through long, slow cooking – grey, muddy and quite delicious, best mopped up with the herb-dusted bread Kastoori bhatura. The specials include green banana curry; a corn and coconut milk assembly with a ground peanut sauce; drumstick curry eaten in much the same way as artichoke leaves, fiddly but worth it; and karela bharela, a profoundly savoury stuffed bitter vegetable. Various specialities are particular to Sunday. The Sunday Special thali priced at £6 brings most of them together and underlines Kastoori's reputation for great value.

£16

OPEN
LUNCH WED–SUN
DINNER EVERY DAY

HOURS
12.30PM–2.30PM
6.00–11.00PM

CREDIT CARDS
MASTERCARD VISA

SERVICE
OPTIONAL

SET-PRICE LUNCH
£8

SET-PRICE DINNER
£13

FACILITIES
SEATS 82
WHEELCHAIR ACCESS
(ALSO WC)

NEAREST TUBE STATION
TOOTING BEC/TOOTING BROADWAY

KENSINGTON PLACE

201 KENSINGTON CHURCH STREET W8   727 3184

'Echoes with enjoyment'

£34

OPEN
EVERY DAY

HOURS
12.00–3.00PM
6.30–11.45PM
SUN
7.30–10.15PM

CREDIT CARDS
MASTERCARD
SWITCH VISA

SERVICE
OPTIONAL

SET-PRICE
LUNCH
£13.50

FACILITIES
SEATS 145
WHEELCHAIR
ACCESS (ALSO
WC)

NEAREST TUBE
STATION
NOTTING HILL
GATE

MAP 1

To my mind one of the uplifting sights in London is the long, glazed wall near the top of Kensington Church Street behind which you see – at the appropriate times – an animated performance of people enjoying themselves eating. Geographical location doubtless plays a part, but I like to think that it is chef Rowley Leigh's vivacious but well-grounded cooking, faithful to its triumphs but responsive to the market, that gives the restaurant its unusually broad appeal. Dowagers rub shoulders with secretaries, bankers with pop stars, fools with tarts and no-one really notices or cares too much. This could be a function of the formidable din requiring you to concentrate on your companion's moving lips if you wish to converse. The fact that the restaurant is noisy and the chairs angular obviously does not deter, for Kensington Place is perennially popular. In all senses it is a streamlined operation, one of the most successful at doing away with the folderol that so often accrues to the notion of fine food. Prime ingredients are made affordable by being bought in abundance at the height of their season, making this a great place for eating game. Dishes of the day are offered as a good value set-price lunch (£13.50 for three courses) or à la carte in the evenings. The main list is long on first courses, including some favourites which cannot be dropped: chicken and goat's cheese mousse with olives; griddled scallops with pea purée and mint vinaigrette; griddled foie gras with sweetcorn pancakes. There is always an omelette – maybe wild mushroom – salads and interesting soups. Main courses find inspiration at home – for example cod with parsely sauce – or in the Mediterranean – for example roast haunch of rabbit with pancetta. Stalwarts among the desserts are crème brûlée; lemon tart (famously good); baked tamarillos with vanilla ice cream and steamed chocolate pudding with custard. Service usually manages to cope cheerfully but some find it cause for complaint. While cooking standards may occasionally waver under pressure, the quality of ingredients does not. Owners Nick Smallwood and Simon Slater are, at time of writing, in the process of planning a new, large restaurant in Chelsea.

KENSINGTON PLACE really offers too many wines to justify the spartan price-order-only layout of its list, especially as the wines themselves are so nomadic: the 80ish bottles are drawn from no fewer than 12 different countries, so the sensible course would be to sort it by style. Those out for a junketing should know that this is the cheapest place to drink vintage Krug (£75). At the opposite end, Giuntini's Parrina is a characterful, rustic red at a house wine price, and there is lots of variety below £20 for wallet-width watchers.

KLEFTIKO

163 CHISWICK HIGH RD W4   0181-994 0305

'Xenophile – from the Greek, meaning to like strangers'

The eating area outside Kleftiko has for over a year been severely disrupted by some quite dramatic excavations. The imaginative and long-suffering owner has decorated the boarded-up earthworks to look like a Greek village house with a trompe l'oeil view through a window on to sparkling blue sea. It makes a witty comment on whatever it is the council have been dredging up from underneath Chiswick High Road and a landmark which will be missed if the work is ever completed. Kleftiko is big on authentic Greek atmosphere and it is an atmosphere you can enjoy from as early as 8am should you require breakfast or a cup of coffee. At an early visit you are likely to see the owner's wife toiling away preparing the traditional Greek and Cypriot dishes. In the evenings the restaurant is packed and with the timing of the Keystone cops waiters dash about, in and out, conveying a hectic but good-natured urgency. A relaxing way to order, a sort of dress rehearsal for a Greek holiday, is The Supreme Meze at £15 a head. A vast array of dishes arrives which has included dolmades, taramasalata, tuna fish salad, black-eyed beans, broad beans, grilled haloumi cheese, followed by chicken kebabs, meatballs too redolent of cinnamon, and particularly good lamb cutlets, tender and delicately flavoured, cooked with a finesse seldom to be found in back garden barbecues. There are cheaper, briefer mezes and also a long, comfortingly predictable à la carte. The eponymous kleftiko, aromatically spiced, is a speciality. The lumpy stucco walls are covered not only with all the usual Greek artefacts but also a large number of paintings, sizable – sometimes alarming – modern canvases which add an extra dimension to the spirit of this enterprising establishment. You can also find Kleftiko at 85 Bush Road, Kew Gardens, Surrey (0181-940 3182).

£20

OPEN
EVERY DAY

HOURS
8.00AM–11.30PM

CREDIT CARDS
AMEX DELTA
DINER'S
MASTERCARD
SWITCH VISA

SERVICE
12½%

SET-PRICE LUNCH
£8.50

SET-PRICE DINNER
£9.50

SUNDAY BRUNCH

FACILITIES
SEATS 80
TABLES OUTSIDE
SEAT 60
WHEELCHAIR
ACCESS (ALSO
WC)

NEAREST TUBE STATION
TURNHAM GREEN

LAHORE KEBAB HOUSE

2 UMBERSTON STREET E1   481 9737

'To get to the bottom of the meaning of balti'

£9 BYO

OPEN
EVERY DAY

HOURS
12.00PM–12.00AM

CREDIT CARDS
NONE

SERVICE
OPTIONAL

FACILITIES
SEATS 70

NEAREST TUBE STATION
ALDGATE EAST/
WHITECHAPEL

MAP 1

The balti craze trickling south from the Midlands has failed to make much impact in London, perhaps because restaurants were already serving the same sort of one-pot cooking under the heading karahi dishes. However, the true spirit of balti cooking – its speed, cheapness, unpretentiousness and delectability – can be found at the estimable Lahore Kebab House off Commerical Road in Whitechapel. In greasy spoon surroundings – this is definitely a café, not a restaurant – you are served kebabs, karahi dishes, curries and biriyanis cooked to order over open flames which have a vitality of flavour found lacking in most grander places. Chicken tikka, which can be purchased for the princely sum of £2, comes in for particular praise for its juiciness and vibrant spicing. Lamb chop curry, chicken karahi, tarka dal and quail have also been singled out. There are usually also dishes of the day which might feature offal. Bread fresh from the tandoor is brought and replenished unasked. You will be in and out quickly, probably making way for someone in a queue. To prolong the event you can order a dessert of kheer – cardamom-flavoured rice pudding. But as Lahore Kebab House is open noon to midnight 365 days a year, it is easy to find relatively quiet times. It is unlicensed but not averse to customers bringing their own alcohol.

THE LANSDOWNE

90 GLOUCESTER AVENUE NW1   483 0409

'Help yourself to great food'

£20

OPEN
LUNCH TUES–SUN
DINNER EVERY DAY

HOURS
MON
6.00–11.00PM
TUES–SAT
12.00–11.00PM
SUN
12.00–3.00PM
7.00–10.30PM

CREDIT CARDS
NONE

SERVICE
OPTIONAL

SET–PRICE LUNCH
£15 (SUN ONLY)

Pub conversions are beginning to divide into two categories: those that are run as restaurants with reservations, waiter service and credit cards taken and the others who hang on to the pub ethos, take no bookings and insist that food is ordered at the bar, paid for up front and with cash or cheques. The Lansdowne is firmly in the second category, complete with few concessions to comfort in the ad hoc decor, but with good enough food to compensate for whatever you might find tiresome in those strictures. Menus change daily. The following describes a typical meal: chilled leek and potato soup (in other words vichyssoise) was generously served in a large bowl, hugely welcome on a hot day; a rough, juicy country terrine came with home-made relish and pickles, a large salad and good bread; half a lobster flavoured with tarragon came with boiled new potatoes, coleslaw and cucumber salad and at £8.50 was considered a snip; prune and almond tart, and strawberries, meringues and cream were much enjoyed. Some other dishes available that meal time were lasagnette (pasta ribbons with fluted edges) with courgettes, chilli and garlic and a Cos salad; spiced, stuffed aubergine with couscous and tzaziki; rib-eye steak with chips, aïoli and watercress salad. You get the picture. On this same hot day a three-pint jug of Pimms at £12 was extraordinarily tempting.

FACILITIES
Seats 70
Tables outside seat 30
Wheelchair access

Nearest Tube Station
Chalk Farm

Map 1

LAUNCESTON PLACE

1A Launceston Place W8   937 6912

'What is going on?'

Prettily located in a Kensington backwater, the look of the interior, which divides into a series of intimate dining rooms, discreetly lit and hung with paintings, is quintessentially upper-middle-class English, the sort who have not yet discovered living in lofts. What also seems English in a less desirable way this year is a casual, who-gives-a-hoot approach both to the preparation of some dishes in the thoroughly modern menu and the service. To offer griddled foie gras with sourdough bread and chilli jam, but deliver peach chutney because there is no chilli jam, and two huge slices of grilled bread overwhelming two mimsy slices of foie gras is dereliction of duty; as is grey, not entirely fresh, cod served with tapenade and roast tomatoes; as is fatty, well-done roast leg of lamb when the request had been for it pink. At the height of the hot summer to offer pumpkin risotto and a hot cream of broccoli soup, both distinctly autumnal in feel, signals a lack of someone thinking or caring. The relationship between Launceston Place and its brother Kensington Place (q.v.) seems all the more tenuous. It is sock-pulling-up time.

£33

Open
Lunch Sun–Fri
Dinner Mon–Sat

Hours
12.30–2.30pm
7.00–11.30pm
Sun
12.30–3.00pm

Credit Cards
Amex Delta
Mastercard
Switch Visa

Service
Optional

Set-Price
Lunch & Dinner
£13.50 & £16.50

Facilities
Seats 85
Private rooms
seat 12 & 30
Wheelchair access

Nearest Tube Station
Gloucester
Road/High
Street
Kensington

Map 2

LAURENT

£17

OPEN
MON–SAT

HOURS
12.00–2.00PM
6.00–11.00PM

CREDIT CARDS
AMEX DELTA
MASTERCARD VISA

SERVICE
OPTIONAL

FACILITIES
SEATS 36
WHEELCHAIR
ACCESS

**NEAREST TUBE
STATION**
GOLDERS GREEN

MAP 1

428 FINCHLEY ROAD NW2   794 3603

'Simply the best couscous'

Doing one thing but doing it well is the principle behind this endearing family-run, simply decorated restaurant. The speciality is couscous, which comes in five versions, including vegetarian or fish couscous, priced from £6.60 (vegetarian) to £10.25 (complet). This last delivers a fluffy heap of coucous grains, vegetables, and grilled lamb chop, brochette and good quality merguez sausage. The harissa (hot sauce) seems home-made and is properly powerful. Start with brique à l'oeuf, an envelope of fried filo pastry with an egg enclosed, and finish with ices, crème caramel or crêpe Suzette. There is a short list of North African wines, but for the same price you might prefer a Côtes du Rhône. Laurent offers a takeaway service which is a thought for parties, occasions that the muffling, absorbing nature of coucous suits very well.

LEITH'S

£36

OPEN
EVERY DAY

HOURS
7.00–11.30PM
SUN
6.30–10.00PM

CREDIT CARDS
AMEX DINER'S
JCB MASTERCARD
SWITCH VISA

SERVICE
12½%

**SET-PRICE
DINNER**
£26.50

FACILITIES
SEATS 75
PRIVATE ROOMS
SEAT 4–40
WHEELCHAIR
ACCESS

**NEAREST TUBE
STATION**
NOTTING HILL
GATE

MAP 1

92 KENSINGTON PARK ROAD W11   229 4481

'And now we bid adieu to the hors d'oeuvres trolley'

Changes are afoot at the long-established Leith's, once – about 26 years ago – considered pioneering for opening in Notting Hill Gate. The owners of Leith's School of Food and Wine, Caroline Waldegrave and Christopher Bland, plus the restaurant's chef and manager, Alex Floyd and Nick Tarayan, have bought the restaurant from Prue Leith. The changes which will take place – opening for weekday lunch and, shock! horror! the abolition of the hors d'oeuvres trolley but the substitution of a plate of hors d'oeuvres – are happening too late for this review to accommodate. However, since Alex Floyd will continue as chef we can comment on his cooking which is contemporary, deft and intelligent in terms of balance and the match-making of what are well-sourced ingredients. His talent seems expressed most volubly in the two-course menu of the week where he is not constrained to provide favourites such as the Leith's duckling (served for two). Two dishes which give a flavour of these menus are feuilleté of roast salmon and scrambled eggs with anchovy butter sauce and roast pork cutlet with black pudding and cream celery sauce. Test meals have revealed Floyd as a dab hand with fish, mentioning sea bass with olive oil and garlic mash as proof. Desserts too – the province of patissier Michael Strong – come in for praise, as should the ambitious vegetarian menu, some of it suited to vegans, which Leith's also pioneered. Criticisms are directed at the anachronistic overbearing service, the sterility of the design and decor in the overlit interconnecting rooms and the high prices. With so much else now on offer in Notting Hill Gate, they are prices that beckon to the corporate customer rather than the individual. However, these elements may also change under the new regime. I hope so. Stop press news is that 15% service charge is reduced to 12½%.

LEITH'S IS PROBABLY the best place to drink decent claret: vintages have been carefully screened, nothing is too old or too young, and extravagance is encouraged by a generous price structure. Those worth pushing the boat out for are Pichon Lalande 1978 at £65 and Latour 1970, which at £150 is £345 less than at Le Pont de la Tour (q.v.). The better domaines of Burgundy show strongly, too. No other region is given the same amount of elbow room, and Australia certainly deserves more. Along the way, attractive sightings include Domaine de Trevallon, Masi's Valpolicella-like Toar, and Mumm's Crémant de Cramant (recent bottlings are labelled Mumm de Cramant). Differently sized parties will appreciate the range of differently sized bottles. Those responsible for the sectional introductions must have attended Leith's School of Exclamatory Writing, but know their wines.

LEMONIA

89 REGENT'S PARK ROAD NW1   586 7454

'Greek/Cypriot food with its finger on the pulses'

The secrets of restaurant success are here on display. Dedicated family-linked ownership, genuine warmth of welcome, carefully prepared dishes – some outside the usual formula – and eminently reasonable prices for food and wine bring customers piling in. It is not only locals who choose this pub-to-taverna conversion in Primrose Hill when they want to go out for a Greek meal or celebrate an anniversary of one kind or another (there is a party room upstairs); people come from afar, causing even greater parking problems in the area. The fact that in winter the nourishing soup trahana (champion for children and invalids) made from cracked wheat and yogurt is

£20

OPEN
LUNCH SUN–FRI
DINNER MON–SAT

HOURS
12.00–3.00PM
6.00–11.30PM

CREDIT CARDS
MASTERCARD VISA

SERVICE
OPTIONAL

SET-PRICE LUNCH
£7.95

SET-PRICE DINNER
£10.50

FACILITIES
SEATS 150
TABLES OUTSIDE
SEAT 60
PRIVATE ROOM
SEATS 30
WHEELCHAIR
ACCESS (ALSO
WC)

NEAREST TUBE
STATION
CHALK FARM

MAP 1

available and the above-average number of dishes based on dried beans and pulses (ideal for vegetarians) are indicative of a love and understanding of Greek/Cypriot food beyond its purely commercial applications. A lively turnover of large numbers of customers – the restaurant seats 150 – enables fish to be sold at a good price. Look to the blackboard for the daily fish specials and also the seasonal vegetable dishes which are lovingly prepared. The abundant meze at £10.50 a head is a famously good deal. Noise at peak times is a problem, but there is the option of the quieter Limani (in the original premises) opposite.

THE LEXINGTON

45 LEXINGTON STREET W1   434 3401

'Laid-back atmosphere and evening prices'

£27

OPEN
LUNCH MON–FRI
DINNER MON–SAT

HOURS
12.00–3.00PM
6.00–11.30PM

CREDIT CARDS
AMEX DINER'S
MASTERCARD VISA

SERVICE
OPTIONAL

SET-PRICE
DINNER
£10

FACILITIES
SEATS 45
PRIVATE ROOMS
SEAT 20
WHEELCHAIR
ACCESS

NEAREST TUBE
STATION
PICCADILLY
CIRCUS/OXFORD
CIRCUS/
TOTTENHAM
COURT ROAD

MAP 5

Chefs at The Lexington come and go, some of them, unfortunately, talking of lollo rosso in the salads. Last year's chef was Mark Holmes (now at Scotts). This year it is Andy Farquarson. However, the menu in shape and form stays pretty constant at Martin Saxon's agreeably laid-back West Soho establishment. Starters – a vegetable soup, a composed salad or two, often dill herrings and sometimes crostini – are followed by midway dishes served in two sizes, two prices. There is usually a risotto, a mussel dish and always The Lexington paysanne, a salad of leaves, duck confit, lentils, vegetable crisps and quail's eggs which originally migrated from The Square (q.v.) to settle here. Typical main courses are seared salmon with risotto; crusted cod with baked vegetables; rump of lamb Provençal; stuffed, roasted quail. There is always a chocolate-based dessert plus a flavoured burnt cream, sorbets, tarts and perhaps tiramisu. Execution of the dishes is fine; not earth-shattering but professional. The only disappointments this year were in the set-price evening menu (£10 for two courses and coffee) where mulligatawny soup tasted like tinned tomato and the roast pork with a grain mustard cream sauce was served pink. In the evening a pianist plays and it feels a little bit like New York. Such casual service would not be found in that city, though. The wine list is reasonably priced and creatively assembled. Upstairs in this Georgian terrace house are two romantic rooms available for private parties.

THE LOBSTER POT

3 KENNINGTON LANE SE11   582 5556

'A theatrically nautical and French setting for fine fish'

A list including portholes, aquaria, nets, shells, French staff in striped shirts and a chef in a fisherman's smock may frighten some, and mentioning that all the above and more are crammed into a tiny space seems sure to bring on cabin fever. Hervé Regent runs a very eccentric ship but maintains the standards of fish quality that would be demanded in Brittany or Normandy. He cooks aromatic fish soups which expand – as la bouillabaisse Brettone – into main-course stews made with John Dory and eel; finds unusually good prawns and squid; does a roaring trade in plateaux de fruits de mer (£10.50/£21) and lobster; and offers his other fish (sole, skate, sea bass) with rich sauces – those on a regime would be hard-pressed to avoid cream, butter or garlic unless they send in a special request to the Breton chef. More of a drawback to most of us will be the prices: there is a stipulation of at least £23 each being spent in the evenings (£15.50 for lunch) and one £20.50 set-dinner menu had six supplements. Fish is a scarce resource which should not be sold cheap and this is a small restaurant to which most customers come expecting to spend a long evening, but more flexibility would be appreciated. Is there no one in Kennington who might like a quick shellfish plate and a glass of wine at the beginning of the evening, or a lobster salad as a late-night treat?

£35

OPEN
TUES–SAT

HOURS
12.00–2.30PM
7.00–10.45PM

CREDIT CARDS
AMEX DELTA
DINER'S JCB
MASTERCARD
SWITCH VISA

SERVICE
12½%

SET-PRICE LUNCH
£14.50

SET-PRICE DINNER
£20.50

FACILITIES
SEATS 24
WHEELCHAIR
ACCESS

NEAREST TUBE STATION
KENNINGTON

MAP 1

LONDON HILTON ON PARK LANE – TRADER VIC'S

22 PARK LANE W1   493 8000

'Escapism'

A basement restaurant tricked out as if the Kon-Tiki had become a luxury cruise ship, where potent cocktails and no glimmer of daylight conspire to blur the time of day, is just the place for when you want to escape real life. At lunch time, Trader Vic's offers set-price menus at £13 and £15 for three courses and coffee (plus 15% service), providing a reasonably priced opportunity to realize that behind all the corny scene-setting there is competent cooking of well-sourced ingredients. Choosing from the carte, it is hard to resist a selection of what are called tidbits and finger food to eat while drinking Mai Tais

£35

OPEN
LUNCH SUN–FRI
DINNER EVERY DAY

HOURS
12.00–3.00 PM
6.30–11.45PM

CREDIT CARDS
AMEX DELTA
DINER'S
MASTERCARD
SWITCH VISA

SERVICE
15%

COVER CHARGE
£1 (LUNCH)
£1.50 (DINNER)

**SET-PRICE
LUNCH**
£13 & £15

**SET-PRICE
DINNER**
£25–£31

FACILITIES
SEATS 160
WHEELCHAIR
ACCESS (ALSO
WOMEN'S WC)

**NEAREST TUBE
STATION**
GREEN PARK/
HYDE PARK
CORNER

MAP 3

or London Sours. Into individual butterfly-shaped dishes of cocktail sauce and mustard you can dip items such as spiced chicken wings, crab Rangoon deep-fried in wonton skins, BBQ spare ribs and the excellent glazed duck goujons. The Chinese wood-fired oven, its design dating, they say, to the Han Dynasty, cooks beautifully the Indonesian rack of lamb served with a peanut butter sauce, the brochette of scallops or Chateaubriand. From the section entitled Trader Vic's Traditions, sirloin of beef with teriyaki sauce is an excellent piece of meat in a sauce that, for teriyaki, is dignified and quite restrained. For those wanting noodly Polynesian dishes there are various assemblies such as Jack's chow mein with seafood, chicken and pork (also appearing on the set-price menu). Fruit or ices or fruit in yet another cocktail make the best dessert.

LOU PESCADOU

241 OLD BROMPTON ROAD SW5   370 1057

' 'Allo sailor'

£24

OPEN
EVERY DAY
(EXCEPT SUN
DURING JULY &
AUG)

HOURS
12.00–3.00PM
7.00PM–12.00AM

CREDIT CARDS
AMEX DELTA
DINER'S
MASTERCARD
SWITCH VISA

SERVICE
15%

COVER CHARGE
£1

**SET-PRICE
LUNCH**
£9

FACILITIES
SEATS 65
TABLES OUTSIDE
SEAT 19
PRIVATE ROOM
SEATS 40
WHEELCHAIR
ACCESS

**NEAREST TUBE
STATION**
EARLS COURT

MAP 2

There seems to have been a trade-off at this nautically themed Provençal fish restaurant located in an unsalubrious stretch of the Old Brompton Road: reliably sound cooking for universal friendliness. Where staff were once haughty and unhelpful to some they have become to a man charm itself, but the standards of food preparation lurch up and down. Pissaladière, which should be – and has been – melting onions on flaky pastry criss-crossed with anchovies and dotted with olives, was a heap of fried onions on a small pizza base. Moules marinière were opened in a broth that had all the appeal of washing-up water. However, crab salad has been described as blamelessly fresh; turbot and sea bass, simply grilled, of good quality but the sauces slightly amateurish; and the tarte aux pommes minute the ideal indulgent dessert for completing a basically healthy meal. Choosing oysters or the plateau Pescadou is one way round the dichotomy. Pasta is usually well cooked. For those not wanting fish, there are steaks and daily specialities such as ossobuco and filet de porc au miel et au citron. No bookings and the egalitarian, beside-the-seaside nature of the menu – pizza or St Pierre, omelette or oysters; the choice is yours – are attractive distinguishing features of Lou Pescadou. A £1 cover charge – covering commercial mayonnaise masquerading as aïoli – and 15% service charge are less appealing. They hike the price of the £9 three-course, set-price lunch.

MAGNO'S BRASSERIE

65A LONG ACRE WC2   836 6077

'A new lease of Covent Garden life'

From The Adelphi (15 mins) to Wyndhams (10 mins), the walking distance from Magno's to London's West End theatres is given at the foot of the pre-theatre menu (tables to be relinquished by 8pm). This two-course-and-coffee deal at £9.95 is a popular attraction, but the place continues to fizz thereafter with an agreeably mixed crowd. The menu is fundamentally French but includes pastas and risottos, dishes of no known derivation such as prawn Caesar salad, and references to the Greek part-ownership in assemblies such as spiced vegetables, nuts and raisins in filo pastry served with tzatsiki. Dishes from the carte which have come in for praise are brandade de morue en canapé au basilic, the salt cod purée being compared favourably to that found at Bibendum (q.v.); ravioli of wild mushrooms with its creamy sauce seemingly intensified with the flavour of porcini; duo de canard aux poires caramelisées, jus au gingembre, the twinning being grilled breast and leg confit; couscous d'agneau et merguez à l'harissa where the lamb verging on mutton suited well the fiery sausage and sauce. Crème brûlée had an untoward gluey quality but tarte aux fraises was comme il faut. Service is French and friendly. Magno's, having gone through some dull patches in its long existence, is currently one of the better bets in Covent Garden.

£32

OPEN
LUNCH MON–FRI
DINNER MON–SAT

HOURS
12.00–2.30PM
5.30–11.30PM

CREDIT CARDS
AMEX DINER'S
MASTERCARD VISA

SERVICE
12½%

SET-PRICE
LUNCH
£13.50 & £16.50

SET-PRICE
DINNER
£9.95

FACILITIES
SEATS 60
WHEELCHAIR
ACCESS

NEAREST TUBE
STATION
COVENT GARDEN

MAP 4

MA GOA

244 UPPER RICHMOND ROAD SW15   0181-780 1767

'And Mr, Miss and Master Goa'

Family values are enshrined in this Goan restaurant in Putney. Mrs Kapoor, who learned her cooking skills from a Goan 'auntie', is in the kitchen; Mr Kapoor (formerly manager of Shezan in Knightsbridge) and their son and daughter run front of house with grave courtesy (the older generation) and friendliness (the younger). The menu has evolved and matured and become more authentically Goan since the restaurant opened in the summer of '93. The best way to begin a meal is to share the starter platter which brings piquant shrimp balchao, fried patties made of lentils and minced lamb, spiced potato-stuffed deep-fried poppadom parcels, and strips of stir-fried lamb's liver. It means missing the nareal and curd soup, based

£18

OPEN
TUE–SUN

HOURS
12.30–2.30
7.00–11.00PM
SUN 1.00–9.00PM

CREDIT CARDS
AMEX DELTA
MASTERCARD
SWITCH VISA

SERVICE
10%

SET-PRICE
LUNCH
£7.95

FACILITIES
SEATS 50
WHEELCHAIR
ACCESS (ALSO
WC)

NEAREST TUBE
STATION
EAST PUTNEY

NEAREST BR
STATION
PUTNEY

MAP 1

on corn and coconut flavoured with turmeric and asafoetida, but at £2.75 you could order that as well. Palm vinegar, fenni (fermented juice from the coconut palm or cashew tree) and mustard oil are some of the ingredients of a true vindaloo, served here using pork which the mainly Catholic Goans enjoy. Sorpotel, a particularly pungent mixture made from pork, liver, blood and rind, is soon to be introduced and probably will be by the time you read this. Cafreal, a Goan chicken dish with a green masala, is also in the pipeline. I can warmly recommend borrego pankhawalla, spiced, marinated lamb chops barbecued over charcoal and served on thinly sliced salad; coconut and coriander galinna, chicken first burnished on the grill then cooked with coconut milk, chillies, ginger and garlic garnished with roasted coconut pieces, served in a hundee, a terracotta pot which sits in the charcoal; Ma's sada pullao, basmati rice cooked in vegetable stock and garnished with fried onions; and the vegetable dishes and dal of the day.

MALABAR

27 UXBRIDGE STREET W8   727 8800

'An easily comprehended Indian restaurant'

Malabar has hit on a winning formula – an easily deciphered Indian menu served in surroundings that invoke the restaurant's previous incarnation as Italian – and so, sensibly enough I suppose, they seem to find no reason to change it. The slightly more unusual dishes continue to hold allure: the chargrilled devilled chicken livers; tamarind-marinated venison; jeera chicken cooked with roasted cumin; sliced banana cooked with ginger and spices. Main courses which have come in for favourable comment this year are the hot and garlicky karahi king prawns and sag gosht, full of complex flavours. However, kaddu – fried pumpkin – managed to be bland and bitter at the same time. Indian desserts on offer are kheer – rice pudding, and kulfi – iced reduced milk flavoured in this instance with almonds and pistachios, but bought in rather than home-made. Vegetarians can order a thali, served like everything else on authentic but rather jarring steel plates. Malabar attracts a regular, probably chiefly local clientele. Its unthreatening, quite upbeat atmosphere makes it a place where women seem happy to eat together or alone, not a common sight in the average Indian restaurant. There is a short wine list which includes the Indian fizzer Omar Khayyám Brut.

£24

OPEN
EVERY DAY

HOURS
12.00–3.00PM
6.00–11.30PM

CREDIT CARDS
MASTERCARD
SWITCH VISA

SERVICE
12½%

COVER CHARGE
80P

SET–PRICE
LUNCH & DINNER
£15

FACILITIES
SEATS 56
PRIVATE ROOM
SEATS 20

NEAREST TUBE
STATION
NOTTING HILL
GATE

MAP 1

MAMTA

692 FULHAM ROAD SW6   371 5971

'Go West to go East'

The far reaches of the Fulham Road are a faintly surprising place to find an Indian vegetarian restaurant, and the area supplies a clientele that might not fit your preconception of meat-shunners – the voices are so loud – but it probably corresponds quite accurately to the new breed of traveller to India. Surroundings are dull, painted a monotonous brown, but perhaps all the better for discovering complexity in the food, with each dish seemingly possessed of autonomous spicing; no tastes duplicated in the course of a meal despite a relatively limited range of ingredients. To start there is a range of vegetarian snacks which include deep-fried bhajia; steamed idli (rice flour cakes) served with a spicy sambal; patra, aravi leaves spread with chick pea paste rolled into pinwheels; uttapam, resembling a thin, savoury crumpet; crisp spheres of fried puri containing soft and sour fillings; and dramatic dosa, large pancakes of fermented rice and lentil flour batter, served plain or with a potato stuffing – more generously filled than you find in India. Among the vegetable dishes, the chef's specials, despite some dopey titles, hold allure. A La Carte Mombai is an excellent potato curry; Shimla Green is spinach tactfully cooked and spiced; Aubergine Sparkle contains aubergine slices which hold their shape in a rich sauce; Undhiu (available Wednesdays and Saturdays) is a highly satisfactory mix of vegetables with crisply fried gram flour balls flavoured with fresh fenugreek. Raitas, chutneys and breads are all carefully prepared. Service can be slow but is anxious that you should like the food and not be frightened by too much chilli-heat.

£20

OPEN
LUNCH WED–SUN
DINNER EVERY
DAY

HOURS
12.30–3.00PM
6.00–11.00PM

CREDIT CARDS
AMEX DINER'S
MASTERCARD VISA

SERVICE
OPTIONAL

**SET-PRICE
LUNCH**
£4.95

**SET-PRICE
DINNER**
£7.25 & £11.50

FACILITIES
SEATS 42
WHEELCHAIR
ACCESS

**NEAREST TUBE
STATION**
PARSONS GREEN

MAP 1

MANDARIN KITCHEN

14 QUEENSWAY W2   727 9012

'The appeal is obvious when the food arrives'

Although the hangar-like room and curt service do not suggest it, someone here has a zeal for good food and good seafood particularly. Live lobsters and crabs are transformed into various Chinese recipes: with ginger and spring onion; or black bean sauce; or chilli and noodles. The choice of sea bass, monkfish, eels or carp depends on the market. If the bass are in and priced to your liking, to have one steamed with

£26

OPEN
EVERY DAY

HOURS
12.00–11.30PM

CREDIT CARDS
AMEX DINER'S
MASTERCARD
SWITCH VISA

SERVICE
OPTIONAL

SET-PRICE
LUNCH & DINNER
£8.90

FACILITIES
SEATS 120
WHEELCHAIR
ACCESS

NEAREST TUBE
STATION
QUEENSWAY

MAP 1

shredded pork (more like bacon), mushrooms, ginger and spring onions is a treat. There are also stewed oysters, fried squid, prawns 'with an unexpected taste' and some interesting meat dishes mixed in with the mundane. Everyone should eat jellyfish and cucumber at least once – some might even enjoy the fish's slight snap. The same cannot be said of sea cucumber, a.k.a. sea slug.

MANDEER

21 HANWAY PLACE W1   323 0660

'Peas are given a chance'

£18

OPEN
MON–SAT

HOURS
12.00–3.00PM
5.30–10.00PM

CREDIT CARDS
AMEX DELTA
DINER'S
MASTERCARD
SWITCH VISA

SERVICE
12½%

FACILITIES
SEATS 60
PRIVATE ROOM
SEATS 30

NEAREST TUBE
STATION
TOTTENHAM
COURT
ROAD/GOODGE
STREET

MAP 4

Good vibrations start at the top of the stairs as you leave the grime and hustle of Tottenham Court Road behind and look down on a statue of Buddha. Once into the restaurant, soothing Indian music, brass light fittings twinkling with fairy lights and gentle waiters reinforce a mood of hippy idealism which is as it should be since Mandeer opened in 1967 at the height of flower power. For nearly 30 years the restaurant has been serving exemplary Southern Indian and Gujerati vegetarian food at eminently reasonable prices. For the uninitiated one of the thalis – set meals – are a good starting point. Devotees will know the delights to be found in sev puri – its mix of crisp and soft, sour and sweet, wet and dry all in one mouthful – patra, dal vada and dosa, and that is just for starters. Curried vegetable dishes that have come in for particular praise this year are panir matter, a mixture of home-made cheese and peas in an onion-based sauce, the black-eyed beans (beans of the day) in a subtle, creamy sauce and the Gujerati dal, spiced with mustard and fenugreek, served at soup consistency, to be mopped up by breads or rice. There is a wide range of desserts encompassing the various results of boiling down – condensing – milk. To drink there is lassi, sweet, salt or plain, but Mandeer is also licensed. At lunchtimes there is also a self-service buffet. Should you be suffering any health problems such as sore throat, malaria, loss of hair, rheumatism or skin eruptions, ayurvedic remedies are sold at the same address.

MANTANAH THAI CUISINE

2 ORTON BUILDINGS PORTLAND RD SE25 0181-771 1148

'Get out the A-Z'

£22

OPEN
TUES–SUN

HOURS
TUES–SAT
6.30–11.00PM
SUN
6.30–10.30PM

CREDIT CARDS
AMEX
MASTERCARD VISA

SERVICE
OPTIONAL

SET-PRICE DINNER
£12.95 & £16

FACILITIES
SEATS 40
WHEELCHAIR
ACCESS

NEAREST BR STATION
NORWOOD
JUNCTION

Vaut le detour is a description the Michelin Guide bestows on certain restaurants and it is one applicable to Mantanah unless, of course, you already live in South Norwood, in which case you are blessed in your local Thai restaurant. The family who own it and who also do the cooking aim to provide something original and, in their word, 'native' for their customers. Consequently, on the long menu you find recipes not offered elsewhere, a fascinating separate section of dishes from the north and north-east of Thailand including the charcuterie for which that region is famous, and a comprehensive, innovative vegetarian list. Dishes which the owners say are particular to the restaurant include Golden Triangle – this sort of fanciful name intersperses transliterations from Thai – spiced chopped chicken and prawns with fragrant rice wrapped in crisp rice pastry, served with pickled cucumber sauce; Emerald Palace, a vegetarian steamed rice cake with Chinese leek stuffing accompanied by soya sauce and browned garlic; Highland Tribes Curry, a slow-cooked pork curry from the north, flavoured with roasted peanuts and pickled garlic; Midnight Curry, a coconut milk-based chicken curry using pumpkin for sweetness and shredded lime leaves for a piquant note. There have also been enthusiastic reports for gong pao, charcoal grilled butterflied king prawns 'enhanced immeasurably by a sweet, syrupy tamarind sauce'; yum pra meuk, a 'superb' squid salad with well-balanced flavourings, and tom kar hed, a thickish mushroom soup with galangal, lemon grass and chilli, apparently champion for clearing the sinuses. Staff are knowledgeable and helpful with the ordering in the sense of suggesting what might go with what – useful when faced with a list of 128 dishes. The drinks list is a weak link: limited beers and an unenlightened selection of wines.

McCLEMENTS BISTRO

2 WHITTON ROAD TWICKENHAM   0181-744 9610

'Lucky Twickers'

£25

OPEN
MON–SAT

HOURS
12.00–2.30PM
7.00–11.00PM

At the time of writing this small restaurant near Twickenham (BR mainline) station is the only venture of John McClements and his chef Phil Rickerby, the other restau-

CREDIT CARDS
MASTERCARD VISA

SERVICE
OPTIONAL

SET-PRICE LUNCH
£10

SET-PRICE DINNER
£16

FACILITIES
SEATS 45

NEAREST BR STATION
TWICKENHAM

rant at nearby Twickenham Green having been closed for refurbishment. A much-needed face-lift in terms of decor has taken place at Whitton Road, with the nips and tucks provided by large watercolours, ornate mirrors and more flattering lighting. Someone has suggested that the menu here is much more sophisticated than the address, but why should residents of Twickenham and thereabouts not be the grateful recipients of robust, creative, enlightened cooking with an emphasis on the delicious possibilities of offal? Meals (offered at a set price) start with home-made bread and pot of pâté made from gizzards. First courses include black pudding en croûte with mustard sauce (a constant on the menu); Provençal fish soup with rouille; brochette of bacon-wrapped scallops on sorrel; croûte of red mullet with aïoli; grilled squid with chillis and garlic; and risotto with wild mushrooms and shavings of Parmesan. Portions are generous, especially in the main dishes – tête de porc with sauce piquant; stuffed lamb's heart with lamb's tongue and tripe Provençal; vol-au-vent filled with lamb's sweetbreads and a sherry sauce; cassoulet (as good as you would expect); saddle of venison with a confit of chestnuts, fennel and onions; and (another menu fixture) assiette du boucher with trotter, oxtail, ox tongue and sweetbreads. Vegetables are modestly priced at £1. As would probably happen in a restaurant of this style in France, desserts wind the meal down rather than conclude it with a fanfare. Tarte Tatin has been feeble in impact and a chocolate Marquise ordinary although rich. The selection of French cheeses is probably the answer. Service is friendly and, importantly, committed to offal.

LE METRO

28 BASIL STREET SW3   589 6286

'Come on down, Mr Right'

£23

OPEN
MON–SAT

HOURS
12.00–2.30PM
6.00–11.00PM

CREDIT CARDS
AMEX DELTA
DINER'S
MASTERCARD
SWITCH VISA

SERVICE
OPTIONAL

SET-PRICE LUNCH & DINNER
£12.30

The tendency noted last year for this basement wine bar/restaurant beneath L'Hotel (part of The Capital Hotel) to fill up with women who smoke and shriek has not gone away. However, the Silk Cut sisters can be avoided, unless of course you want to join in, and the strengths of the place concentrated upon. These are, quite simply, the food, which comes from the kitchen of Philip Britten at The Capital (q.v.) and the wine list, with the facility of most of it available by the glass (see below). A customer who observed that the food was probably better than it needed to be (a sad and I hope unheeded observation) hugely enjoyed a salade tiède of chicken livers, kebabs of rare tuna alternating with peppers, and the pudding of summer berries steeped in Port. Other dishes favourably commented upon were honey-glazed duck on a bed of stir-fried shreds of vegetables rich in soy and ginger, and the well-chosen British cheeses with which a nice glass of red was finished. The fact that drinks were priced at happy-hour prices (half the usual price) despite the meal lasting beyond the deadline of 7.30pm was also appreciated. When they can get this so right, you wonder why the Levin family had so many problems with The People's Palace (q.v.).

ALL BUT the half dozen or so low-turnover grandees of Le Metro's 60-wine cellar are available by the glass, a fact which at a stroke lifts this from being a good list to an unbeatable one. As was remarked last year, why is this not more widely copied? You can, for example, kick off with Schloss Johannisberg's delicate QbA Riesling, move on to Turckheim's thick, floral Gewürztraminer, and finish off with Guigal's gamey Côtes du Rhône, and still drive home. And if a bottle is what you're after, the prices are far from off-putting.

MIJANOU

143 EBURY STREET SW1   730 4099

'Nothing of her doth fade, but doth suffer a sea-change…'

There is something rich and strange about Sonia Blech's cooking, indeed there are rich and strange elements about the entire operation she and her husband run at 143 Ebury Street. For example, why is the door firmly locked at times when the dining room is full of staff and customers? And what are those people doing depicted on the wall to the left as you enter? This piece of art in the style of stained glass mixes medieval figures clothed or unclothed save for what looks like a bathing cap. The taste and ideas are entirely the couple's own, no playing to the gallery. As an epithet, idiosyncratic is the immediate choice and not necessarily a criticism: the kitchen and its entire workings on full view and Neville Blech's special system for matching his excellent wines to the wife's food are both likeable quirks. So, too, is putting so much work into set lunches – priced at time of writing at £12 for two courses or £15 for three – which show no stinting on the combinations and complexity for which this senior woman chef is known.

FACILITIES
SEATS 40

NEAREST TUBE STATION
KNIGHTSBRIDGE

MAP 2

£42

OPEN
MON–FRI

HOURS
12.00–2.00PM
7.00–11.00PM

CREDIT CARDS
AMEX DELTA
DINER'S
MASTERCARD VISA

SERVICE
OPTIONAL

SET-PRICE LUNCH
£13.50

SET-PRICE DINNER
£38.50

FACILITIES
SEATS 30
TABLES OUTSIDE
SEAT 14
PRIVATE ROOM
SEATS 20
WHEELCHAIR
ACCESS

From the set menu a simple-sounding roast chicken came elaborately and deliciously stuffed, served with a delicate sauce of puréed mushrooms and buttery cracked wheat. The fish soup that preceded it was necessarily plainer, but also generously made. On the à la carte, descriptions grow longer, as in a saddle of venison with elderberry, juniper gin and a Tatin of apples and shallots; wild boar noisettes served with a ragout of Toulouse sausages, green lentils and spatzle. The latter had a strong, savoury appeal, although an economical cook might think it quite enough to offer either boar and the delicate little spatzle dumplings or Toulouse sausage and lentils. The inspiration is French, but the manner is entirely Mrs Blech's own. Some of the dishes are so manifold that they are difficult to imagine from studying the menu: it is wise to identify the effect you would like and consult the senior staff who know exactly what is cooking.

THIS LIST has to double as the sommelier whom the restaurant cannot afford (which is a problem, if my last visit is anything to go by: a half-full bottle was dropped and smashed over our table, with no replacement being offered, and an invitation to comment upon one of my later choices was met with a conversation-stopping, 'Well, you've chosen it, haven't you?'). That is why dishes on the menu are cross-referenced with bin number suggestions from the wine list – the actual names would be more useful – and why there are so many divisions by style. Treated in isolation, the wine list is a gem. The stylistic sections look unwieldy but are actually easy to use and there's now a conventional index if you're still flummoxed, the less familiar labels have pithy, informative notes, and the wines have clearly been chosen by someone who knows their stuff, as well as being fairly priced.

MING

£25

OPEN
MON–SAT

HOURS
12.00–11.45PM

CREDIT CARDS
AMEX DINER'S
JCB MASTERCARD
VISA

SERVICE
OPTIONAL

35–36 GREEK STREET W1   734 2721

'A Chinese menu to explore'

Anyone numbed by the repetitiousness of Chinatown's Cantonese menu will be relieved to find Ming on the other side of Shaftesbury Avenue in Soho proper. To get to grips with the long and varied list of mainly northern Chinese dishes offered by owner/manager Christine Lau and Taiwanese chef Jack Chang, look for the phrase Ming Special, which leads to items such as Mongolian lamb served in a lettuce leaf wrap; Beijing fish soup; crab on a bed of soft noodles; shredded duck with winter green; Tibetan garlic lamb; beef flank slow-cooked with star anise, known as Empress beef; and another slow-cooked family-style dish based on pork, Mr Edward's pork. What strikes me as a great breakthrough is the good use made of vegetables. At Ming, asparagus, fennel, kohl rabi, spinach and cauliflower (a Chinese restaurant first?) are offered along with Chinese vegetables and incorporated into monthly specials such as steamed white fish with salted turnip julienne; casserole of vegetables with tofu; kohl rabi with mixed seafood, prawns and scallops or with shredded lean pork; fresh soya beans, tree mushrooms, button mushrooms, spring onions and carrots stir-fried with shrimps. There is a £10 lunch and pre-theatre menu and the Ming Bowl Menu, a list of one-dish meals based on rice, noodles or the soft, white Northern bread called mantou. The general consideration shown towards an Occidental clientele extends to the wine list which has been composed by former restaurateur David Wolfe.

SET-PRICE LUNCH & PRE-THEATRE MENU
£10

SET-PRICE DINNER
£19.80

FACILITIES
SEATS 70
TABLES OUTSIDE
SEAT 8

NEAREST TUBE STATION
LEICESTER
SQUARE/
TOTTENHAM
COURT ROAD/
PICADILLY CIRCUS

MAP 5

MITSUKOSHI RESTAURANT

14–20 REGENT STREET SW1   930 0317

'A superior Japanese restaurant with prices to match'

What a boon Japanese restaurateurs are to property developers with that tricky basement space to sell off. Lack of natural light or an outlook seems not to be on their list of disadvantages: indeed, above-ground establishments like to screen out such distractions in favour of bland interiors that focus attention on what is on the table. Mitsukoshi Restaurant below the Mistukoshi store is arranged in just such a way, with partitions, soft lights and an anonymous sort of luxury which has something in common with the look of first-class airport lounges. Thank heavens the food and service are rather more distinctive. Set menus are steeply priced (£30–£50 at dinner, £15–£50 at lunch), but bring a properly balanced banquet of lovely things on unmatched china. Three trimmed French beans arranged on a crescent-shaped plate with a tiny chicken roll and an arrangement of aspic and fish that looked like a Liquorice Allsort would fulfil many people's worst fears, but after it had been replaced with sashimi thickly cut from fish of perfect freshness, followed by light tempura of vegetables and a whole little sole, and then the beef dish shabu-shabu cooked in

£50

OPEN
MON–SAT

HOURS
12.00–2.30PM
6.00–10.30PM

CREDIT CARDS
AMEX DINER'S
MASTERCARD VISA

SERVICE
OPTIONAL

SET-PRICE LUNCH
£15–£50

SET-PRICE DINNER
£30–£50

FACILITIES
SEATS 92
PRIVATE ROOMS
SEAT 4–24

NEAREST TUBE STATION
PICCADILLY
CIRCUS

MAP 3

broth at the table with two savoury sauces to accompany the finely cut meat, plus vegetables and noodles cooked in the pot and the cooking liquor to drink as soup, the issue would not be one of calorific satisfaction. You might, however, question the cost (£41 each) or be unresponsive to Japanese food. Among fans Mitsukoshi is counted as one of the best of London's grand Japanese restaurants, achieving the kind of excellence in ingredients, nuances of flavour and variation of textures that turns them on. The etiquette about choosing a saki cup and then having to fill your neighbour's while he or she returns the attention (hint: take someone with a similar drinking speed) is observed. Women in kimonos with male juniors (conventional dress) wait at the tables with grace and courtesy, and will keep up a conversation if encouraged. As with other Japanese restaurants included in the guide there has either been a move towards offering more seasonal and unusual recipes, here called Chef's Suggested Menus, or perhaps to translating what had previously been thought of interest only to fellow countrymen.

MONKEYS

1 CALE STREET SW3   352 4711

'The business is game'

Tom Benham (who cooks) and his French wife Brigitte (who runs front of house) are a long-standing fixture on Chelsea Green in this rather oddly named and themed – there are simian references in pictures and prints – but comfortable, attractive Anglo-French restaurant. The fixed-price lunch menu is something of a bargain and enhanced by plats du jour – Monday, salmon fish cakes; Tuesday, roast chicken and bread sauce; Wednesday, braised oxtail and dumplings and so forth – but in the evening Monkeys is a place to luxuriate in a meal. At the fixed price of £35 it might begin with their speciality of foie gras terrine, move on through scallop salad with lentils and centre on game in season, which is cooked with consummate skill and timing born of long practise, and garnished traditionally. A champagne sorbet provides a pause for the palate after which come a good cheese selection and rich English country house puddings. This is a meal for when you want to make an evening of it. There is a cheaper menu at £22.50 and a carte. Pricing is generally confident but includes mineral water, cover charge, vegetables – usually served in austere French quantity – or salad. Despite the name, it is a highly civilized place.

£45

OPEN
MON–FRI

HOURS
12.30–2.30PM
7.30–11.00PM

CREDIT CARDS
DELTA
MASTERCARD
SWITCH VISA

SERVICE
OPTIONAL

SET-PRICE LUNCH
£15

SET-PRICE DINNER
£22.50 & £35

FACILITIES
SEATS 50
PRIVATE ROOM
SEATS 12

NEAREST TUBE STATION
SLOANE
SQUARE/SOUTH
KENSINGTON

MAP 2

MON PETIT PLAISIR

33 HOLLAND STREET W8   937 3224

'The romance of the bistro'

In a pretty Kensington backstreet, this small restaurant with its old-fashioned ad hoc decoration complete with night-lights, copper pans and old posters successfully meets people's expectations of the look of a French bistro. The short menu, enhanced by dishes of the day announced on a blackboard, plays along gamely. Cassolette d'escargots were presented in a little dish with six holes for the snails bubbling in their garlic butter. A salad with chicken livers, bacon and a poached egg was fine, if slightly pedestrian. Boned rabbit stuffed with Agen prunes was sliced into beautiful, small, black-and-white slices contrasting with tournedos aux morilles which was a towering piece of well-cooked, pink meat in a rich sauce with (reconstituted, dried) morilles. Fish dishes include sole meunière and étouffée de St Jacques au safran. Vegetables maintain an almost impeccable French accent, being a choice of epinards à la crème, gratin Dauphinois, pommes allumettes plus salads, green or mixed, and a 'farandole' of mixed vegetables. Desserts enjoyed were chocolate Marquise of a high standard and a light, fragrant orange mousse. Comfortably off (it is not cheap) local residents seems to find their pleasure here; the restaurants rather lacks energy or drive but there are plenty of other places for that sort of thing. There is a pretty forecourt for warm-weather eating.

£28

OPEN
LUNCH MON–FRI
DINNER MON–SAT

HOURS
12.00–2.15PM
7.00–10.30PM

CREDIT CARDS
AMEX DELTA
DINER'S
MASTERCARD
SWITCH VISA

SERVICE
OPTIONAL

**SET-PRICE
LUNCH**
£13.95

FACILITIES
SEATS 25
TABLES OUTSIDE
SEAT 12
WHEELCHAIR
ACCESS

**NEAREST TUBE
STATION**
HIGH STREET
KENSINGTON

MAP 2

MON PLAISIR

21 MONMOUTH STREEET WC2   836 7243

'Some things never change but the world around them does'

This Monmouth Street address where the (original) front room decorated with fading French travel posters, faux-brick wallpaper and blue glass soda siphons personified every English person's notion of what a simple French restaurant should be like, did it about 40 years before Café Flo and Café Rouge got in on the act. But the themed bistro chains have inevitably diluted the impact of Mon Plaisir, despite the kitchen's efforts to offer more than cliché cooking. Chansons seemingly on a loop, the slightly sniffy service when owner Alain Lhermitte or his son Philippe are not around to supervise, and lack, as they would say in France, of charm, make one

£32

OPEN
MON–SAT

HOURS
12.00–2.00PM
5.50–11.15PM

CREDIT CARDS
AMEX DELTA
DINER'S
MASTERCARD
SWITCH VISA

SERVICE
12½%

**SET-PRICE
LUNCH & DINNER**
£13.95
(DINNER PRE-
THEATRE ONLY)

FACILITIES
SEATS 95
PRIVATE ROOM
SEATS 30

**NEAREST TUBE
STATION**
COVENT GARDEN/
CHARING CROSS

MAP 5

more unforgiving about a crass onion-based sauce around a good piece of fillet of beef, petits pois à la Française served cold, a dull first course salade maraîchère frothing with lollo rosso, and a risotto with asparagus spears being served as a cold rice salad done up in a ribbon of pastry, the sort of dish you dread being handed at a picnic. These items were served one Saturday night in high summer when the restaurant was half empty. Mon Plaisir responds better to bustle, more likely to exist weekday lunch times or before theatre when set-price menus can ameliorate the bill and encourage enjoyment of the well-chosen wines. Simple dishes such as rillettes, entrecôte Bearnaise, calf's liver, pommes allumettes, the garlicky spinach purée and the selection of cheese are the wisest choices.

MOSHI MOSHI SUSHI

UNIT 24 LIVERPOOL STREET STATION EC2   247 3227

'Raw fish and rice brief-at-counter'

£14

OPEN
MON–FRI

HOURS
11–30AM–9.00PM

CREDIT CARDS
MASTERCARD VISA

SERVICE
OPTIONAL

FACILITIES
SEATS 54

**NEAREST TUBE
STATION**
LIVERPOOL
STREET

MAP 1

This Japanese restaurant perched high in the refurbished Liverpool Street station, London's accidental answer to the Quai d'Orsay, is a train spotter's paradise in a temple of franchises. It is also heaven for sushi lovers. There are a few small tables but most of the action takes place at the bar where, sitting at a high stool, you watch the food come past slowly on a conveyor belt. Dishes are different colours, the colours denoting the price of the contents, and you help yourself to miso soup and whichever sushi or sashimi appeals. Shokuhin sanpuru, models of food fashioned in resin, in the window and charts on the wall help you to identify what is what. Some, such as prawns, salmon and salmon eggs, will be familiar, others such as 'gizzard shad' and sea urchin less so. Jars of pickled ginger and bottles of soya sauce are put on the counter for customers to help themselves. At the end of the meal the waitress counts up your empty dishes to figure out the bill. The quality of food is high and behind the clamour of city folk you hear the authentic tat-tat-tat-tat of blade on wood coming from the sushi chefs. In addition, there is a list of five ekiben, boxed lunches for takeaway, similar to those sold at Japanese railway stations and on Japanese trains. If you use them, be sure to break the chopsticks afterwards lest a devil find them and use them for evil purposes, like creating further delays on the Eastern Region or Naming you at Lloyd's. So successful is Moshi Moshi Sushi that a branch in Clerkenwell is planned.

MR KONG

21 LISLE STREET WC2   437 7341

'A chap who can be counted upon'

Mr Kong, where reassuringly two of the owners are also the chefs, is one of the few consistently good Cantonese restaurants in volatile Chinatown. I have it on reliable authority that the chef from Fung Shing (q.v.) eats here in his time off. That there is a regular clientele of Westerners can be inferred from the camaraderie which exists between the staff and some customers; not so usual in this area which is a magnet to transient tourists and out-of-towners. The menu is long and made longer by the list of Chef's Specials, which is where to look if you like the more recherché dishes such as braised duck web with baby clam in the pot (excellent, by the way, with a deeply savoury aniseedy gravy); stuffed fish maw with abalone, prawn paste and steamed vegetables; staty ells (sic) which are in fact crisp dry-fried pieces of eel on a skewer – satay – served with an eerie, earthy sauce. The main menu is strong on seafood and also on chicken dishes – try a half Emperor or Mandarin chicken, or for a more subtle flavour steamed chicken with seasonal greens. In place of the starters provided as a sop to Westerners try sliced pork, salted eggs and vegetable soup (served for a minimum of two) or a baked lobster or crab with black beans and chilli or steamed fresh scallops. For lunch there are Cantonese roasts including a hearty Roasted Meat Combination. Dessert is slices of orange brought automatically to the table. There is a wine list.

£25

OPEN
EVERY DAY

HOURS
12.00PM–1.45AM

CREDIT CARDS
AMEX DINER'S
JCB MASTERCARD
VISA

SERVICE
10%

**SET-PRICE
LUNCH**
£8–£11

**SET-PRICE
DINNER**
£15–£21

FACILITIES
SEATS 115
PRIVATE ROOM
SEATS 40
WHEELCHAIR
ACCESS

**NEAREST TUBE
STATION**
LEICESTER
SQUARE

MAP 5

LE MUSCADET

25 PADDINGTON STREET W1   935 2883

'French cooking as it used to be'

The interior of Le Muscadet, housed in a rather unprepossessing block of flats off Baker Street, invokes the sort of restaurant you expect to stumble upon in every small town in France and now only occasionally do. Shades of pink picked up in Arcadian tapestry and too many dried flowers sets the style. The menu is written on a blackboard but recited mellifluously to all customers, usually by the owner, Burgundian M. François Bessonard (who started in London with the plushy Le Bressan in Kensington several decades ago). He is a man of fundamental bonhomie but looks capable of superior behaviour if he did

£34

OPEN
LUNCH MON–FRI
DINNER MON–SAT

HOURS
12.30–2.30PM
7.30–10.45PM

CREDIT CARDS
MASTERCARD VISA

SERVICE
12½%

FACILITIES
SEATS 36
WHEELCHAIR
ACCESS

not like the cut of a customer's jib. Dishes are classics of French provincial cooking, competently and confidently prepared, not shrinking from the dark, rich sauces we associate with professional rather than domestic traditions. Asparagus with sauce Hollandaise; croustade de champignons; escargots de Bourgogne; moules marinière Dieppoise are typical first courses. The main courses the restaurant describes as specialities include escalope de foie gras frais au madère; turbot au vin rouge échalotes confites and magret de canard aux myrtilles. Cailles farcies aux champignons sauvages has been much appreciated, not least for someone else having boned the little creatures. A dash of balsamic vinegar in the sauce was one of the few concessions to fashion. Another was soya sauce and sweet spices contributing to a marinade for tuna. The cheese trolley is not to be missed. It offers a wonderful selection divided into strong cheeses, including some Burgundian varieties, goat's cheeses and blue cheeses, all French. It has been observed that the generosity of this display makes up for paper tablecloths and paper napkins, which are a bit of a let-down in a restaurant of this kind and this cost.

MUSEUM STREET CAFÉ

47 MUSEUM STREET WC1   405 3211

'If you don't finish your greens, you might not get dessert'

£30

OPEN
MON–FRI

HOURS
12.30–2.30PM
6.30–9.30PM

CREDIT CARDS
AMEX DELTA
MASTERCARD
SWITCH VISA

SERVICE
OPTIONAL

**SET-PRICE
LUNCH**
£15

**SET-PRICE
DINNER**
£21

FACILITIES
SEATS 35
WHEELCHAIR
ACCESS (ALSO
WC)

**NEAREST TUBE
STATION**
HOLBORN/
TOTTENHAM
COURT ROAD

MAP 3

Avisitor to this austere restaurant who compared it to a Swedish open prison added that there was a prevailing sense that pleasure here is not to be taken lightly. That said, there is pleasure usually to be found in the modern cooking which homes in on the appeal of chargrilling and on good baking. The menus are relatively short – a bit more choice at lunch time than in the evening but change every day at both meal times. A typical meal might start with a resourceful soup – Spring Tonic, a purée of spinach, watercress, rocket and chervil, was much enjoyed, particularly as the garnish of soured cream performed its mellowing effect on the acerbic flavours – follow with chargrilled veal chop – one has been reported as substantial and succulent – and move on to an indulgent dessert such as Valhrona chocolate cake with whipped cream or orange and poppy-seed cake. Desserts are invariably a high point. The sourcing of ingredients and the details of the meal such as aperitifs, breads, coffee, teas, infusions, chocolate truffles, dessert wines are all carefully and well attended to.

Surroundings are plain, with the kitchen, quite rightly, the focal point; chairs are hard, tables are small, the floor is lino, paintings are sort of minimalist-pointillist, and smoking is outlawed, all of which make Museum Street Café, in the opinion of many, more suited to a working lunch than an easygoing, sparkling evening out.

THERE ARE MORE wines worth trying in this short, two-dozen-strong list than in some lists five times its size, and each has a useful descriptive note. The mark-ups are still restrained: nothing will cost you more than £32 (Jaboulet's Hermitage La Chapelle 1982, which should be at its peak), and almost half the bottles are available either by the glass or by the half-bottle.

NAMASTE

30 ALIE STREET E1   488 9242/702 1504

'An Indian star in the East End'

Some media recognition is starting to accrue to chef Cyrus Todiwala, which is more significant than it might at first seem. Although going out for an Indian remains one of the most popular national pastimes, there has been little effort made either within the catering industry or by the press to identify, say, the Antony Worrall-Thompson of Indian cooking. Todiwala's decision to market his exceptional in-house pickles and chutneys – try raw mango, hot and sweet carrot, brinjal (aubergine) and Rajasthani wild boar – has attracted notice. Doubtless the next step will be an enterprising publisher commissioning a cookery book. The plain and, apart from the front courtyard, almost atmosphere-free East End premises give no clue to the interesting cooking on offer. Todiwala, a Parsi by birth, explores not only regional dishes with a particular emphasis on Goa – he worked as chef at the Taj group's Fort Aguada hotel there – but casts his net far wider than is usual for ingredients. Thus, dishes might be orchestrated around langoustines, sea bass, squid, conger eel, wild boar, venison, pheasant, goose and more. The weekly-changing speciality menu is where to find them. This list also features creative vegetable assemblies and Gujerati and South Indian snack food based on pulses. My advice is to base your meal on the weekly specialities, embellishing the order with a Goan, South Indian and/or Parsi dish from the main list. Goan galinha xacutti and the Parsi way with lambs' kidneys and liver are well worth

£22

OPEN
LUNCH MON–FRI
DINNER MON–SAT

HOURS
12.00–3.00PM
6.00–11.00PM

CREDIT CARDS
AMEX DELTA
DINER'S
MASTERCARD
SWITCH VISA

SERVICE
OPTIONAL

FACILITIES
SEATS 75
TABLES OUTSIDE
SEAT 8
WHEELCHAIR
ACCESS

**NEAREST TUBE
STATION**
ALDGATE/
ALDGATE EAST

MAP 1

trying. Breads are good. Effort has been made to compose a wine list with some relevance to spiced food. In mid-November 1995, Todiwala will be moving to 16 Prescott Street E1 to launch Café Spice. The premises will frame his cooking more flatteringly, while ensuring that he stays loyal to the City area which provides him with a lively lunch-time trade.

NICOLE'S

158 NEW BOND STREET W1   499 8408

'Good food by design'

£35

OPEN
MON–SAT
DINNER MON–FRI

HOURS
10.00AM–6.00PM
6.45–10.45PM

CREDIT CARDS
AMEX DELTA
DINER'S
MASTERCARD
SWITCH VISA

SERVICE
12½%

COVER CHARGE
£1

FACILITIES
SEATS 70

NEAREST TUBE STATION
GREEN
PARK/BOND
STREET

MAP 3

The fact that this restaurant is part of Nicole Farhi's stylish New Bond Street shop inevitably to some extent shapes the likely clientele, but after a slightly shaky start with uncoordinated service, Nicole's has become a separate entity; a very reckonable restaurant in its own right. This became clear when eating one evening – success quickly led to extended opening hours – when the dishes chosen had that extra dimension of deliciousness which professional cooks, rather than chefs, can achieve. The distinction may strike you as empty, but Simon Hopkinson (guiding light at Bibendum q.v.) describes himself as a cook, not a chef, and I would say women are more likely to embody it. Tellingly, Annie Wayte, who cooks here, trained with Sally Clarke at her eponymous restaurant (q.v.). Ingredients are carefully sourced and couturier-like attention is paid to the detail of dishes. Healthiness is given a nod but mercifully many of the dishes would be turned away at the door of a Californian spa. Menus evolve rather than radically change. The style can be inferred from items such as smoked haddock chowder (cullen skink put together with the right accessories); grilled marinated vegetable salad (beautifully done); grilled halibut with roasted baby gem; scallops with spicy lentils; chump chop of lamb with baked sweet potatoes; pan-fried duck breast with watercress and pear salad; rhubarb beignets with ginger ice cream; lemon sponge pudding with lime syllabub; blood orange jelly with Grand Marnier cream. Desserts generally are disconcertingly tempting to those whose aim is to be forever size 8. The wine list has all but three of the still wines available by the glass, allowing both experimentation and interesting frugal drinking. A long bar on a raised section at the back of the understated basement room is ideal for quick meals or eating alone. For quiet, easy parking, and time to unwind and enjoy three courses, go for dinner.

ODETTE'S

130 REGENT'S PARK ROAD NW1   586 5486/8766

'A girl of many moods'

O dette has many moods: gregarious when the weather is
warm and tables move onto the street; brisk in the light-
flooded conservatory at the back; reclusive in the downstairs
wine bar; and romantic in the main room of the restaurant
decorated in dark green with lighting reflected glowingly from
dozens of gilt-framed mirrors. It suits the locals on business or
on dalliance and has held on to its reputation as North
London's most alluring restaurant for many years. Chef Paul
Holmes strives to divert and to entice, but sometimes it is
effort rather than delectability that is apparent. On what I
later discovered was the chef's night off (which should be no
excuse), a warm tartlet of artichokes and mint looked and
tasted drab and was swamped by the toothpaste flavour of
mint. A mixture of crab, avocado and apple was a mush
sandwiched inside oily leaves of filo pastry. In general there is
a bit too much chopping and changing with ingredients. The
same evening the top seemed to have fallen off the soya sauce
bottle when making seared beef with black beans and asparagus. However, there are simpler ideas and much has worked
well, for example, risotto with broad beans and basil; a much
better tart of celeriac garnished with pissenlit and radicchio;
fillets of hare in an intense sauce flavoured with juniper berries
and a trace of Chinese five-spice. Desserts maintain the
tempo, as you can infer from coconut jelly, macerated prunes
and Madeira custard; white chocolate, banana and sesame
praline truffle; hot pear and honey butter brioche 'pizza' with
crème fraîche. There are Spanish cheeses to have with
another bottle from the extensive wine list. The £10 three-
course lunch is a bargain and downstairs has one of the best
wine bar menus in London.

ODETTE'S has done a good job with this list, but not as good
as the effusive notes and general air of self-congratulation
would have you believe. Everything seems to have been sourced
from Bibendum (the wine merchant, not the restaurant), a good
rather than definitive supplier. Most areas are covered and high
spots are Natter's Sancerre and Dumazet's Viognier, a sort of
cut-price Condrieu. The fine wines at the back are seldom
drawn from correspondingly fine vintages, and mark-ups
throughout are on the hefty side.

£32

OPEN
LUNCH EVERY DAY
DINNER MON–SAT

HOURS
12.30–2.30PM
7.00–11.00PM

CREDIT CARDS
AMEX DINER'S
MASTERCARD VISA

SERVICE
OPTIONAL

**SET-PRICE
LUNCH**
£10

SUNDAY BRUNCH

FACILITIES
SEATS 60
TABLES OUTSIDE
SEAT 12
PRIVATE ROOMS
SEAT 10 & 30

**NEAREST TUBE
STATION**
CHALK FARM

MAP 1

OGNISKO POLSKIE

55 EXHIBITION ROAD SW7   589 4635

'A world apart'

£26

OPEN
EVERY DAY

HOURS
12.30–3.00PM
6.30–11.00PM

CREDIT CARDS
AMEX DINER'S
MASTERCARD VISA

SERVICE
OPTIONAL

**SET-PRICE
LUNCH & DINNER**
£7.50

FACILITIES
SEATS 70
TABLES OUTSIDE
SEAT 30
PRIVATE ROOM
SEATS 35

**NEAREST TUBE
STATION**
SOUTH
KENSINGTON

MAP 2

Ognisko is the spacious, lofty restaurant of The Polish Hearth Club, open to non-members and anyone seeking a dining experience with a difference. The look personifies faded grandeur and has the air of being suspended in time – possibly some 50 years ago. The view is over gardens and a large terrace where meals are served on sunny days. Pink tablecloths and gold chairs have an air of impermanence, as if hired for a party, perhaps one to celebrate the release of The Prisoner of Zenda. The menu is long and interesting and for a moment Polish seems like an easy enough language to master: zupy is soups, desery is desserts, but then things get considerably more complex. Fortunately all is carefully translated. Start with herrings in soured cream and dill or blinis with smoked salmon, Sevruga caviar and cream where the blinis are strongly flavoured with fermented rye or one of the soups, all carefully made and sustaining, particularly the borscht with kolduny dumplings. There are fish dishes but somehow large helpings of items such as knuckle of pork Bavarian style, a ham hock the size of a boar's head in a dark red sauce; dumplings stuffed with meat or cheese and potatoes which come glazed with melted fat; roast goose served with gnocchi and red cabbage; and dessert pancakes filled with sweet cheese seem the appropriate order. You are in a world out of step with modern moods and modes and the space, calm and politesse invite long conversations, digressions, digestion. There is an uneventful wine list and, in any case, vodka, plain or flavoured, seems the right thing to drink to the stirring music of triumphal marches and polkas.

OLD DELHI

48 KENDAL STREET W2   723 3335

'India, Persia and Acker Bilk'

£26

OPEN
EVERY DAY

HOURS
12.00–3.30PM
6.00–11.30PM

CREDIT CARDS
AMEX DELTA
DINER'S
MASTERCARD VISA

SERVICE
15%

Despite what has been described as disagreeably fulsome service, this on-the-face-of-it Indian restaurant near Marble Arch is worth seeking out for its Iranian specialities – ownership is by an Iranian family – and the quality of the ingredients used. Because Indian food is available everywhere, it is tempting to gravitate towards the Persian dishes. In the first course kufteh, balls of minced lamb with rice and fresh herbs in a tomato sauce, are outstanding. Mirza-ghasemi, egg and aubergine mashed with garlic and spices, has a smoky taste due, to some extent, to charred onions. Such dishes could be contrasted with chicken tikka, prawn puri or aloo chat. In the main course the Specialities of the House include gaimeh, a combination of lamb, split yellow peas, spices, including cinnamon, and dry limes; sultani, chargrilled, sliced and also minced lamb served with saffron rice; and fesenjune, chicken in a sweet and sour pomegranate and walnut sauce, a sauce which is surprising to start with but can become burdensome due to its overpowering quality. One good way to slacken its impact is to mix it through one of the (expensive) Persian rice assemblies such as zereshk polo, basmati mixed with dried barberries and saffron. To finish the meal, have a water ice flavoured with rose water and finely grated pistachios. Wines are confidently marked up. Since you are charged 15% for the U. Heep Esq. approach of the staff, my advice is just to ignore it and enjoy the unusual aspects of the cooking. Also, turn a deaf ear to the Muzak which has been known to mix Acker Bilk's 'Stranger on the Shore' with the main theme from Dvořák's *New World Symphony* with a bit of Pachelbel's 'Canon' thrown in.

FACILITIES
SEATS 56
WHEELCHAIR
ACCESS

NEAREST TUBE
STATION
MARBLE ARCH

MAP 1

OLIVERS ISLAND

162 THAMES ROAD W4   0181-747 8888

'The conventions of modern food produced with élan'

£25

OPEN
LUNCH SUN–FRI
DINNER EVERY
DAY

HOURS
12.00–3.00PM
7.00–10.30PM

CREDIT CARDS
DELTA DINER'S
MASTERCARD
SWITCH VISA

SERVICE
OPTIONAL

FACILITIES
SEATS 75
TABLES OUTSIDE
SEAT 10
PRIVATE ROOM
SEATS 35–40
WHEELCHAIR
ACCESS (ALSO
WC)

Strand-on-the-Green is an attractive part of west London to which folks gravitate in order to have a pint by the river. There is now also the possibility of a good meal at Olivers Island, a restaurant with no watery view which takes it name from the nearby island in the Thames where Oliver Cromwell is supposed to have sought refuge. At first sight the menu is one you will feel you have read somewhere before – that modern mix which includes Caesar salad, a Thai starter, fish and chips, rump of lamb and something with wilted rocket – but Aussie chef Darren Farr cooks it with brio, the impact of his abilities overcoming the mundane wine-bar decor and longueurs in service. Sautéed field mushrooms with fresh herbs and a sprinkling of lemon zest on brioche taste dark and earthy the way they should. Deep-fried salt-and-pepper squid with aïoli, though something of a mix of metaphors, is delicious. Quite aggressive salt-and-peppering also distinguishes the roast corn-fed chicken served with sautéed potatoes and salsa verde. Roast loin of lamb with spicy couscous – almost more spices, nuts and sultanas than grains – comes with excellent marinated vegetables described as chutney. Dessert has featured sticky date pudding; rhubarb crumble; chocolate truffle cake. Wines are reasonably priced.

OLIVO

21 ECCLESTON STREET SW1   730 2505

'Vindication of the Mediterranean diet'

£30

OPEN
LUNCH MON–FRI
DINNER MON–SAT

HOURS
12.00–2.30PM
7.00–11.00PM

CREDIT CARDS
AMEX ACCESS
MASTERCARD VISA
SWITCH DELTA

SERVICE
OPTIONAL

COVER CHARGE
£1.35

**SET-PRICE
LUNCH**
£13.50 & £15.50

FACILITIES
SEATS 43
WHEELCHAIR
ACCESS

**NEAREST TUBE
STATION**
VICTORIA

MAP 2

**NEAREST TUBE
STATION**
GUNNERSBURY

**NEAREST BR
STATION**
CHISWICK

Booking well ahead is essential for both lunch and dinner at this Italian/Sardinian restaurant decorated in shades of Cycladic blue and Dijon-mustard yellow which, when eating-out fashion changed and came down in favour of healthy olive oil-slicked food, cannily took the place of the rather prim French restaurant Ciboure whilst ownership remained the same. Reasonable prices – particularly at lunch time – are one explanation for its popularity, but the cooking is a lure despite the original chef Giorgio Locatelli having decamped to Zafferano (q.v.) via The Red Pepper (q.v.). The £1.35 cover charge delivers a bowl of golden olive oil and some good breads. First-course salads are interesting and enterprising: salad of endive, artichoke, Parmesan and truffle oil; marinated fresh anchovies with grilled courgettes; buffalo mozzarella salad with aubergines. Pasta dishes are well assembled. One hit this year was fresh black tagliatelle with a ragu of cuttlefish which seemed to have been 'seasoned' with bottarga (dried mullet roe), which would have been a Sardinian way of going about things. The chargrill plays a central role in the main course, most items, including fish (usually accompanied by a rocket salad), being cooked that alluring way. Desserts, probably more ordered at dinner, are also more interesting at that meal time. Sebada, a traditional Sardinian confection, is a warm pastry shell filled with soft cheese and trickled with honey. There is usually a cheese tart made either with ricotta or mascarpone and an ice cream or frozen yogurt. The wine list promotes developments in Italian wine-making and offers a good range of bottles under £20. Tables are closely packed. The decor can sometimes be sunnier than the attitude of the staff.

Olivetto, an upmarket pizzeria and pasta sister restaurant opens at 49 Elizabeth Street SW1 (730 0074) just after the *Guide* goes to press.

192

'The heartbeat of Notting Hill'

Ignoring the ever-increasing numbers of bistros, brasseries, trattorie, diners, restaurants and pub conversions in Notting Hill Gate, 192 sails on, drawing to it a Dorian Gray crowd who seem happy to model the same black wardrobe, have the same conversations at the same red tables and eat the same sort of modern food as they have done for years. Expansion a couple of years ago has attracted other types, but the core clientele remains spookily unchanged. Chef Albert Clarke by no means leads the pack who have fed and watered the twenty- and thirty- and perhaps even fortysomethings here, a pack which includes Alastair Little, Rowley Leigh, Adam Robinson, Rose Gray (no relation), Maddalena Bonino, Margot Clayton and Dan Evans. Comments on Clarke's cooking complain of vapidity in the seasoning and slips with timing resulting in unwelcome details like al dente potatoes and practically raw asparagus. However, there is a great deal of choice – perhaps too much choice – in the daily-changing lunch and dinner menus and you can get lucky as someone did with beautifully cooked, succulent cod with a tomato, black olive and basil sauce. Seasonal salad and fish cakes are popular staples on the list. Desserts come in for praise. The colour scheme seems deliberately noxious but the mirror strip at eye-level height when seated (a now much-copied restaurant detail) is a great help in checking out who is sitting where with whom. The wine list is, and always has been, one of the strengths of the establishment. Prices are restrained and there is a better than usual selection offered by the glass (in two sizes). Service is amiable if sometimes sedate in pace.

CRISP PRESENTATION, a good ratio of New World to Old, and plentiful wines by the glass (standard and large) reveal this to be one of those clued-up, modern-minded lists. But this has more, because alongside the expected attractions in the sub-£20 bracket (Olivier Leflaive's command of Burgundy's lesser appellations is evidenced here) is a handful of 'grand wines' which have been subjected to a most generous pricing policy. Arlot's magnificent white Nuits-St-Georges (£32) and the rare white wine of Château Margaux (£26) are both cheaper here than in their retail outlets.

£28

OPEN
MON–SUN

HOURS
12.30–3.00PM
7.00–11.30PM

CREDIT CARDS
AMEX DINER'S
MASTERCARD
SWITCH VISA

SERVICE
OPTIONAL

**SET-PRICE
LUNCH**
£9.50
(SUN £12.50)

FACILITIES
SEATS 100
TABLES OUTSIDE
SEAT 10
WHEELCHAIR
ACCESS

**NEAREST TUBE
STATION**
NOTTING HILL
GATE

MAP 1

ORSINO

119 PORTLAND ROAD W11   221 3299

'Finding its bearings'

£26

OPEN
EVERY DAY

HOURS
12.00PM–12.00AM

CREDIT CARDS
NONE

SERVICE
OPTIONAL

**SET-PRICE
LUNCH**
£11.50 & £13.50

FACILITIES
SEATS 100
PRIVATE ROOM
SEATS 25

**NEAREST TUBE
STATION**
HOLLAND PARK

MAP 1

Tapering in shape and painted pinky-peach, Orsino looks like a finger pointing north. On to Neasden! Or maybe not yet, for it has taken the team responsible for Joe Allen and Orso restaurants around the world some time to achieve consistency in their latest branch. The bush telegraph (that's Shepherd's Bush, home of BBC TV) has been much more complimentary of late. Pasta with several elements and wafer-thin pizzas are an important part of the menu, now correctly cooked and sauced and, in the cases of linguini with fennel, tomato and pine nuts or leek and ricotta tortellini, very satisfying. Suckling pig is another popular choice which is cooked so that it is very succulent, but – when last sampled – had no crispness to the skin. The set menu of three courses for £13.50 until 6.30 every day represents good value in the area; you do not need to go far to fare worse either monetarily or in standards of service. The smart waiters (and waitress or two) serve a damn fine cup of coffee. Quibbles are the small servings of antipasti as most customers take these as starters and, as ever, the policy of only dealing in cash or cheques.

ORSO

27 WELLINGTON STREET WC2   240 5269

'Has its fans, has its critics'

£28

OPEN
EVERY DAY

HOURS
12.00PM–12.00AM

CREDIT CARDS
NONE

SERVICE
OPTIONAL

**SET-PRICE
LUNCH**
£11.50 OR
£13.50 (SAT &
SUN ONLY)

FACILITIES
SEATS 100

**NEAREST TUBE
STATION**
COVENT GARDEN

MAP 4

Reasons for liking Orso: apart from Christmas Eve and Christmas Day it is open every day from noon to midnight (last orders); it is easy to eat lightly and healthily, selecting first-course salads, wafer-thin pizzas, grilled fish; the Italian menu and the cooking methods are unfussy; there is often a glamorous crowd there and nearly always a bustle and buzz; if you are famous or a regular you are likely to get preferential treatment; the Italian wine list (see below). Reasons for not liking Orso: it is in a basement, part of which is decorated with white lavatory tiles; some dishes are little more than assemblies and sometimes clumsy ones; it has been known to use stale oil in deep-frying; what once seemed thrillingly innovative – colourful pottery plates, bruschetta, vegetables served tiède dressed with olive oil and lemon, arugula, grilled rabbit, stylish desserts such as Pecorino with pear, handsome waiting staff –

are now commonplace; dictatorial attitudes towards bookings and a lack of finesse in turning over tables; if you are neither famous nor a regular you are likely to imagine others are being treated better; no credit cards taken. Orso has its fans and its critics. My most recent meal on a Sunday evening when the A team, both in the kitchen and front of house, seemed to have been given the night off, comprised squid which had been fried in what smelled like industrial oil and a dish of veal escalope in a lemony sauce which could have come from a Sixties museum, and put me in the second camp. Useful in the Covent Garden area Orso still is, especially the good-value set-price menu.

THE PRODUCERS featured on Orso and Orsino's (q.v.) list (Italians to a man – Maculan, Tedeschi and Jermann, among others) deserve better than to be crammed together with no indication of their location or winemaking style, and an opportunity to instil a little education has been missed. But this is a good selection, and it would be even better if it didn't suffer the usual Italian handicap of being light in half-bottles. Those who think Frascati is little more than alcoholized water should try Pulcini's thick-textured single-vineyard offering, Colle Gaio.

OSLO COURT

CHARLBERT STREET NW8   722 8795

'Remember grilled grapefruit?'

Oslo Court in St John's Wood occupies a special place in the hearts of north London diners. Situated on the ground floor of a characterless block of flats across from Regent's Park, the restaurant has been in existence for close on a quarter of a century. In its culinary heyday, when owned by the Yugoslavian Katnic family, it was the recipient of a star in the Egon Ronay guide. A former Ronay inspector (now a famous chef) speaks to me mistily about crab à la Rochelle, duck bosnaka, salmon trout Mama Zora and the outstanding wine list. What once might have been proudly described as a Continental menu remains the order of the day under the current Spanish ownership. Crab à la Rochelle (with a brandy sauce) is still offered, as is that dinner-party dish of the Sixties – pink grapefruit grilled with brown sugar and sherry, which is probably hard to find anywhere else in London. Duck Montmorency, veal Holstein, steak Diane and other period pieces beckon proudly, but a wide range of fresh fish which can be served simply grilled is another important

£32

OPEN
MON–SAT

HOURS
12.30–2.30PM
7.00–11.00PM

CREDIT CARDS
AMEX DELTA
DINER'S
MASTERCARD
SWITCH VISA

SERVICE
OPTIONAL

SET-PRICE LUNCH
£18

SET-PRICE DINNER
£25

FACILITIES
SEATS 100

NEAREST TUBE STATION
ST JOHN'S WOOD

MAP 1

element in the menu. A certain atmosphere of never-mind-the-quality-feel-the-width attaches to the huge range of vegetables offered, the Technicolor dessert trolley, the large plate of petits fours and the pink rose for the lovely lady, but the clientele, most of them regulars, appreciate the value implicit in the set-price deal – in spite of the disingenuous menu message, 'extra charge will be added for expensive dishes' – and responds well to the brusque ministrations of service of the old school.

OSTERIA ANTICA BOLOGNA

23 NORTHCOTE ROAD SW11   978 4771

'Assagi the appetite'

£25

OPEN
EVERY DAY

HOURS
12.00–3.00PM
6.00–11.00PM
SAT
12.00–11.30PM
SUN
12.30–10.30PM

CREDIT CARDS
AMEX
MASTERCARD
SWITCH VISA

SERVICE
OPTIONAL

COVER CHARGE
70P

**SET-PRICE
LUNCH**
£7.50

FACILITIES
SEATS 75
TABLES OUTSIDE
SEAT 12

**NEAREST BR
STATION**
CLAPHAM
JUNCTION

MAP 1

All-wood restaurant interiors are rare in London but here we have one in a Clapham osteria which, for one customer, brings to mind a place where Gepetto might have carved out his son Pinocchio. If so, Gepetto was a popular chap, as the place is usually packed. Last year's observation that the menu is genuinely interesting, sometimes more so than the food itself, still holds. Assagi, the dozen small dishes which can be ordered like meze either to start or to compose a meal, come as described, but can be slightly slipshod in detail, such as a routine tomato sauce over the involtino made of aubergine rolled round scamorza cheese and pancetta, and a strange taste to the centre of the boiled octopus served with rocket, olive oil and chillis. Pastas are interesting and some of the garnishes have a baroque quality suited to the traditions of Emilia-Romagna. In the main course, or middle dishes as they put it, the capretto alle mandorle, goat cooked with a rich tomato and almond pesto, is the house speciality. Other main courses which have been liked are polpette alla pastora, lamb meatballs cooked with fresh and salted ricotta, tomatoes and basil, and a daily special, gambotta di pollo arrostizzate, chicken cooked with luganega sausage, fennel, aubergine and fresh herbs. Home-made desserts – which are a high point – include torta moretto, dark chocolate cake filled with espresso cream served with cream and warm chocolate sauce, and schiacciata di noci e mele, warm apple and walnut cake served with fresh cream. The wine list repays study and exploration and there is a fine selection of dessert wines by the glass. Celebrating the regionality of Italian food is, of course, commendable but in homing in on Bologna the owners have set their sights high, perhaps too high for the combination of this kitchen coping with the crowds who pour in.

OVERTONS

5 ST JAMES'S STREET SW1   839 3774

'A fish restaurant swimming with the tide'

The revamp in 1993 – both culinary and decorative – of this long-established St James's fish restaurant seemed at the time to escape the notice of the staff and management. They went on behaving in the brusque and misogynistic way that is doubtless considered appropriate for English fish restaurants. It made it difficult fully to appreciate chef Nigel Davies' modern fish cooking or even the 'Overtons Traditional Dishes' he was perhaps constrained to offer as an alternative. New management is now in place and it seems pleased to be presenting Davies' short, sprightly, oft-changing menus. Thoughtfully composed and subtly dressed salads make light first courses. Petals of salmon gravadlax with the frills reddened by the juice of beetroot has the pleasing accompaniment of stalks of asparagus and salsify. A salad of wood pigeon is finished with roast parsnips and truffled meat juices. Main courses are, as it were, fully inclusive and even the modish accompaniment of a black bean and spring onion risotto does not outshine the most important consideration – the freshness and perfect cooking of the fillet of cod. For meat lovers there are items such as roast loin of pork with sweet potato rösti and oyster mushrooms. Desserts are a short selection but crème brûlée fulfils most of the requirements of a sweet treat – satin-smooth and brittle at one and the same time. The bar area panelled in pale wood and dotted with prints leads to the restaurant where the decorative colours of royal blue and English mustard converge most strikingly in a carpet decorated with sea creatures.

£33

OPEN
MON–FRI

HOURS
12.30–2.45PM
7.00–10.45PM

CREDIT CARDS
AMEX DINER'S
JCB MASTERCARD
SWITCH VISA

SERVICE
12½%

**SET-PRICE
LUNCH & DINNER**
£21.75 OR
£26.50

FACILITIES
SEATS 60
TABLES OUTSIDE
SEAT 40
PRIVATE ROOM
SEATS 20
WHEELCHAIR
ACCESS

**NEAREST TUBE
STATION**
GREEN PARK

MAP 3

LE PALAIS DU JARDIN

136 LONG ACRE WC2   379 5353

'Fast, furious, French and full'

Perhaps because of its anonymous ownership this successful oyster bar and brasserie in Covent Garden gets less media attention than, say, Quaglino's (q.v.), but its appeal can be inferred from the considerable expansion this year in the Covent Garden premises and plans for a new bumper outlet – 550 seats – in Brompton Cross, near the Conran shop. The front part of the premises – a café and shellfish bar – gives no hint of the huge, humming machine of a restaurant that lies

£26

OPEN
EVERY DAY

HOURS
10.00–12.00AM

CREDIT CARDS
AMEX DINER'S
MASTERCARD VISA

SERVICE
12½%

FACILITIES
SEATS 370
TABLES OUTSIDE
SEAT 20
WHEELCHAIR
ACCESS (ALSO
WC)

NEAREST TUBE
STATION
COVENT GARDEN/
LEICESTER
SQUARE
MAP 4

behind the grand central bar. The atmosphere is very French, seething with energy and in a hurry to feed as many people as possible in the shortest possible time. This is a palace which is for the people; prices are reasonable, acoustics are such that one can hear oneself speak and the accoutrements of the table – big white linen napkins, shining large glasses – deliver that frisson of anticipation upon sitting down which is one of the joys of restaurant going. The menu is written in French (with translations) except when it comes to fish cakes and bangers and mash, two of the cheapest main courses at £6.95 including chips with the fish cakes and a lentil and onion gravy with the sausages. Once into French, the tone becomes positively flowery as in filet de venaison 'en robe' et timbale de champignons sauvages et poireaux; brodquin d'agneau et mousse d'aubergine, sauce ratatouille; filet de boeuf en croustade de Stilton et chou rouge, sauce Porto, this last a seemingly popular dish ordered by both neighbouring tables at one test visit. Fruits de mer are fairly priced as evidenced by various ways with mussels at £3.50 and whole lobster served cold with mayonnaise at £10.50.

PEARL

22 BROMPTON ROAD SW1   225 3888

'Not of great price, but not cheap either'

£35

OPEN
EVERY DAY

HOURS
12.00—3.00PM
6.00—11.30PM

CREDIT CARDS
AMEX
MASTERCARD VISA

SERVICE
OPTIONAL

SET-PRICE
LUNCH
£13.80

SET-PRICE
DINNER
£20

FACILITIES
SEATS 72
PRIVATE ROOM
SEATS 40

NEAREST TUBE
STATION
KNIGHTSBRIDGE

MAP 2

The location and consequent clientele, made up in part of tourists and businessmen, seem to militate against this rather faceless Chinese restaurant making the impact that its menu suggests it could. Chef Chan Ping joined the restaurant from Hong Kong in September 1994 and you get the feeling that if it were Kowloon outside and not Knightsbridge Green the cooking would be geared up a few notches. The set menus composed of the most banal dishes are something of a giveaway. However, the à la carte bristles with interesting Cantonese dishes, often described as à la Kwangtung, plus other regional specialities, and the fact that it is written in Chinese characters as well as English and that there is a section devoted to shark's fin and abalone dishes, including Emperor's prime (braised whole abalone at £45 each), points to use by the Chinese themselves. The highlights of a test meal were a first course of snow prawn balls, a cluster of noodles in batter encasing prawns; sea bass with black bean sauce, impressively fresh fish in a not overwhelming sauce, delicately dissected at the table;

and braised aubergine in sea spice, the vegetable distinctly flavoured with powdered shrimp and chilli. Service is attentive and civil but it is probably up to the customer to find the pearls in the experience of eating here through careful study of the long menu and enterprising ordering. Hotel foyer-style Muzak does nothing to counteract the atmosphere of blandness.

THE PEASANT

240 ST JOHN STREET EC1   336 7726

'More Watteau than What Ho'

With so many restaurants now punctuating St John Street, it is perhaps to the point to say that this converted pub (formerly The George & Dragon) is towards the Islington end, more Sadler's Wells than Barbican if you like. It is a conversion with few frills beyond the original Italianate mosaic floor – revealed in the stripping down – and the moulded ceiling where a fan turns to only desultory effect in summer. Tables are bare, napkins are paper, staff are casually dressed but work hard; The Peasant is popular and deservedly so. The food cooked by a team headed by John Pountney is excellent. The handwritten, daily-changing menu offers many temptations. A meal for two, much enjoyed, started with the small size of antipasti which for £5 brought an ample, well-assorted assembly of proper pepper salami, anchovies, olives, grainy, slightly tart hummus, lightly pickled celery and cucumber, strips of fried courgette flavoured with mint; and salt cod fritters with sorrel accompanied by a purée of red peppers reduced to a pigmented mush. Main courses were moist tender chicken brochettes tasting as if marinated in mango chutney served with noodles tossed with cucumber, pepper, coriander, carrot and lemon grass, and merguez sausages with borlotti, broad and butter bean salad (actually a first course) where the detail of peeled broad beans belied the restaurant's name but impressed hugely. Chocolate mousse cake with fresh, dark cherries was relished for dessert but the wistful conclusion to the lunch was the desire to go back to try the pancetta dish; the soup made with radish leaves, potatoes and bread; the hake baked in batter; the lentils with spinach and gremolada; the five-spice ice cream with plums; the pudding wines; the three grappas in tasting size for £6… Even the coffee is good. Noise levels can get high and you might be alarmed by the amount of smoke, but this peasant has a sophisticated palate.

£24

OPEN
LUNCH MON–FRI
DINNER MON–SAT

HOURS
LUNCH
12.30–2.30PM
DINNER
6.30–10.45PM

CREDIT CARDS
MASTERCARD
SWITCH VISA

SERVICE
12 ½%

FACILITIES
SEATS 80
WHEELCHAIR
ACCESS (ALSO
WC)

**NEAREST TUBE
STATION**
ANGEL/
FARRINGDON

MAP 3

THE PEOPLES PALACE

ROYAL FESTIVAL HALL, SOUTH BANK SE1   928 9999

'A room with a view'

£28

OPEN
EVERY DAY

HOURS
12.00PM–3.00PM
5.30–11.00PM

CREDIT CARDS
AMEX DELTA
DINER'S
MASTERCARD
SWITCH VISA

SERVICE
OPTIONAL

**SET-PRICE
LUNCH**
£10.50 & £13.50

FACILITIES
SEATS 180
WHEELCHAIR
ACCESS (ALSO
WC)

**NEAREST
TUBE/BR
STATION**
WATERLOO

MAP 3

This new restaurant in the Festival Hall opened in the Spring of '95 to a storm of restaurant critical censure. There were a few anodyne write-ups but from most restaurant correspondents – including myself – I think the negative reaction was based on a strong sense of disappointment and even bewilderment. The owners are the Levin family, owners of the very creditable Capital Hotel Restaurant (q.v.) and The Greenhouse (q.v.), the consultant chef is Gary Rhodes (star of stove and TV screen), who put The Greenhouse on the culinary map, the chef is Stuart Busby, who has worked with Rhodes over a period of time, and the restaurant has an unparalleled riverside situation. The largely inept food surrounded by gimmicky promotional silliness (starting with the name), such as offering to accept payment in any currency at that day's exchange rate, seemed such a travesty of what could and should be the most exciting restaurant within the South Bank arts complex. That title is not a difficult one to win. Reports of improved cooking, the efforts to keep prices down plus the undeniable magic asset which the restaurant possesses – the panoramic view of the river and the North bank – will probably soon sway the vote in favour of the Peoples Palace. Staff still stare at the computerized tills and scratch their heads. Few concert-goers as yet seem to have discovered the restaurant's bar as the most civilized place in the building in which to have a drink.

LE PETIT MAX

97A HIGH STREET HAMPTON WICK   0181-977 0236

'Bonne continuation'

£25.50 BYO

OPEN
TUE–SUN

HOURS
7.00–11.00PM
SUN 3.30–4.30PM
8.00–9.30PM

CREDIT CARDS
NONE

SERVICE
10%

**SET-PRICE
LUNCH & DINNER**
£23.50

The Hampton Wick branch of the Renzland twin's oeuvre (c.f. Chez Max) is by day a caff called Bonzo's, by night, with the tea urn heaved off the counter, a centre of French cuisine bourgeoise. This bit of background is to explain some of the strictures of eating here: booking is a pain since you usually have to leave messages and field the reply; tables are cramped, there is no space to spare, and conversations are perforce overheard; no credit cards are taken. However, there is the advantage of no liquor licence, so that even with corkage at

£2 the evening out will be something of a bargain with the menu at £23.50 (with some supplements) plus 10% service charge for three substantial courses. The first course of Picandou farm goat's cheese baked with shallots and olive oil, served with Provençal vegetables and rocket salad, is, they say, their only 'vegetarian' dish. Presumably the onion soup is made with beef stock. Coming from another direction altogether pan-fried foie gras with Sauternes sauce is first rate and the salad Lyonnaise, here sporting sausage, potatoes and fried strips of parsnips – very rarely encountered in France – with a heap of frisée, was much liked. Fillet of Aberdeen Angus beef is a fixture on the menu. Other meats might be noisettes of lamb; ballotine of guinea fowl; roasted Bresse pigeon, all suitably garnished. There is also a fish dish or two, such as délice of peppered halibut with a red wine sauce, or tronçon of brill with herb beurre blanc. Service comes with flourishes of the French language. At one meal every diner embarking on his or her main course was wished 'Bonne continuation'. You might think that delightful or you might think it ridiculously affected.

FACILITIES
SEATS 34
TABLES OUTSIDE SEAT 16
WHEELCHAIR ACCESS

NEAREST BR STATION
HAMPTON WICK

LE P'TIT NORMAND

185 MERTON ROAD SW18   0181-871 0233

'Tres typique'

The red-checked tablecloths, the curl of the script in which the day's dishes have been chalked up, and the chatter of tables of French customers are enough to make you forget that you are in the sleepy south-west suburb of Southfields. Le P'tit Normand serves the sort of bistro food of France that is a treasured memory: rillettes; boudin noir; big bowls of moules; boeuf bourguignon; rognons de veau and chocolate desserts. The results are just as authentic as one would wish, and generously served. The wines tend to be the work of superior growers in the secondary areas. Sometimes the manager manages single handed, which is quite a feat, as the menu must be explained, the large selection of cheeses identified and apportioned and incoming guests welcomed. Most of his customers know the score and so the mood remains good humoured. What jolts the diner out of the delusion that this is a detour off the autoroute is the bill. Sunday's set lunch at £11.95 is the economical option.

£28
OPEN
LUNCH MON–FRI
DINNER MON–SAT

HOURS
12.00–2.30PM
7.00–10.30PM

CREDIT CARDS
AMEX DELTA
DINER'S
MASTERCARD VISA

SERVICE
12½%

SET-PRICE LUNCH
£9.95
SUN £11.95

SUNDAY BRUNCH

FACILITIES
SEATS 35
PRIVATE ROOM SEATS 20
WHEELCHAIR ACCESS (ALSO WC)

NEAREST TUBE STATION
SOUTHFIELDS

MAP 1

PIED À TERRE

£52

OPEN
LUNCH MON—FRI
DINNER MON—SAT

HOURS
12.15—2.15PM
7.15—10.30PM

CREDIT CARDS
AMEX DELTA
DINER'S JCB
MASTERCARD
SWITCH VISA

SERVICE
INCLUDED

SET-PRICE
LUNCH
£18.50 & £35

SET-PRICE
DINNER
£35

FACILITIES
SEATS 40
PRIVATE ROOM
SEATS 12
WHEELCHAIR
ACCESS

NEAREST TUBE
STATION
GOODGE STREET

MAP 4

34 CHARLOTTE STREET W1   636 1178

'Let the chef take the strain'

At a recent lunch at Pied à Terre a publisher was overheard saying that he had just commissioned a book from the chef Richard Neat. Plucky the domestic cook who embarks on Neat's intricate, dexterous, ingenious, complicated, labour-intensive recipes which are, in part, the reason one might go to a high falutin' restaurant rather than eat at home. Neat, who trained with Raymond Blanc, Joel Robuchon and Marco Pierre White, creates pictures on the plate, but these are pictures with substance, flavour and sometimes hidden depths. He works with luxurious ingredients, but also elevates the more humble, interesting contributor like skate, salt cod, sardines, pig's head, pig's trotters, duck gizzards and hare. Sauces often take the form of purées, their edges dotted with a parsimonious vegetable garnish. Dinner here is a no-messing-about £35 inclusive for two courses. To try the style more economically, there is a set-price lunch at £18.50 for three courses with a choice of two items in the first and main course. From this deal, first courses of scallops in a smoked salmon sauce and boned quail with parsley sauce, leeks and wild mushrooms were dainty portions, much liked but quickly consumed. To follow, Dover sole fillets were arranged sinuously, almost surrealistically, on a bed of boulangère potatoes and a sliver of apple with the proposed spinach and French beans puréed into a sauce. Chump of lamb was another masterly miniature in a sea of pea green with individual peas bobbing round the edge. Dessert did not fill the gaps as it too was a fairy portion: a blob of vanilla ice with sugar-dusted biscuits, although one plate did have two blueberries as part of the garnish instead of just the one. Desserts à la carte are usually sumptuous. The interior of the restaurant slowly evolves and improves. At the front of the restaurant there is now a bar area where Neat rather disconcertingly tends to lurk after service.

A STERN, SERIOUS selection (mainly French) with an evident determination to offer the very best – hence such labels as Trimbach's Clos Ste-Hune, Dujac's Clos St-Denis, Drouhin's Marquis de Laguiche Montrachet and Vega Sicilia's Unico. A baker's dozen of 'rare and mature' wines are grouped together, but are hardly any grander than the 'regular' listings. There is still precious little for those wishing to stay below £20 a bottle.

POISSONERIE DE L'AVENUE

82 SLOANE AVENUE SW3   589 2457

'Fresh fish with old-fashioned values'

£38

OPEN
MON–SAT

HOURS
12.00–3.00PM
7.00–11.45PM

CREDIT CARDS
AMEX DINER'S
MASTERCARD
SWITCH VISA

SERVICE
15%

**SET-PRICE
LUNCH**
£16.50

FACILITIES
SEATS 90
TABLES OUTSIDE
SEAT 14
PRIVATE ROOM
SEATS 18
WHEELCHAIR
ACCESS

**NEAREST TUBE
STATION**
SOUTH
KENSINGTON

MAP 2

Established over 30 years ago, the Poissonerie has every reason nowadays to feel surrounded and beleaguered by the various restaurants that have sprung up and are springing up in the area some call Brompton Cross. Perhaps in defensive action, but forfeiting what had become an exceptional asset – an old-fashioned look – the façade has been remodelled on glazed modern lines. The interior, much expanded since the restaurant's inception, remains wood panelled with tables well spaced. A set-price menu at lunch time – £16.50 for three courses – throws down a challenge to, say, Bibendum, and certainly helps keep in check a bill which otherwise tends to plump up with separately priced vegetables and 15% service charge. The carte is long and, reflecting the amenity of La Marée, the fish shop next door in the same ownership, is supplemented by dishes of the day. These tend to provide the less hallowed species such as gurnard, the fish which croaks plaintively when caught, and mackerel, but in my view the temptation here is to go for a dish such as middle-cut of turbot simply grilled accompanied by an interesting vegetable such as salsifis or fennel sautéed in olive oil with pine kernels. Fancier cooking can be relegated to the first course with its dishes such as the light croustade of fresh crab with spinach or ravioli of lobster and salmon – slightly tough pasta – in an excellent tomato sauce. There are nice old-fashioned endings in the savoury of angels on horseback or the dessert of oeufs à la neige au caramel. Waiters are formal but not so well schooled as to convey to one another who ordered what. La Poissonerie also has an oyster bar.

LE PONT DE LA TOUR

36D SHAD THAMES SE1   403 8403

'The heart of the Gastrodrome'

£40

OPEN
EVERY DAY

HOURS
RESTAURANT
12.00–3.00PM
6.00PM–12.00AM
SUN
6.00–11.00PM BAR
& GRILL
11.30AM–12.00AM
SUN
11.30AM–11.00PM

It has been said about this sleek restaurant which launched the Butlers Wharf 'Gastrodrome' that you pay the same at Le Pont de le Tour as at Bibendum (both Conran enterprises) for half the amount of food. That is as maybe but certainly the style of the menu and the nature of the dishes are similar – chef David Burke worked with Simon Hopkinson at Bibendum (q.v.). The observation may have been post-rationalization when studying a bill. Even with the service charge now reduced from 15% to 12½% prices are the sort that only very successful City traders, who flock over here at lunch times, would dismiss lightly. However, when the cooking takes off from being just agreeably simple approaches to good ingredients into the realms of dishes like grilled oysters with champagne sabayon and matchstick frites and you combine that seductive assembly with the view of the Thames and Tower Bridge and the magnificent wine list, it begins to seem worth it. Other dishes coming in for praise this year are roast saddle of rabbit with tarragon, bacon and mustard dressing; fillet of beef with foie gras croûte and cèpes; and vegetable dishes (priced separately) of scrubbed new carrots and inky-black field mushrooms. If you do not mind eating early or late the pre- and post-theatre menu at £19.50 for three courses is one way of 'economizing'. The bar and grill (no bookings) attached to the restaurant is another thought if it is a seat by the riverside with just some oysters or a Caesar salad you are after.

WELL OVER 50% of this massive wine list is what I'd call silly-price items, and in these circumstances it is hard to appreciate the marvellous completeness of the coverage. For instance, the gratitude one feels in finding Willi Opitz's sweet Austrian masterpieces diminishes on seeing that they average more than £100 a half-bottle. However, unlike Bibendum (q.v.) and Le Gavroche (q.v.), Le Pont de la Tour does help the customer to locate affordable bottles by grouping them into three fully annotated sections at the front (<£20, <£50, <£55). This should become standard practice with lists of this magnitude.

POONS

4 LEICESTER STREET WC2　　　　　　437 1528

'Money-wise, Poons helps you breathe more easily'

One of the challenges of compiling a guide is to do justice to those admirable places that remain the same. Striving to write something radically different might do a place like Poons a disservice. Its specialities are as before in nature and quality: the wind-dried foods with or without rice (with is better) and rich casseroles or hotpots. The sister restaurant in Lisle Street does similar dishes in more cramped conditions. A recent, speedy supper there of wind-dried food on rice, pork casseroled with dried shrimp and stir-fried leaves tasted beautiful and came to only £12 for two. Meanwhile, back at Leicester Street, the fried or soup noodles still make a satisfying quick meal; staff still seem well-disposed toward single customers, though the latter would be pushing their luck at times when the queue is heading towards Leicester Square; the refurbishment is an improvement; the bowls from long-gone restaurants remain; prices continue keen. Shocking to say, there is another school of thought which praises the likes of sweet corn soup, chicken with lemon sauce and fried rice. 'Brilliant value,' they say, ganging together to tackle the set meals.

SERVICE
OPTIONAL

SET-PRICE LUNCH & DINNER
£14 (FOR 2 PEOPLE)

FACILITIES
SEATS 120
PRIVATE ROOM
SEATS 26

NEAREST TUBE STATION
LEICESTER SQUARE

MAP 4

PORTO BELLO

67 WORNINGTON ROAD W10   0181-960 9669

'An end to the beastliness of the home barbecue'

This Portuguese restaurant is a relative newcomer previously called Oporto and located behind one of the cake shops of the same nationality on the Golborne Road. Through the courtyard is a rather fancy blue lounge and a plainer bar that is liked by the Iberian locals. The obvious option is to perch outside in fair weather and order from a long list of good things done to a turn on the open-air charcoal barbecue: chicken, steak and various fish including fresh sardines and scabbard fish. But the cooking by other methods is also interesting, and very reasonably priced, offering the national staple, salt cod, in several recipes, or clams with a hot sauce or good quality cold shellfish. The bread, mayonnaise and salads are ordinary, whereas the bargain house wines always seem to go down a treat. The disappearance of the immense BBQ grill and the Brazilian dishes are due to a change of ownership, but standards do not seem to have suffered, so that eating here is a sensible option for West Londoners wary of lighting their own fires.

£16

OPEN
EVERY DAY

HOURS
12.00–11.30PM

CREDIT CARDS
DELTA DINER'S
MASTERCARD
SWITCH VISA

COVER CHARGE
50P

FACILITIES
SEATS 47
TABLES OUTSIDE
SEAT 15

NEAREST TUBE STATION
LADBROKE GROVE/
WESTBOURNE
PARK

MAP 1

PRINCE BONAPARTE

80 CHEPSTOW ROAD W2   229 5912

'A pub with broad appeal'

The good ol' boys who used to drink in the pubs in and around Westbourne Park Road look on in stunned amazement as one by one their locals fill up with trustafarians eating

£20

OPEN
EVERY DAY

HOURS
12.00–2.45PM
6.30–10.30PM
SUN
7.30–10.00PM

CREDIT CARDS
AMEX DELTA
DINER'S
MASTERCARD
SWITCH VISA

SERVICE
OPTIONAL

SUNDAY BRUNCH

FACILITIES
SEATS 85
PRIVATE ROOM
SEATS 35

NEAREST TUBE
STATION
NOTTING HILL
GATE/
WESTBOURNE
PARK

MAP 1

oysters. At Prince Bonaparte, one of the pub conversions of the area – along with The Cow (q.v.) and The Westbourne – there is enough space and the right attitude to accommodate what have been described as 'real' people as well as the young who have been inspired to discover pubs anew as a great place to hang out and to eat well. The partners at the Bonaparte are Phillip Wright, a gifted New Zealand chef, Mark Harris, a handsome manager, and my sister, Beth Coventry, who made her name with English food at Green's in Duke Street, St James's (q.v.). The menu, inspired by travel and tradition, changes daily. At any one time it might include dishes as diverse as Thai tiger prawn noodle soup; spinach, roast red onion and feta salad; pesto and asparagus spaghettini; steak sandwich with aïoli; Spanish pork stew with cornbread; and Beth's fish cakes with tartare sauce and broccoli. Manchego (Spanish sheep's cheese) with quince jelly and rocket or desserts such as Egyptian orange and almond cake, home-made ice cream, or steamed marmalade pudding with custard follow on. The cooking is first rate. Well, I would say that, wouldn't I? But others agree and thousands vote with their feet. Although no bookings are taken, the sweep of the space is such that there is usually not a problem in finding space at one of the hand-made wooden tables. Evenings can get noisy. Lunch times are the time for deep, meaningful conversation.

PRINCE OF CEYLON

39 WATFORD WAY NW4   0181-203 8002

'A serendipitous discovery'

£20

OPEN
EVERY DAY

HOURS
12.00–3.00PM
6.00PM–12.00AM

CREDIT CARDS
AMEX DELTA
DINER'S
MASTERCARD
SWITCH VISA

SERVICE
OPTIONAL

SET-PRICE
LUNCH & DINNER
£7.50

FACILITIES
SEATS 60
WHEELCHAIR
ACCESS (ALSO
WC)

Sri Lanka, like many South-East Asian countries, reflects in its cooking influences from traders and conquerors. There are legacies and remnants from the Dutch (notably egg and butter-based cakes), the Portuguese (more sweet things), the British (doubtless a nice cup of tea), Malays, Arabs and the vegetarian dishes of the neighbouring South Indians. Sri Lankan food, available in a handful of restaurants in London, none of them centrally located, offers a diverting change from the repetitive menus of most Indian, or more probably Bangladeshi, restaurants. Prince of Ceylon in Hendon was the first to open to serve the Sri Lankan community. The menu offers a wide range of the specialities from which you should be sure to choose: hoppers, lace-edged, bowl-shaped pancakes made from fermented rice flour, crisp on the exterior, spongy within; pittu, steamed cylinders of rice flour mixed with coconut; and godamba, a kind of roti bread made with wheat flour, eggs and coconut oil. This gives you a basis of starch which you enliven with devilled meats (chicken livers are excellent), curries of fish and meat and sambals, a version of chutney of which the onion-based seeni sambal is my favourite. There are also excellent vegetable dishes including a memorable cashew nut curry. The menu has been revised to be more descriptive than in the past, which is merciful given the waiting staff's reticent approach to the art of communication. The interior is slightly gloomy. Colombo Ikea was one description.

NEAREST TUBE STATION
HENDON CENTRAL

QUAGLINO'S

16 BURY STREET SW1   930 6767

'Glamour for the masses'

This stylish ocean liner of a restaurant designed by Terence Conran Associates is set to be eclipsed, in size that is, by the next Conran enterprise, Mezzo in Wardour Street, open at the time this edition is published. Meanwhile the buzz goes on and although getting a table is slightly easier than it used to be, it is usually you the customer who has to fit in with the restaurant's plans rather than vice versa. Gliding, insofar as one is capable, down the sweeping staircase from the bar to the restaurant spread below is a thrill, and whatever happens subsequently in London – now suddenly the home of huge restaurants – it should be remembered that Quaglino's in its current manifestation was the first to emulate the big Parisian brasseries with their joyful atmosphere of egalitarian eating. The original Quag's, opened in 1929, apparently attracted royalty, the rich and the famous. Looking around in 1995 you might well say where are the Mountbattens, Windsors and Duff-Coopers de nos jours? The best way to enjoy the place is to go in a large party and create your own world in which you might be able to hear each other speak. Otherwise you may find yourself, as we have done, next to chain-smoking estate agents who say things like, 'I'm viewing it as a suck-it-and-see situation' or on the other side a disgruntled about-to-be-ex-wife confiding to her companion that at least she had seen his insurance policies. The menu keeps trucking, not settling into a formula. Crustacea make the best starter. Avoid the spicy Thai fish salad based on chunks of grilled tuna, liverish in colour. Dishes printed in red are specialities, at least one of them vegetarian, which change

£34

OPEN
EVERY DAY

HOURS
12.00–3.00PM
5.30PM–1.00AM
SUN
5.30–11.00PM

CREDIT CARDS
AMEX DINER'S
MASTERCARD VISA

SERVICE
12½%

SET-PRICE
LUNCH
£12.95

SET-PRICE
DINNER
£12.95
(5.30–6.30PM
ONLY)

FACILITIES
SEATS
RESTAURANT 338
ANTIPASTI BAR 90
PRIVATE ROOM
SEATS 40
WHEELCHAIR
ACCESS (ALSO
WC)

NEAREST TUBE
STATION
GREEN PARK/
PICCADILLY

MAP 3

regularly. Roast chicken, bacon and stuffing is prettily presented, a far cry from the English Sunday lunch dish. It is good to find salt beef, served here with braised peas and a stinging dollop of mustard. Items from the grill and rotisserie – visible through the glass wall of the kitchen – are usually well timed. Desserts look showy and taste good. The lower echelons of service, denoted by their garb, seem forbidden to speak or be helpful outside their prescribed duties. Branded products on sale at the entrance, including some naff jewellery, are rather sad. Couldn't they have resisted that little extra bit of profit?

THE AIM OF Quaglino's 'basic' list seems to be to introduce drinkers to the bright, youthful tastes of different grape varieties grown in different parts of the world – the list is arranged by grape variety – and in this it is a complete success. Don't miss Bonny Doon's Muscat Canelli, a dessert wine made with grapes that, prior to fermentation, have been tossed in the freezer alongside the Birdseye packets. The champagne line-up looks to have strayed from a more expensive list, so one hopes for consistency in the quality of the house NV (£5.95 a glass). The wines on the fine-wine list are for the most part overpriced and overyoung, but a good range of digestifs is offered by the glass.

THE QUALITY CHOP HOUSE

94 FARRINGDON ROAD EC1   837 5093

'Le Caprice for the working classes'

A surprise of the best kind: the outside has preserved the look of a caff which serves egg and chips whilst inside an atmosphere of good living prevails. Chef/proprietor Charles Fontaine, who spearheaded a restaurateurs' move to Farringdon, has taken pains to maintain the integrity of the interior of what once was presumably an Edwardian chop house but subsequently became, as the etched-glass frontage announces, a 'Progressive working class caterer'. High-backed pews enclose long tables which couples must share. Branded bottles of sauce stand proudly on small shelves, one for each table. Decorative colours of brown and cream provide the traditional, undemanding backdrop. Fontaine was for a time chef at Le Caprice (q.v.) and his menu at The Quality is a not dissimilar lively mix of dishes with something for everybody. It is a delightfully 'class-

£25

OPEN
LUNCH SUN–FRI
DINNER EVERY
DAY

HOURS
12.00–3.00PM
6.30–11.30PM

CREDIT CARDS
NONE

SERVICE
OPTIONAL

SUNDAY BRUNCH

FACILITIES
SEATS 48

**NEAREST TUBE
STATION**
FARRINGDON

MAP 3

less' menu but were you looking for cloth-cap leanings true to the café's antecedents, they are there in the offer of eggs, bacon and chips; sausages (from Toulouse), mash and onion gravy; corned beef hash and a cup of traditional English tea to finish. Quite another sort of meal could start with roast snails ('classic, fat and rich' according to one report) with garlic butter, move on to steak tartare with chips and French beans and finish with crème brûlée ('as well made as any with a delicately thin crust'). There are also dishes which are the sine qua non of the modern menu: Caesar salad; Bang Bang chicken; salmon fish cake and sorrel sauce; confit of duck, some of them originally introduced to London society by Fontaine. The intimacy enforced by the seating arrangement seems to work for the good of the atmosphere; everyone pulling together towards a feeling of enjoyment. The drinks list is as well sourced and egalitarian as the menu. There are beers and ciders as well as a short, well-chosen selection of wines and champagnes. A Delord Frères VSOP Armagnac after the meal will help deflect the creeping paralysis that sets in after sitting for an hour or so on the hard benches.

QUINCY'S

675 FINCHLEY ROAD NW2   794 8499

'An enthusiastic welcome on the wilder shores of Finchley'

It is quite possible you will forge a relationship with owner David Wardle even while making a booking at this little north London restaurant of long standing. He is a genuinely dedicated restaurateur. On the floor he dashes hither and thither; a finger in every pie, a cheery word for everyone and, as a result, the clientele is often composed of loyal regulars. Chef David Philpott's monthly-changing menu is offered at £24 for three courses, coffee and petits fours. Test meals this year have commented favourably on fish soup with a resoundingly tasty rouille; marinated salmon, delicate and soft, offset by the sharp crunch of pickled cucumber; fillet of lamb with 'tapinade' jus; and courgette flan, with this last turning out to be a pleasant creamy dollop, green with finely shredded courgette. Less impressive items were the vegetarian main course of leek and onion sausage with lentil salsa, mashed potato and tarragon butter, which turned out to be a formless mass with no textural definition surrounded by more flabby accoutrements; and rice pudding with apple and sultana compote which lacked skin

£33

OPEN
TUES–SAT

HOURS
7.00–11.00PM

CREDIT CARDS
AMEX
MASTERCARD VISA

SERVICE
OPTIONAL

SET-PRICE DINNER
£24

FACILITIES
SEATS 30
PRIVATE ROOM
SEATS 16
WHEELCHAIR
ACCESS

NEAREST TUBE STATION
GOLDERS
GREEN/FINCHLEY
ROAD

MAP 1

(some people like skin on rice pudding) and, in nanny-knows-best fashion, the compote already stirred into the pudding. Quincy's is a sound local Franglais bistro with the decorative effects which that phrase might imply: in a converted shop with lace curtains at half mast, posh silver candlesticks are set on scrubbed pine tables; the dark-green walls are decorated with junk-shop finds such as Millet's *The Angelus*.

RAGAM

£18

OPEN
EVERY DAY

HOURS
12.00–3.00PM
& 6.00–11.30PM

CREDIT CARDS
AMEX DINER'S
MASTERCARD VISA

SERVICE
10%

FACILITIES
SEATS 34
PRIVATE ROOM
SEATS 20
WHEELCHAIR
ACCESS (ALSO
WC)

**NEAREST TUBE
STATION**
WARREN ST/
GOODGE ST/
GREAT
PORTLAND ST/
TOTTENHAM
COURT ROAD

MAP 4

57 CLEVELAND STREET W1   636 9098

'Have a South Indian breakfast for lunch'

Ragam, near the Middlesex Hospital, continues to please with its kind prices, sweet waiters, simple surroundings and its undoctrinaire approach to Indian food which allows a menu of Keralan vegetarian dishes to be offered alongside a list of chicken, egg, meat and seafood curries. Whatever your proclivities where diet is concerned, some of the Southern Indian dishes should be part of an order. The pancakes and steamed buns made of, variously, rice, lentil and gram flour, enlivened with chutneys and sambal, under the headings dosa, utthappam and vadai, are intriguing to newcomers to the cuisine, delightful to Keralan travellers who might pitch up at noon to make that most satisfying of late breakfasts out of them, complete with the hot pepper soup, rasam. A meat masala dosa, filled with minced meat as well as potatoes, may be unorthodox, but it is very good. Fish – try king prawn fry – egg and vegetable curries follow on more seamlessly as main courses than does meat but lamb dopiaza has been praised for the same feeling of freshness to the cooking that applies to the Keralan dishes and the vegetable assemblies. One fan of Ragam thinks that a new carpet would not come amiss, but wonders whether the prices could subsequently be kept so low.

RANSOME'S DOCK

£26

OPEN
LUNCH EVERY DAY
DINNER MON–SAT

35–37 PARKGATE ROAD SW11   223 1611/924 2462

'A bright star in what some natives call Battarsia'

The dock itself is a bit dull, as Thames inlets have a way of being, and the houses in between shut the river off from view, and that is about that in terms of qualifications. Ransome's Dock the restaurant is a well-run establishment which serves good to great food and offers an attractive wine list. The mixture of seasonal, comforting or fashionable items on the menu seems just right, and execution is precise; salad garnishes are dressed correctly and scrambled eggs made to order (not such a big deal, the domestic cook will think, but many restaurants can't be bothered). Steak and chips – sometimes immense pont neuf frites – delicately spiced potted shrimps and daily fish specials are always on the carte. There is a liking for the lighter kinds of game such as rabbit, guinea fowl and for foods of particular provenance (Northumberland kippers, Norfolk smoked eel and Rocombe Farm ice cream from Devon). Accompanying elements have been properly thought out and the prices are very fair, considering the care that goes into everything. It would be a pity to peak too soon in a meal and have no room for desserts such as cheesecake of raisin and chocolate or treacle tart prepared by Vanessa Lam. The same commendation on value can be given to the large wine list the chef/proprietor Martin Lam selects. Also on offer are varietal apple juices, lively ginger beer and children's portions. 'And we have our own water,' enthused the manageress, explaining that there is an artesian well below and that the premises was once an ice house. If Ransome's Dock continues to prosper as it deserves and if, as she also said, there are two levels below the dining room, it might be an idea to move the loos below, so that there is a view across the entire cobalt-blue-painted room.

A GLANCE at the first page of this wine list and you know that you're in the hands of someone who knows and loves their wine: cleverly varied house selections, all under £15, serious champagnes at tempting prices (Veuve Clicquot, Krug, Billecart-Salmon), quirky sparklers (try Seppelt's sparkling Shiraz with your pudding) and a brace of almacenista sherries from Lustau. The list is arranged so far as is practicable by grape variety, and each section is packed with interest. All France's regions yield good bottles (the Rhône features more prominently than Bordeaux, always a sign of a conscientiously-put-together list) while the New World is represented by a surprising diversity of grapes and styles. Completing matters are 14 dessert wines – 15 if you count the sparkling Shiraz – each of which is utterly individual.

HOURS
11AM–11.00PM
SAT
12.00PM–12.00AM
SUN
12.00–3.30PM

CREDIT CARDS
AMEX DELTA
DINER'S
MASTERCARD VISA

SERVICE
OPTIONAL

SET-PRICE LUNCH
£11.50

SUNDAY BRUNCH

FACILITIES
SEATS 65
TABLES OUTSIDE
SEAT 25
WHEELCHAIR
ACCESS (ALSO
WC)

NEAREST TUBE STATION
SLOANE SQUARE

NEAREST BR STATION
BATTERSEA PARK

MAP 2

RASA

'Sowing coconut palms in Stoke Newington'

£17

OPEN
EVERY DAY

HOURS
12.00–2.30PM
6.00PM–12.00AM

CREDIT CARDS
AMEX DELTA
DINER'S
MASTERCARD
SWITCH VISA

SERVICE
OPTIONAL

FACILITIES
SEATS 42
TABLES OUTSIDE
SEAT 20
WHEELCHAIR
ACCESS (ALSO
WC)

**NEAREST BR
STATION**
STOKE
NEWINGTON

MAP 1

Anyone who has visited Kerala and travelled along the Quilon-Alleppey backwaters will fall on Rasa as somewhere, speaking in culinary terms, almost better than home from home. Owner Das Padmanabhan is a native of Cochin, the capital of Kerala, and is a tireless proselytizer for the cuisine of this most lovely part of Southern India. Blessed with natural prosperity in terms of foodstuffs and spices and benefiting from the influences of various traders and settlers who, over time, have included 'Syrian' Christians, Jews, Arabs, Chinese, Dutch, French and, of course, the English, Keralan cuisine is to my mind the most subtle and appealing in all the subcontinent. The menu at Rasa is entirely vegetarian, some parts of it familiar from other Indian vegetarian restaurants, but among the specialities you will find the appams (a.k.a. hoppers) and idiappams which are not widely available. Appams, resembling a bowl-shaped pancake crossed with a crumpet, are made from fermented rice flour batter thinned with coconut milk. Cooked in something like a small wok, they emerge with a spongy base and crisp lacy edge. Served with a mild creamy potato curry (pal) they are heavenly, and, indeed, eaten by Keralan Christians at Easter. Another special is kappa and kadala curry, two contrasting, separately spiced mixtures based on cassava and chick peas. Lovers of dosas will discover nadam dosa, round, thick pancakes made of rice and black gram batter mixed with onions, chillis and tomatoes, served with a lentil sauce and coconut and ginger chutney. Hindu tea shops in the South make it as a breakfast dish. The list of curries has more discoveries: moru kachiathu, a sweet and sour mixture of mangoes and green bananas cooked in yogurt with chillis, ginger and fresh curry leaves; rasa kayi, a spicy mixed vegetable curry from Karnataka; papaya parippu, green papaya and split peas cooked in a fresh green masala; bagar baingan, a Hyderabadi aubergine assembly. The Keralan rice, plain or flavoured with tamarind, lemon or coconut, and the various breads, including the Malabar paratha fashioned like a coir mat, supply a delicious foundation for these dishes. To start the meal, choose from the various crisp delights extracted from grains, pulses and vegetables and do not miss pappadavadai, poppadoms taken to new heights of crunchiness, and the home-made pickles and chutneys. Desserts include sweet, nutty mixtures, kulfi (condensed milk ice cream) in various flavours and gulab jamun (spongy puffs in rosewater syrup). Both the menu and the staff give helpful guidance towards composing a revelatory meal. Rasa is small and simply, brightly decorated. Smoking is not allowed, but even smokers have been known to forget all about their habit when eating here.

REBATO'S

169 SOUTH LAMBETH ROAD SW8   582 8089/735 6388

'Tiptoe through the tapas'

Something of the effect of the British package holiday on Spain is encapsulated in Rebato's, located in the Little Iberia that is South Lambeth. In the restaurant decorated with Spanish floor tiles, arched cream walls, hanging artificial plants and dark landscape paintings the very reasonable three-course table d'hôte menu at £13.95 (plus £1.50 supplements on some dishes) lists Parma ham and melon, avocado with prawns, grilled Dover sole and supreme of chicken Devon alongside gambas al ajillo, huevos flamenca, zarzuela de pescado and chuletas de cordero à la brasa con aïoli. It is doubtless in response to customer demand. The general consensus is that the tapas bar at the front of the premises is more authentic and more fun. Portions are large enough to dine on with ease and paella can be ordered there as well. Copitas of sherry are a good accompaniment, but it is worth studying the wine list.

THIS SPANISH-DOMINATED list differs from that produced by Albero & Grana (q.v.) in that it makes less attempt to introduce the drinker to regional styles. Instead, it showcases the full ranges of two of Spain's most famous houses, Torres and Marqués de Cáceres, together with a good haul of riojas, a quartet of cavas and a dozen brandies. Prices are unbelievably good: with well-chosen house wines at £1.50 a glass.

RED PEPPER

8 FORMOSA STREET W9   266 2708

'Pizzas and pizazz'

A traditional wood-burning pizza oven lifts this Maida Vale pizzeria on to a higher plane, as does the care taken with first courses, pasta dishes and desserts, the reasonable, good

£28

OPEN
LUNCH MON–FRI
DINNER MON–SAT

HOURS
12.00–2.30PM
7.00–11.00PM

CREDIT CARDS
AMEX DINER'S
MASTERCARD VISA

SERVICE
OPTIONAL

**SET-PRICE
LUNCH & DINNER**
£13.95

FACILITIES
SEATS 70

**NEAREST TUBE
STATION**
STOCKWELL

MAP 1

£20

OPEN
LUNCH FRI–SUN
DINNER
EVERY DAY

HOURS
12.30–2.30PM
7.00–11.00PM
SUN
12.30–3.30PM

CREDIT CARDS
DELTA
MASTERCARD
SWITCH VISA

SERVICE
OPTIONAL

FACILITIES
SEATS 60
TABLES OUTSIDE
SEAT 10
WHEELCHAIR
ACCESS

**NEAREST TUBE
STATION**
WARWICK AVENUE/
MAIDA VALE

MAP 1

Italian wine list and the input of consultant chef Giorgio Locatelli, currently cooking at Zafferano (q.v.). Few London restaurants can boast a wood-fired oven – Sol e Luna in Covent Garden and The River Café (q.v.) are two that come to mind – and it does produce a better pizza. Adding some toppings in two stages, some baked on, some used as garnish, also helps as textures and flavours are differentiated. The menu changes regularly, but features always imaginative first-course salads such as thin-sliced wind-dried tuna with rocket, fresh tomato and French beans or endive, orange slices and salami; usually a fish dish, such as sautéed scallops or stuffed calamari with tomatoes and basil; and perhaps a bruschetta, such as one topped with sautéed chicken livers and truffled olive oil. Filled pastas which have pleased include agnolotti filled with pumpkin and ricotta in a walnut sauce and ravioli stuffed with potatoes and mint in a purée of red peppers. Calzone, where the disc of dough is folded over the filling, is a particularly good, seemingly less bready way of going about having a pizza. For dessert, tiramisu, grown-up in its restraint with sweetness and lapped with an espresso coffee sauce, is notable. Surroundings are plain, almost brutal. The place is popular and usually packed, but Latin-lover waiters slink to efficient effect.

THE RITZ – LOUIS XVI RESTAURANT

150 PICCADILLY W1   493 8181

'The chateau on the edge of Green Park'

£62

OPEN
EVERY DAY

HOURS
12.30–2.00PM
6.00–11.15PM
SUN
6.30–10.30PM

CREDIT CARDS
AMEX DELTA
DINER'S
MASTERCARD
SWITCH VISA

SERVICE
OPTIONAL

**SET-PRICE
LUNCH**
£29

**SET-PRICE
DINNER**
SUN–THURS £43
FRI–SAT £49

Since the Mandarin Oriental Hotel Group took over management of The Ritz, service has been rejuvenated and improved but, perhaps inevitably, prices have jumped up. Last year's guide noted that the four-course dinner at The Ritz at £39.50 was something of a bargain given the extravagant surroundings. That same meal is now £49 (£43 from Sunday to Thursday). There are many other – too many other – set-price arrangements including pre- and post-theatre meals and a menu gastronomique which results in a card cumbersome to deal with. The kitchen under David Nicholls also seems to find it cumbersome: dishes are less precise this year and also slightly less generous. However, the Louis XVI room is still London's, if not the world's, most stunning belle epoque restaurant interior and the facility of dining on the terrace or in the sunken Italian Garden during warm weather has made it all the more seductive. Luncheon (£29) offers robust daily specialities such as ossobucco, steak and kidney pie, mixed grill and dishes of the day from the trolley (different cuts of lamb or beef apart from Friday's salmon). A hint of Eastern flavour has been noticed since the Mandarin took over. Not only are the flower arrangements often orchids but there are dishes offered such as warm Oriental salad of scallops with chicken oysters, and Chinese-style ravioli filled with scallops, lobster and langoustines, but in the main the food is modern British and perhaps most satisfying when it is least fussed with. Sunday lunch is a nice time to enjoy The Ritz, and note that there is an enterprising Sunday brunch (£16) offered in The Palm Court, also the perfect setting for afternoon tea.

LEAFING THROUGH The Ritz wine list has made me *very unhappy*. Big names at unreal prices, that's all it is. Champagne starts at £39.50; Sauternes/Barsac at £67; port at £76 (none offered by the glass). Claret outnumbers the Rhône by 43–2; and two is the number of bottles offered for less than £20. An English wine and a Rosé d'Anjou. Both delicious, no doubt.

FACILITIES
SEATS 120
TABLES OUTSIDE
SEAT 60
PRIVATE ROOMS
SEAT 20–50
WHEELCHAIR
ACCESS (ALSO
WC)

NEAREST TUBE
STATION
GREEN PARK

MAP 3

RIVA

169 CHURCH ROAD SW13   0181-748 0434

'Become a regular'

Few restaurateurs are such dedicated enthusiasts as Andrea Riva. He is never away from his restaurant when it is open and when it is closed he might be tracking down ingredients and researching dishes in his native Lombardy. His chef, Francesco Zanchetta, is from the north-eastern region Friuli Venezia Giulia adjacent to the former Yugoslavia. Although so many restaurants are nowadays in thrall to that tragic area for their staff, the presence of its calm, competent, milkmaid-demure girls here is particularly fitting. I make no bones about knowing Andrea Riva since most of his customers are regulars and benefit from his extras and arbitrary imports such as translucent, tinged-with-pink-like-a-sunrise, herb-sprinkled slices of pork fat which his brother sends over, served wrapped round a breadstick, a cheese which he claims is from Bosnia or wines which are not on the list but which he, with justification, likes. A favourite first course is brodetto dell'Adriatico, a little minestra of clams, shrimps, cuttlefish in a broth spiked with garlic and rounded out

£28

OPEN
LUNCH SUN–FRI
DINNER MON–SUN

HOURS
12.00–2.30PM
7.00–11.00PM

CREDIT CARDS
DELTA
MASTERCARD
SWITCH VISA

SERVICE
10%

FACILITIES
SEATS 50
TABLES OUTSIDE
SEAT 8
WHEELCHAIR
ACCESS

NEAREST BR
STATION
BARNES

MAP 1

with butter. Tris di carpacci assembles slices of raw beef decked with artichokes and grana (hard cheese), slices of home-cured goose served with chicory, oranges and nuts in an oil and lemon dressing and a sublime version of vitello tonnato with a stock-thinned sauce. Historically, pasta is not of great importance in Lombardy although risotto and polenta are, a fact reflected in Riva's menu. Try risotto with saffron and scampi or pizzettina gialla, the pizza base made with maize topped with smoked mozzarella, asparagus and egg. Fava (broad) beans, soft polenta, barley pancakes and pizzoccheri, a pasta dish from Valtellina, made with buckwheat flour layered with cabbage, potatoes and cheese, are some of the regional garnishes in the main courses which might focus on sea bass, best end of lamb, roast kid, calf's liver or breaded veal cutlets. Desserts are a strong point, as is apparent from warm zabaglione served over ice cream; prugne cotte e mirtilli alla grappa, prunes and blueberries in grappa with cinnamon ice cream; and crostone al Gorgonzola e miele, cheese on toast with chestnut honey. Dessert wines and grappe are irresistible. The underplayed look of the long, narrow, ochre room is all part of the cumulative seductive effect.

THE RIVER CAFÉ

THAMES WHARF RAINVILLE ROAD W6   381 8824

'Just keeps rolling along'

The magnificence of the food here is not in question. Sometimes it is a simple magnificence true to Tuscany, often the source of inspiration for The River Café's star chefs, Rose Gray and Ruth Rogers. In Tuscany there is not such an enthusiasm for a succession of courses or for subjugating ingredients to the cook's will as is found further north. Pasta is not such a big thing either, which can be literally true at The River Café when its cooks send out a tiny portion of delicious spinach gnocchi with the merest suggestion of butter as a sauce. Chargrilled or wood-oven-roasted meats plainly accompanied and served in large portions are the backbone of The River Café menu, and certain to satisfy if they match your mood and you are prepared for the prices. A recent menu managed £22 for 'veal roasted with porcini, sage and white wine with Scottish chanterelles'. The veal was not British and the mushrooms were not particularly expensive in shops at the time so the price seemed quite a premium. Praise is due this restaurant's brilliant bread salad and bread soup, and ice creams of its own making.

£40

OPEN
LUNCH EVERY DAY
DINNER MON–SAT

HOURS
12.30–5.00PM &
7.30–11.00PM
SUN 1.00–5.00PM

CREDIT CARDS
AMEX DELTA
MASTERCARD
SWITCH VISA

SERVICE
12½%

FACILITIES
SEATS 98
TABLES OUTSIDE
SEAT 50
WHEELCHAIR
ACCESS (ALSO
WC)

**NEAREST TUBE
STATION**
HAMMERSMITH

MAP 1

Some customers are flummoxed by service they describe as casual and inconsistent. A summer visitor reports being reduced to 'Doing a Winner' (which means waving one's napkin to attract attention, an action the British public and British waiters usually despise) after asking three times for a bottle of water. Evidently this is not a restaurateur-run business and no one seems to have suggested to the well-meaning young staff that it is useful to scan the tables to see what might be needed or to pause as you pass to give your customer a chance to ask. It is curious too that the bread is so ordinary: a French restaurant of similar class would bake every day, and The River Café has its own wood oven. Now that the book of the Café is available, sceptics can try their hand at reproducing the recipes at home. They will miss out on the cool beauty of the restaurant's long dining room and may find that Gray and Rogers' clear flavours cannot be reproduced as simply as they imagined.

IN LAST YEAR'S GUIDE this Italian list was praised for its notes which 'convey flavours and philosophies with uncommon intelligence'. Where have they gone? Instead, we have an unannotated document divided into Vini Frizzante, Vini Bianchi and Vini Rossi, and arranged solely by price. This would be acceptable for a more modest collection, but the River Café list is good enough to blow its own trumpet. All the wines are well chosen and sensibly priced. Those prepared to fork out £28 for a Valpolicella – there can't be many, I know – are in for a treat, for it is Giuseppe Quintarelli's Monte Ca Paletta.

ROYAL CHINA

13 QUEENSWAY W2   221 2535

'Probably the best dim sum in London'

If Peter Stringfellow were to open a Chinese restaurant, I dare say it would look something like this. But doubtless Hong Kong is full of places that resemble Stringfellow's club. The walls are black and shiny with waves, clouds and flying ducks picked out in white and gilt. Staff are plentiful and formally dressed. If you make a booking – which is wise – turn up on time. (Note: you cannot book for the justifiably popular weekend dim-sum.) The menu is an eight-page booklet of Cantonese cuisine including family Chaochou dishes, some of which are included in the short menu of nine dishes tantalizingly printed only in Chinese characters. The list, which is

£28
OPEN
EVERY DAY

HOURS
12.00–11.15PM
SUN
12.00–10.30PM

CREDIT CARDS
AMEX DELTA
DINER'S
MASTERCARD
SWITCH VISA

SERVICE
12½%

SET-PRICE
DINNER
£20

SUNDAY BRUNCH

FACILITIES
SEATS 100
PRIVATE ROOM
SEATS 15

NEAREST TUBE
STATION
QUEENSWAY/
BAYSWATER

MAP 1

perhaps overpowering to the uninitiated, is actually well balanced between luxury items and everyday food. Yan-Kit So, author of the peerless *Classic Food of China* (Macmillan, £25), makes the following suggestions: to start, Shanghai dumplings, sautéed on one side, steamed on the other; the tender baby squid with garlic and spicy salt; seafood golden cups, four crisp cups containing well-seasoned and moist pieces of scallop and prawn, worth the outlay. In the main course, steamed eel with black bean sauce, where the slippery skin of the eel in its oily sauce cut by the black beans and the fragrance of dried orange peel is heaven for eel lovers; half of braised duck with superior soya sauce, deeply savoury but not overwhelmed by star anise, served on the bone, Chinese style; the Fuchou dish of bean curd topped with diced seafood, a sophisticated peasant dish; sautéed Chinese broccoli with ginger, each slice perfectly proportioned, half-stalk, half-leaf; omelette with pickled turnip and Chinese chives (listed in Chinese characters only, but worth trying to order), crisp on the outside, baveuse inside; finally the rice steamed in a clay pot which is cooked to order. In her view, Royal China serves the most sophisticated and authentic dim sum in London.

Although they claim not to be linked there are certain shareholders in common and certainly a name, decor and menu style in common with Royal China in Putney at 3 Chelverton Road SW15 (0181-780 1520/788 0907) but research suggests Queensway has the definite edge in cooking.

RSJ

£27

OPEN
MON–SAT

HOURS
12.00–2.00PM
6.00–11.00PM
SAT
5.45–11.00PM

CREDIT CARDS
AMEX DELTA
MASTERCARD
SWITCH VISA

SERVICE
10%

SET-PRICE
LUNCH & DINNER
£15.95

13A COIN STREET SE1   928 4554

'A Loire unto themselves'

March 1995 marked the fifteenth anniversary of RSJ and also its winning of the 1995 *Wine Magazine*/Muscadet 'Most Sympathique Restaurant' Award. This award, for which I have been one of the judges, depends on the degree of success of the ten nominated restaurants in fulfilling various criteria which cover welcome, service, quality and variety of food and wine, and value for money. One of the most extensive lists of Loire wines in the world – see below – is doubtless no handicap to winning a prize sponsored by Muscadet. RSJ is also well placed geographically for grateful customers. The owner deserves special mention for spotting this opportunity in the market long before most. Dishes tend towards the over-complex, with sometimes not altogether felicitous pairings, as exemplified by smoked chicken and lobster salad, mango salsa; mash (sic) salad and roast woodland pigeon with penne pasta, cèpe mushrooms, smoked bacon, shallots and pigeon jus; and mille fruille (sic) of mixed berries, pear bavarois, raspberry coulis. However, there has been praise for mushroom risotto with Parmesan crackling – chefs have discovered that grated Parmesan will melt in a frying pan into a kind of cheese mat – and superb quality fillet of beef on Dauphinoise potatoes with a 'confit' of vegetables. RSJ has seating at three levels. Someone, who in May shivered in the basement, pointed out that the weather in the streets never penetrates there.

FACILITIES
SEATS 90
TABLES OUTSIDE
SEAT 12
PRIVATE ROOM
SEATS 20
WHEELCHAIR
ACCESS

NEAREST TUBE
STATION
WATERLOO

MAP 3

THIS EXTRAORDINARY LIST is devoted to the wines of the Loire and proves beyond question how versatile and various they can be: most people will assume that this is crisp, dry white territory, but here reds and sweeties are just as numerous (17 Chinons, 13 Bourgueils, and 20 Coteaux du Layons). The Chenins of Vouvray and Savennières quite properly outnumber the less individual Sauvignons of Pouilly-sur-Loire and Sancerre, and equally properly have received plenty of bottle age. There is even a 20-year-old Muscadet for the super-adventurous with £40 to burn. Prices are fair, and RSJ must be one of only two restaurants (the Tate Gallery, q.v., being the other) where one can buy wines from the 1970s at less than £20 a bottle. The layout will make most sense to those who already know their way around, but the tasting notes are educational, appetizing, and, on occasion, witty.

RULES

35 MAIDEN LANE WC2   836 5314

'Don't leave it to the tourists'

£28

OPEN
EVERY DAY

HOURS
12.00PM–12.00AM

CREDIT CARDS
AMEX DELTA
MASTERCARD
SWITCH VISA

SERVICE
12½% PARTIES
OF 7 OR MORE

Claiming, no doubt truthfully, to be London's oldest restaurant (established 1798), Rules is run as a highly efficient modern business right down to a Remanco system (computerized till) complete with electronic game boys for the waiting staff. However, this anachronistic air of efficiency – given the seductive, plushy, picture-panelled, historic surroundings – and the theme-park look of the laminated menu need not deter, for they serve to keep prices eminently reasonable and do not seem to militate against efforts being made in the kitchen to deliver well-sourced, well-prepared traditional British dishes with an

**SET-PRICE
LUNCH**
£7.95–12.95

**SET-PRICE
DINNER**
£12.95 (MON–FRI
5.00–6.00PM
ONLY)

FACILITIES
SEATS 140
PRIVATE ROOMS
SEAT 8–46
WHEELCHAIR
ACCESS

**NEAREST TUBE
STATION**
CHARING CROSS

MAP 4

emphasis on furred and feathered game. To list guinea fowl under this last heading is stretching a point, but eating outside the season for true game birds – August to February – the braised guinea fowl served for two in an oval copper saucepan, with wild mushrooms, brioche dumplings packed with herbs and forcemeat wrapped in cabbage, was thought to be almost regal in presentation. Steak, kidney and oyster pudding served in an individual basin with an oyster perched on the somewhat gooey suet crust also pleased a party who had come to the sensible conclusion that Rules came into being long before the advent of the health lobby, and therefore ordering, say, poached wild salmon with a basil and sun-dried tomato mayonnaise would be to miss the point. Puddings are properly hearty and include a steamed treacle sponge with custard and Sauterne crème caramel with Armagnac prunes. The wine list is short and reasonable. A magnum of the house red, Sandeman claret, at £16 is not a bad start. My tip for Rules is go for late weekday lunch between 3pm and 5pm when any starter and main course can be had for £7.95 (£12.95 at weekends). With the right company you can act out the Prince of Wales and Lillie Langtry, two habitués of the past.

ST JAMES'S COURT HOTEL – AUBERGE DE PROVENCE

41 BUCKINGHAM GATE SW1   821 1899

'A yearning for Provence'

£40

OPEN
LUNCH MON–FRI
DINNER MON–SAT

HOURS
12.30–2.30PM
7.30–11.00PM

CREDIT CARDS
AMEX DELTA
DINER'S
MASTERCARD
SWITCH VISA

SERVICE
OPTIONAL

**SET-PRICE
LUNCH**
£24.50

**SET-PRICE
DINNER**
£32

Looking round at the mock hacienda-style decor in the restaurant that is this Taj-owned hotel's evocation of L'Ousteau de Baumanière (workplace of consultant chef Jean-André Charial) one visitor remarked that it was 'like a living room in a very satirical Alan Ayckbourn play'. Given that it would be anyway difficult to capture the spirit of one of Europe's prettiest restaurant settings in the Alpilles of Provence within a former Edwardian mansion block near Victoria Station, perhaps the hopelessness of the try can just be seen as endearing. It is a comfortable restaurant with tables well spaced and offers attentive, efficient service. The kitchen, led by chef Bernard Briqué, is altogether more successful in importing the flavours of Provence: the basil, olives, olive oil, pine nuts, aubergines and tomatoes that convey the role played by the sun. From the weekly-changing lunch menu, roulade de sole et poivrons rouge à l'aïoli was seaside fresh with the textures of the fish and the red pepper mousse it encased beautifully balanced. A crêpe of lamb, aubergine and goat's cheese was more modest but no less successful. At lunch when the fixed-price menu is £24.50 for three courses, there is a supplement of £1 if cheese is chosen in place of dessert. Since this might deter some from roaming among the stunning display of more than 25 varieties from every region of France – almost reason enough to come here – my advice to the management would be to round up the price to £25 and encourage grazing; cheese is, after all, an ephemeral commodity. The advice holds for dinner when cheese is a supplementary £2 on top of a £30 menu price. Charial's interest in vegetarian cooking, instilled during a trip to India, is evident in the menu. Provençal wines, some produced by the Baumanière, are the sensible choice. Despite the holiday associations, this is a restaurant better suited to business discussions than dalliance.

ST JOHN

26 ST JOHN STREET EC1   251 0848

'Nose to tail eating'

St John, located in a former smoke-house near Smithfield meat market, is the new venture for chef and architect manqué Fergus Henderson, previously working at The French House Dining Room (q.v.). 'Nose to tail eating' and a picture of a pig sectioned into its culinary cuts are the messages on the menu and within a deliberately plain but interesting list Henderson goes further than most in his espousal of offal. For example, he will salt and dry pig's liver and serve thin slices in a well-dressed salad with radishes, a tangle of whole chives and hard-boiled egg. In its tough, chewy way, having something of the sustaining quality of biltong, salted, dried pig's liver is good. Duck's neck is stuffed using some of a duck's other bits and pieces to make a coarse sausage-shaped pâté. The pork pie served with home-made chutney – a gourmet Branston – is notable for the delicious, shimmering jelly between meat and pastry case. Marrow bones are roasted and served with a lively parsley salad. However, there are also dishes for the gastronomically tremulous, quite often celebrating an ingredient such as sabre, a deep-water white fish, which seems a new discovery. And vegetarians are not ignored. Vegetable side dishes are carefully cooked, generously served. St John is one of the few restaurants that gets green salad right. Desserts include

£25

OPEN
LUNCH MON–SUN
DINNER MON–SAT

HOURS
12.00–3.00PM &
6.00–11.30PM
(12.00–3.30PM
SUN)

CREDIT CARDS
AMEX DELTA
DINER'S
MASTERCARD
SWITCH VISA

SERVICE
OPTIONAL

FACILITIES
SEATS 120
TABLES OUTSIDE
SEAT 40
PRIVATE ROOM
SEATS 20
WHEELCHAIR
ACCESS (ALSO
WC)

NEAREST TUBE STATION
FARRINGDON

MAP 3

something based on chocolate, something based on lemon, an ice and usually a steamed pudding. Henderson seems to me to have created a new definition of English food which is both timely and bona fide, having no recourse to heritage, whimsy or other marketing ploys. He pushes cannily bought ingredients at the customer with infectious enthusiasm. The what-you-see-is-what-you-get ethos of the menu is carried on into the remorselessly uncluttered refectory decor where the only 'picture' on the white walls is a view of the kitchen at work. Staff are agreeable. As with the food so with wines; there is no traipsing round the globe for sources. The list with a good deal of choice between £8 and £20 is wholly French. Meals are served all day in the ground-floor bar.

ST QUENTIN

243 BROMPTON ROAD SW3   589 8005

'Not the patron saint of vegetarians'

£34

OPEN
EVERY DAY

HOURS
12.00–3.00PM
7.00–11.30PM

CREDIT CARDS
AMEX DELTA
DINER'S
MASTERCARD
SWITCH VISA

SERVICE
12½%

**SET-PRICE
LUNCH & DINNER**
£9 (BEFORE
7.30PM)

FACILITIES
SEATS 80
PRIVATE ROOM
SEATS 22
WHEELCHAIR
ACCESS

**NEAREST TUBE
STATION**
SOUTH
KENSINGTON

MAP 2

There have been a few changes to the dining room at St Quentin. The bar has been moved to the back, making a wider space for tables. No doubt redecoration was necessary too, but only to replicate the old-fashioned French interior of dark wood, mirrors and brass railings. This is old-school territory, from the red canopy outside and the uniforms of the staff to the uncompromising menu. Customers greeted as regulars look old-school, too – old public school, which goes with the territory. Ditto a wine list big on bordeaux, but which does include some good, cheaper options. Trend followers and vegetarians would have to vote with their feet, leaving others to tuck into trotters with foie gras, tripe in the fashion of Caen or an omelette of elvers. The trio are examples from the daily specials, supplementing a classical carte of oysters, oeufs en meurette, goat's cheese salad, a short list of main-course fish, then duck, steak with Roquefort and cuts of lamb or beef for two. The quality of the meat and poultry and confidence of the cookery were obvious in a maverick modern dish, gazpacho with shellfish; in foie gras terrine; a sauté of chicken and spring vegetables; and an anise-spiced, rare-cooked squab pigeon. This meal was much more inspired than one six months before, and was supported by good bread and salad and rounded off with fine patisserie and coffee. The drawback is the expense, but that is not disproportionate when the kitchen is on such form and using the very best ingredients.

SALLOOS

'Good cooking from Pakistan served with strictures'

£35

OPEN
MON–SAT

HOURS
12.00–3.00PM
7.00PM–12.00AM

CREDIT CARDS
AMEX DELTA
DINER'S
MASTERCARD
SWITCH VISA

SERVICE
15%

COVER CHARGE
£1.50

**SET-PRICE
LUNCH**
£16

**SET-PRICE
DINNER**
£25

FACILITIES
SEATS 65
WHEELCHAIR
ACCESS (ALSO
WC)

**NEAREST TUBE
STATION**
KNIGHTSBRIDGE

MAP 2

When told that he is being bossy, the amazing chap in charge here switches to being jovially bossy. His bossiness is as much a feature as the excellence of the tandoori dishes of chops, quails and a tangy seekh kebab made of lamb leg ('not trimmings' instructs the menu) and coriander that he may deign to bring to your table himself. Some temerity is required to ask for the set-dinner menu which enables you to have soup, a tandoori dish plus naan bread, a choice of curries, vegetable dish, pulao rice and dessert for £25 – a bargain by Salloos' standards. The clever curry choice is chicken karahi, which zings with ginger and chilli against a background of subtler spices. Undoubtedly this is one of London's best curried dishes. Pulao rice is near perfect and the kulfi luxurious. Many of the recipes on the à la carte are unique to Salloos. Others, like the bhuna gosht, are elevated. The downside is that the same kitchen is capable of sending out a dreary mixed vegetable dish or over-salting some prawns which were in themselves full of flavour. A complaint would require courage. It is a shame that the atmosphere is not more relaxing, because then the charm of the mews location, a long French wine list and other house specialities such as the leg of lamb (raan masala) or beautiful biriani would make a long evening here attractive.

SAN LORENZO FUORIPORTA

WORPLE MEWS SW19   0181-946 8463

'Advantage Wimbledon'

£35

OPEN
EVERY DAY

HOURS
12.00–3.00PM
7.00–11.00PM
SUN
12.00–3.30PM

CREDIT CARDS
AMEX DINER'S
MASTERCARD
SWITCH VISA

SERVICE
OPTIONAL

COVER CHARGE
£2

**SET-PRICE
LUNCH**
£15.50

A man I met whose lifestyle I hugely admired had a London flat at the top of a tall block in Brewer Street, Soho, and a country house in Putney. Customers of San Lorenzo in Beauchamp Place, Knightsbridge, who share the same enlightened view of rural life can seek out a retreat at San Lorenzo Fuoriporta – meaning beyond the city walls – in Wimbledon. Both restaurants are owned by Mara and Lorenzo Berni, but the country branch is run by their son Ghigo. The approach to the premises is around the back and through a garden whereupon you reach a glamorous, airy space decorated with creamy tiles, large plants and bold artwork. A glance at the menu tells you this is going to be an expensive experience, starting with a

SUNDAY BRUNCH

FACILITIES
SEATS 120
TABLES OUTSIDE
SEAT 65
PRIVATE ROOM
SEATS 30
WHEELCHAIR
ACCESS

**NEAREST TUBE
STATION**
WIMBLEDON

£2 per person cover charge. The wise old crone who told you, 'look after the pennies and the pounds will take care of themselves' was not, I think, meaning for you to order crostino al pomodoro e basilico, basically tomatoes on toast, at 650p (which is how it is expressed). However, the food here is well prepared, the environment is attractive and they are welcoming to children, which makes weekend lunch a happy event. Dishes liked this year include carpaccio di tonno con rucola, translucent slices of raw tuna on rocket in a sharp, lively dressing; pizza al prosciutto di Parma con rucola, a thin, crisp pizza with generous toppings; and taglialata di bistecca alla rucola – yes, rucola is something of a constant – an entrecote steak served sliced with Robespierre sauce, a light, zingy dressing which gives the meat added allure. Vitello alla San Lorenzo, veal with aubergines and cheese made like an old-fashioned bed before the days of duvets, the meat tucked in with gooey layers of aubergine and mozzarella, was, how shall we say, old-fashioned. Desserts are a veritable song sheet of Italian favourites. Hum your way through tiramisu, zabaglione, meringa con frutta di bosca and la passione di San Lorenzo, which is ice cream. Service is professional and attentive.

LES SAVEURS

37A CURZON STREET W1   491 8919
'Calm brilliance'

£55

OPEN
MON–FRI

HOURS
12.00–2.15PM
7.00–10.30PM

CREDIT CARDS
AMEX DELTA
DINER'S
MASTERCARD
SWITCH VISA

SERVICE
OPTIONAL

**SET-PRICE
LUNCH**
£22.50

**SET-PRICE
DINNER**
£38

This Japanese-owned French restaurant quietly goes from strength to strength without chef Joel Antunes forcing his attentions on the public in the way that many 'important' chefs feel they must do. Something of his commitment and capability can be inferred from his decision to change his extensive à la carte menu on a monthly, as opposed to three-monthly, basis. He says, reasonably enough, that some of the seasonal ingredients he cooks, such as grouse, razor fish, abalone, asparagus, courgette flowers and soft berries, are at their best for only a matter of weeks. Antunes has trained with Maximin, Bocuse and Pierre Troisgros in France, and also occupied the position of chef de cuisine at the Oriental Hotel in Bangkok where his fascination with spices and the seasonings particular to the Far East was born. He uses these with discretion but with enough innovation greatly to heighten the excitement of eating. Butter and cream occupy very little shelf space in his fridge; sauces tend to rely on flavoured oils, stocks and juices and transformations on processes such as home-smoking, puréeing, wrapping garnishes into little parcels of impact and contrasting luxurious with homely ingredients. With such a fluid menu it is difficult to recommend particular dishes, but some which stood out at a recent lunch were fritters of eel on a bed of puréed herbs; a carrot soup with Dublin Bay prawns which cleverly steered clear of too much sweetness; a 'tian' of lamb's tongues on white coco beans with Parmesan; breast of guinea fowl served rolled and sliced with morilles plus little deep-fried pastry squares filled with tapenade; a light dessert of intensely flavoured poached pear with yogurt sorbet. The basement dining room has been described as characterless but I rather like its absence of taste imposition. The message is that you are here simply to enjoy very good food.

THIS LOOKS TO BE another overlong listing of grand French wines – though the whole thing could be contained in half the number of pages with no loss of clarity – until one examines the names of the growers (Michelot-Buisson, Graillot, Zind-Humbrecht, Foreau) from which it is clear that shrewd, up-to-the-minute buying has been done. Offering Taylor 1963 by the glass is a nice touch, too. Bargain hunters will search in vain, not least because the Vins Étrangers, instead of providing price modulation, are drawn almost exclusively from the most fashionable and expensive producers.

THE SAVOY GRILL

THE STRAND WC2   836 4343

'A glittering and illustrious cul-de-sac'

Lunch at The Savoy Grill is like a club for which it is difficult to secure membership. The regulars, heavyweights – mostly men with titles – from the worlds of politics, business and the media, hog the tables, allotted by maitre d' Angelo Maresca according to a system of precedence he does not divulge. This review, therefore, concentrates on dinner. At this meal a slightly different sort of prosperous clientele is in evidence: dark suits are leavened by the occasional little black dress. Uniformed staff with grave synchronicity usher customers to their tables, ease them into chairs, tuck them in with napkins and having thus immobilized them, furnish menus. It is a stunning performance whose speed and impeccable teamwork make you realize that if The Savoy was suddenly

FACILITIES
SEATS 50
PRIVATE ROOM
SEATS 10

NEAREST TUBE
STATION
GREEN PARK

MAP 3

£46

OPEN
LUNCH MON–FRI
DINNER MON–SAT

HOURS
12.30–2.30PM
6.00–11.15PM

CREDIT CARDS
AMEX DINER'S
MASTERCARD
SWITCH VISA

SERVICE
OPTIONAL

**SET-PRICE
DINNER**
£28.75 & £32
(PRE-THEATRE
ONLY)

FACILITIES
SEATS 90
WHEELCHAIR
ACCESS

**NEAREST TUBE
STATION**
CHARING CROSS

MAP 4

redesignated as a hospital, it would boast an Accident and Emergency department to die for; no lying around on trolleys in corridors here. Indeed, in their place are huge silver Easter eggs on wheeled cabriole legs, like glittering baroque portable barbecues, which open up to reveal the roast of the day or the wherewithal to flame and sizzle ingredients alongside the tables. The menu, without being too long, has an all-encompassing air, with first courses ranging from Beluga caviar to poached egg, black pudding and bacon, and main courses which include plats du jour of mainly roasts or honey-baked ham as well as chef David Sharland's specialities such as le demi-homard poche, meli-melo de crustacés; les suprêmes de pigeon-neaux sautés aux courgettes, tomates et olives noires. Roasted turbot was tender and firm-fleshed but against its subtle flavour and pearly whiteness the dark bed of lentils was terribly salty. Kidneys were flamed at the table with panache and served with a whiskey grain mustard sauce. The sweet trolley resembles something you might have seen going down the Mall at the Coronation, heavily ornate and loaded with stately fruits and puddings. The mise-en-scène, the flame-throwers, the acres of napery and the gallons of Silvo used seem somehow wasted on the stuffy clientele, but to some extent they are a self-selected sample based on what it costs to be here.

THIS IS A sleeker and more financially sympathetic list than one might expect from a grand hotel. Not surprisingly, its strongest suit is claret, with a number of reasonable buys, but no major region is ignored, and Torres and Mitchelton are reassuring names to encounter lower down the scale. Clos Haut-Peyraguey must sell well because the only alternative dessert wine offered by the bottle is Yquem 1980 at £230.

SEC'S & CHECKS

241 FULHAM ROAD SW3   823 3079

'Let the food, not the design, astonish you'

£30

OPEN
LUNCH MON–SAT
DINNER EVERY DAY

HOURS
12.30–2.30PM
7.00PM–12.00AM

CREDIT CARDS
AMEX
MASTERCARD
SWITCH VISA

'For reasons of good taste' , the waiter said, the owners of this absurdly named restaurant used the non-word sec's in place of what they really wanted, which was sex. Well, good taste in names and in decor is a subjective affair but when it comes to cooking, that can be evaluated according to more or less agreed principles. Chef Mark Williamson, who trained with Marco Pierre White at Harvey's and returned there as head chef for a while after Marco had left, seemed at first to be thrown by the institutionalized zaniness into losing his sense of direction, but he is now performing according to his own very real abilities. The madness of a menu with dishes such as Seared Ox Tongue, Dolmades Sweet Pickle, Celeriac Remoulade, which opened the restaurant, has been left behind. In its place is a list which, although eclectic, understands and respects the natural harmony of ingredients. Flavours are bold, the impact is strong with dishes such as filo ravioli of lobster with champagne sauce; roasted sweetbread, grilled calf's liver and black pudding with onion marmalade and mashed potatoes; Moroccan spiced squab with couscous, roast peppers, garlic and grilled aubergines. These dishes comprised the first and second course of a well-nigh faultless meal at which the only cavil was the untoward 'cakiness' of the date and pecan pudding. But passion fruit crème brûlée was great. Put behind you what has been done in the name of trendy design to that venerable pub The Queen's Elm – in which Sec's and Checks occupies the first floor – and tell yourself that it is a function of restaurants to provide an alternative universe: don't miss out on Mark Williamson's cooking.

SERVICE
12½%

SET-PRICE
LUNCH
£10.50–£13.50

FACILITIES
SEATS 50

NEAREST TUBE
STATION
SOUTH
KENSINGTON

MAP 2

SHAWS

119 OLD BROMPTON ROAD SW7   373 7774/4472

'Bolt hole for the Little Boltons'

Here, on the site that was the Chanterelle, Frances Atkins has set herself the difficult task of selling food founded on classic French cuisine to a population spoilt for choice: near neighbours and competitors include Hilaire (q.v.) and Bibendum (q.v.). The drawing-room style in which the room has been redecorated does not make a strong impression – the scheme is shades of beige – so it is down to the prettily presented cooking to provide colour. Mrs Atkins' CV lists awards from previous restaurants in Bucks and Perthshire, and she prides herself on 'innovative use of fresh produce particularly game… and fish in general'. A plethora of menus signals a large repertory: game terrines; risottos; mousse of smoked haddock; salad of melon, bacon and pine nuts and, in the main course, 'a mignon' of veal and beef on rösti with red cabbage, wild mushrooms and a juniper-scented sauce; breast of guinea fowl stuffed with spinach and served with noodles and a crayfish sauce. There is a danger that the combinations can

£40

OPEN
LUNCH SUN–FRI
DINNER MON–SAT

HOURS
12.00–3.00PM
7.00–12.00AM
SUN
12.00–4.30PM

CREDIT CARDS
AMEX DELTA
DINER'S
MASTERCARD
SWITCH VISA

SERVICE
12½%
(DINNER ONLY)

SET-PRICE
LUNCH
£14 & £17.50

SET-PRICE
DINNER
£26.75 & £29.75

SUNDAY BRUNCH

FACILITIES
SEATS 44
TABLES OUTSIDE
SEAT 10
WHEELCHAIR
ACCESS

NEAREST TUBE
STATION
GLOUCESTER
ROAD

MAP 2

prove so hectic that flavours get out of kilter (for instance, in the latter dish the one flavour that did not register was the guinea fowl's). But the skill is there, as is a praiseworthy determination to give value for money. The sweet course is worthy of co-owner Sir Neil Shaw, chairman of Tate & Lyle.

SHAW'S HAS secured the services of a Master of Wine for the compilation of this shortish list, and his involvement is apparent in both the sure-footed selections and in the educative commentary. The aim throughout has been to ensure that each bottle offers something different: thus if you want an Aussie red, you have a choice between a Shiraz at £14.50 (Capel Vale), a Cabernet at £17.70 (Capel Vale, again), and a Pinot Noir at £21 (Coldstream Hills), all of which makes choosing easy. The dwindling crew of German wine lovers will applaud the appearance of wines from Fritz Haag and Ernst Loosen.

SHREE KRISHNA

182–194 TOOTING HIGH ST SW17   0181-672 4250/6903
'South by South-West; South Indian spices in SW17'

£15

OPEN
EVERY DAY

HOURS
12.00–3.00PM
6.00–11.00PM
FRI–SAT
6.00PM–12.00AM

CREDIT CARDS
AMEX DINER'S
MASTERCARD VISA

SERVICE
10%

FACILITIES
SEATS 120
PRIVATE ROOM
SEATS 60
WHEELCHAIR
ACCESS (ALSO
WC)

NEAREST TUBE
STATION
TOOTING
BROADWAY

MAP

In some sort of sibling relationship to Ragam (q.v.), Shree Krishna serves a similar mix of Keralan (South Indian) vegetarian specialities and conventional Indian dishes. The premises are somewhat lacklustre – a great deal of brown varnish has been applied – but Hindu artefacts and some marquetry panels with religious themes provide decorative distraction. The lighting gives the room an oddly overcast look but the clientele, many of whom seem to be regulars, seem happy to focus on the notably reasonably priced (in fact cheap) food. There is an air of quiet, good-natured concentration, rather like a public exam with a paper for which everyone is well prepared and eager to get on with. Staff patrol the tables like invigilators. The South Indian dishes are mainly variations on a pancake theme, each item subtly different in taste and surprisingly varied in texture, ranging from crisp, light and crunchy to dense, chewy and substantial. Utthappam has a kind of rose window design of green chillies and tomatoes on a rice and lentil flour base resembling a thin crumpet. Adai has a texture reminiscent of American cornbread. Avial, a spiced vegetable stew in a sauce as yellow as a brimstone butterfly, is a fine accompaniment to the dry dishes. The one non-vegetarian speciality is meat masala dosa, a giant spliff of a pancake rolled around minced meat, potatoes and onions. The restaurant claims credit for its invention. Among the breads, green chilli paratha comes in for particular praise.

SINGAPORE GARDEN

83 FAIRFAX ROAD NW6   328 5314

'A ground-floor restaurant which works on several levels'

Studying surrounding tables it becomes obvious that people come here for very different reasons. Some treat Singapore Garden like an upmarket 'Chinky' (an obnoxious expression actually overheard) and seem unaware that Malaysian and Singapore cooking is the house speciality. Others may know, but seem not to care because they are caught up in noisy socializing and neighbour-spotting. Two women setting out to tackle a fair percentage of the chef Mrs Lim's specialities seemed weird enough for fellow diners to ask questions: 'What is that you're ordering?' 'Will you be able to eat it all?' The answer to the first question was chilli mussels, chewy, garlicky soft shell crabs, Singapore laksa soup, the noodle dish fried kway teow, beef rendang and simple stir-fried greens. The answer to the second was yes, every dish was vividly flavoured and too good to leave, with the exception of the beef which needed longer cooking. The daily specials, shellfish or Singapore and Malaysian sections of the menu are the places to find such excitements as chilli crab or the rare, soothing Hainanese chicken rice. Grass jelly is a novel, sober drink.

£26

OPEN
EVERY DAY

HOURS
12.00–2.45PM
6.00–10.45PM
FRI & SAT
6.00–11.15PM

CREDIT CARDS
AMEX DINER'S
MASTERCARD VISA

SERVICE
12½% PARTIES
OF 6 OR MORE

SET-PRICE
LUNCH & DINNER
£16

FACILITIES
SEATS 100
TABLES OUTSIDE
SEAT 10
PRIVATE ROOM
SEATS 50
WHEELCHAIR
ACCESS

NEAREST TUBE
STATION
SWISS COTTAGE

MAP 1

SMOKEY JOE'S DINER

131 WANDSWORTH HIGH STREET SW18   0181-871 1785

'Somewhere with soul near the soulless Arndale Centre'

Charlie Phillips is Smokey Joe. Smokey Joe's is Charlie Phillips. He is the life and soul food of this Caribbean/American takeaway and unlicensed restaurant seating about fifteen. You don't book. You turn up, hope to get a seat, sway to the music, listen to the Phillips' radio broadcasting without pause for breath on topics ranging from levels of unemployment to the government's poor record on everything to the state of his love life and order items such as roti with curry of the day; heroe sandwiches; Bar-B-Q spare ribs; jerk

£12 BYO

OPEN
EVERY DAY

HOURS
12.00–3.00PM
6.00–11.00PM
SAT
12.00–11.00PM
SUN
3.30–10.00PM

pork, tender and hickory smoked; charbroiled corn-on-the-cob, dripping in butter and accompanied by roasted coconut to sprinkle on top; and perhaps the dish of the day. On Monday it is callalloo and saltfish, on Wednesday red bean stew with rice and salad, on Thursday braised oxtail and so on, a system pretty similar to that at The Connaught (q.v.). Desserts include ice cream sundae, carrot cake, and pancakes with ice cream and maple syrup. The food is very good of its kind and Joe is genuinely good natured. It is BYO, and nearly always party time at Smokey Joe's. With advance notice, he will cater for parties of ten to 20 from Monday to Thursday starting after 9pm at a price of £14.90 a head.

SNOWS ON THE GREEN

166 SHEPHERD'S BUSH ROAD W6   603 2142

'Mediterranean flavours at Snow's place'

The rather dank phrase 'useful in the area' has been applied to Snows on the Green but anyone would be pleased to find Sebastian Snow's Mediterranean menu and the evocation, via colour posters, of the lavender fields of Provence in that hinterland between the roundabouts of Shepherd's Bush and Hammersmith. Details in the execution of some of the dishes sometimes need attention: ravioli of anchovy and aubergine as well as being a slight misnomer sported undercooked fried aubergine slices on which the (three only) intensely salty, anchovy-paste-filled pasta envelopes were placed; duck cooked two ways served with canellini beans and caramelized apples featured undercooked and therefore indigestible beans. However, much else pleases: the evilly successful pan-fried foie gras served with a fried egg and balsamic vinegar; vitello tonnato, the meat tender and generously served under a rich coating of tuna sauce garnished with anchovies and capers resting on sliced fresh tomatoes; the caramelized rice pudding served with clotted cream and slivers of stewed plums. Snow's liking for robust assemblies lives on in dishes such as Italian pigeon with Savoy cabbage and black pudding, and pork, bean and sausage stew with sage. Sole with curry, spinach and mussels seems to mark a new departure. Don't take your secrets to Snows on the Green. Tables are close together and the acoustics created by the hard surfaces bounces conversations around. As we go to press, there is news of Sebastian Snow opening a second restaurant in Battersea Square.

CREDIT CARDS
NONE

SERVICE
OPTIONAL

COVER CHARGE
£1

FACILITIES
SEATS 15

NEAREST TUBE
STATION
EAST PUTNEY

NEAREST BR
STATION
WANDSWORTH
TOWN

MAP 1

£28

OPEN
LUNCH SUN–FRI
DINNER MON–SAT

HOURS
12.00–3.00PM
7.00–11.00PM

CREDIT CARDS
DELTA
MASTERCARD
SWITCH VISA

SERVICE
OPTIONAL

SET-PRICE
LUNCH
£13.50

SUNDAY BRUNCH

FACILITIES
SEATS 80
PRIVATE ROOM
SEATS 25
WHEELCHAIR
ACCESS

NEAREST TUBE
STATION
HAMMERSMITH

MAP 1

SOFRA

36 TAVISTOCK STREET WC2 240 3773/3772

'The healthy face of inexpensive eating'

Sofra – now expanded into a small chain of Turkish restaurants and cafés owned and run by the energetic Huseyin Ozer – can sometimes be a victim of its own success. Crowds attracted by the diverse and healthy dishes woven into myriad set-price deals, some of them startlingly cheap, can stretch the capability of the kitchen and the capacity of the staff to near breaking point. And Shepherd Market and Covent Garden, where the two restaurants are located, have crowd-pulling abilities of their own. However, if you eat outside peak times, facilitated by non-stop service from midday to midnight, the event can be rewarding. At Tavistock Street, which has the advantage of stylish, restrained decor without a shred of folksiness, first courses or meze dishes of tabule (sic), a parsley salad dense with flat-leaf parsley; manca, spinach in fresh yogurt with garlic; enginar, a salad of artichoke hearts cooked in olive oil with potatoes, carrots, broad beans and dill; humuz kavurma, chickpea purée topped with diced lamb and pine kernels; sucuk izgara, grilled spicy sausages; and kibbeh, delicate pip-shaped rissoles of minced meat fried in a crisp wheat case, are all distinctively prepared. The meat used in main-course grills is of good quality and sparkily seasoned. Bulgur pilav, when available, and shepherd's salad with extra chilli are good side orders. Desserts comprising sweet pastries, soothing rice puddings and fruit salad roll up on a trolley. Also at 18 Shepherd Street W1 (493 3320).

£24

OPEN
EVERY DAY

HOURS
12.00PM–12.00AM

CREDIT CARDS
AMEX DELTA
DINER'S
MASTERCARD
SWITCH VISA

SERVICE
12½%

**SET-PRICE
LUNCH & DINNER**
£8.45

FACILITIES
SEATS 220
TABLES OUTSIDE
SEAT 4
PRIVATE ROOM
SEATS 100

**NEAREST TUBE
STATION**
COVENT GARDEN

MAP 4

SONNY'S

94 CHURCH ROAD SW13 0181-748 0393

'Opening the Barnes door'

Being either in or out of a restaurant guide would, I imagine, be of little import to Sonny's. Chefs come and go – Redmond Hayward has gone and Anthony Demetre has come – the menu retains a modern British identity, prices stay reasonable and *le tout* Barnes floods in to the attractive long room with its miniature garden framed in glass halfway down and its interesting selection of art. A report of a recent Sunday lunch, an especially popular meal time, approved a mushroom and basil risotto although the flavour of basil was fleeting; a tart of

£28

OPEN
EVERY DAY

HOURS
10.00AM–11.00PM

CREDIT CARDS
AMEX
MASTERCARD VISA

SERVICE
OPTIONAL

**SET-PRICE
LUNCH**
£13.50

FACILITIES
SEATS 100
PRIVATE ROOM
SEATS 24
WHEELCHAIR
ACCESS

**NEAREST BR
STATION**
BARNES

MAP 1

goat's cheese and chard which was weighted in favour of the latter; chargrilled chicken served with properly cooked new potatoes, carrots and beans; chargrilled salmon served with courgettes in a balsamic vinegar dressing and raved about a walnut tart with Chantilly cream. The warm welcome given to children and babies was noted. The above dishes are typical of the style that in the à la carte shows slightly more imagination, as exemplified by main courses of griddled scallops with Serrano ham, garlic, parsley and vegetable minestrone; sautéed neck of lamb with aromatic couscous and a cumin and cauliflower cream; dolcelatte ravioli with warm celery and tomato vinaigrette; and floating island with pistachio ice cream. Service is amiable.

THIS IS A LOVELY miniature of a wine list. Every one of the 35 wines (mainly French and Australian) is recommendable in terms of quality and individuality, and over half may be bought by the glass. Most crowd sensibly within the £15–£20 sector, but the loftier wines are priced in such a way as to encourage you to peer beyond the limits you may have set yourself – Bollinger NV at £30.50, Dujac's fully mature Clos de la Roche 1983 at £35.

THE SQUARE

32 KING STREET SW1   839 8787

'On the move'

£45

OPEN
LUNCH MON–FRI
DINNER MON–SUN

HOURS
12.00–2.30PM
6.00–11.45PM
SUN
7.00–10.00PM

CREDIT CARDS
AMEX DINER'S
MASTERCARD
SWITCH VISA

SERVICE
OPTIONAL

**SET-PRICE
DINNER**
£32 & £38

FACILITIES
SEATS 60
PRIVATE ROOM
SEATS 20
WHEELCHAIR
ACCESS (ALSO
WC)

Chef Philip Howard, who has trained with the Roux brothers, Simon Hopkinson and Marco Pierre White when on form – and reports this year suggest that these days he is consistently – produces particularly delectable food: imaginative without being tricksy, clean cut and well-balanced. You can read from the dishes that he is a chef who, away from his mentors, has found his own path. Without resorting to turning them into milkshakes, he gives soups personality. Seldom are they served as just a bowlful of liquid where one spoonful will be the same as the next. For example, vichyssoise, the classic recipe closely stitched with chives, is served with a cunning little salad based on papery slices of white summer truffle. White asparagus soup comes with warm roasted wild salmon. The first course also always holds interesting salads such as peppered loin of venison with green beans and truffle oil; a perfected salade Niçoise with rosy tuna and mustard-yellow yolk of oeuf mollet;

or a summer mixture of new potatoes, broad beans and prosciutto. Main courses tend to divide evenly between fish and meat, offering perhaps seared scallops with pommes frites, tomato, parsley and garlic; roasted cod with a ragout of leeks and mussels; roast squab with caramelized carrots and meat juices; sauté of calf's kidneys with creamed potatoes and grain mustard. Desserts are delicious, with special mention for port-roasted figs served with cinnamon-dusted beignets, like dough-nuts for grown-ups. As this guide goes to press there is news that The Square is planning to move to premises in Bruton Street in January 1996, when the lease at their distinctive, brashly decorated St James's premises runs out. No doubt the high-profile clientele will manage to cross Piccadilly.

NEAREST TUBE STATION
PICCADILLY CIRCUS/GREEN PARK
MAP 3

THE SQUARE clearly has access to the pin-striped wine merchants in St James's and it offers a suitably up-market, traditional-looking list, strong and long in Bordeaux and Burgundy, and pretty good on the rest of France and, indeed, California. It is the quality of producer that stands out, whether from traditional regions such as Burgundy (Gerard Chavy, Michel Lafarge, Dujac) or from the New World (Kistler, Coldstream Hills, Ridge). There is a nice range of maturity on offer too, and this again applies to New World bottles as well as to Old. No bargains, and champagne prices look particularly steep when one considers that no alternative sparkler is on offer.

STAR OF INDIA

154 OLD BROMPTON ROAD SW5   373 2901

'Fancy a Ruby?'

In 1955 when Star of India opened it offered meat curry or fish curry with chips, rice or – presumably to encourage experimentation with an exotic commodity – half chips/half rice. In 1995, celebrating its ruby anniversary, the food at Star of India, prepared by chef Vineet Bhatia, who two years ago came from the Oberoi Hotel in Bombay, is as telling an indica-tion of how restaurants have evolved and improved over the past few decades as you are likely to find. A good deal of the credit for the restaurant's pre-eminence goes to owner/manager Reza Mahammad, who is passionate about his family's business. Reza is responsible for the Italianate frescoes which decorate the walls, the choice of music and also the live music on the first floor, and for encouraging the chef to break new ground. If

£28

OPEN
EVERY DAY

HOURS
12.00–3.00PM
6.00–12.00PM
SUN
7.00–11.30PM

CREDIT CARDS
AMEX DELTA
DINER'S JCB
MASTERCARD
SWITCH VISA

SERVICE
OPTIONAL

COVER CHARGE
£1

FACILITIES
SEATS 98
PRIVATE ROOMS
SEAT 12–30
WHEELCHAIR
ACCESS

NEAREST TUBE
STATION
GLOUCESTER
ROAD/SOUTH
KENSINGTON

MAP 2

you can involve the winsomely excitable Reza in your ordering it will be all to the good, but here are some of my recommendations. In the first course, baingan-e-bahar, charred aubergine halves filled with spiced cheese and tomatoes flavoured with curry leaves and mustard seeds; karbagah, baby lamb chops cooked in milk with ginger and fennel seeds before being dipped in rice batter and crisply fried, served with a walnut and mint dip. From the section entitled Star Specialities, multani bateyr, de-boned quails stuffed with minced chicken flavoured with dried fruits in a rich sauce; shai batak, duck breast cooked with papaya and ginger in a sauce scented with cloves and cinnamon; subz kesari, a wonderful dish of pithy, salty samphire in a saffron sauce flavoured with star anise and fennel. There is a tandoori section, and one of meat and poultry from which, if you like chilli-hot food, pick lal maas, a Rajasthani lamb dish which uses Ajmeri red chilli paste. There is much else including dum-cooked food, i.e. sealed and cooked in its own juices, a process applied to sea bass as well as new potatoes and chicken biriani. For dessert try lychee and almond kulfi, a condensed milk ice reticent with its sweetness. When you get to know Reza, you will find he is the opposite.

STEPHEN BULL

5–7 BLANDFORD STREET W1   486 9696

'The quality of Mercy'

New chef at Stephen Bull is Mercy Fenton, voted Young Chef of the Year in 1993 and recently cooking at Morels in Haslemere. Perhaps to mark this (still quite rare) situation of a woman in charge, the clinic-white decor of these doctor-land premises has been changed. Two of the walls are now painted in vivid colours: yellow and turquoise. At time of writing Fenton, who has only recently moved in, is cooking a menu familiar from when Steven Carter – now chef at Stephen Bull's Bistro (q.v.) – was running the kitchen. Dishes tried were, on the whole, beautifully executed and it will be interesting to see what changes she brings. Certain items will stay because regulars protest if they disappear. One such is the first course of twice-cooked goat's cheese soufflé, which was as good as ever. Other dishes that typify the menu are mixed leaf salad with crisp duck skin, orange and hazelnuts; tortellini of crab with citron vinaigrette (rather resilient pasta when tried); roast rump of lamb with pearl barley 'risotto' and spinach; seared scallops with

£32

OPEN
LUNCH MON–FRI
DINNER MON–SAT

HOURS
12.15–2.15PM
6.30–10.45PM

CREDIT CARDS
AMEX
MASTERCARD VISA

SERVICE
OPTIONAL

FACILITIES
SEATS 55
WHEELCHAIR
ACCESS

NEAREST TUBE
STATION
BOND
STREET/BAKER
STREET

MAP 3

tomato, red onion and basil salsa served around a fine purée of potatoes delicately flavoured with garlic; saltimbocca with fresh pasta and anchovy cream; demoulded (sic) apricot soufflé with an Amaretto mousseline sauce; variations on a theme of chocolate (not varied enough, says one report). A 60-minute menu at lunch time reflects the pressures on the local business and Harley Street clientele. They come back to let their hair down in the evenings but rush off relatively early to bed.

A MEDIUM-LENGTH LIST, two-thirds French, with plenty of familiar-looking producers. When this happens it means either that it is safe and boring, or so in tune with your own tastes that you want to try everything on it. The latter is the case here, though it would be better still if the Bordeaux and Beaujolais sections were trimmed to make room for a few Italian reds. At £26.50 Bonny Doon's rich, waxy Le Sophiste (a Californian interpretation of white Hermitage), complete with plastic top hat, looks to be the bargain in the bunch.

STEPHEN BULL'S BISTRO & BAR

69–71 St John Street EC1   490 1750

'Extending a warmer welcome'

In the restaurant world one of the signals of success is the horizontal buy-out, where the business next door is swallowed at a gulp. Stephen Bull's Bistro has grown in this way, resulting in a bigger drinking area and a separate seafood counter behind which a chef is stationed shucking shellfish and deftly making sushi. It seems that the arrival of the St John restaurant (q.v.) in the same street has benefited Mr Bull's business by drawing in a species of casual evening customer who drops by at either or both. Service and food have responded well to the competition, the young staff now work smoothly and with a smile. From the seafood bar, to be had as single snacks or elements of a longer meal, come choices such as crab and cucumber; picture-pretty marinated scallops served on their shell with mirepoix-cut salsa; a tray of sushi including the avocado-centred Californian maki roll; and a lovely salad of pickled cucumber and seaweed. With the changes the main menu has become rather fish-fixated, with cooked fish making up half of the main courses. With Jeeves, the *Guide* believes that ingestion of fish benefits the brain cells, but those unconvinced

£25

OPEN
LUNCH MON–FRI
DINNER MON–SAT

HOURS
12.00–2.15PM
& 6.30–11.00PM

CREDIT CARDS
AMEX
MASTERCARD VISA

SERVICE
OPTIONAL

FACILITIES
SEATS 125
WHEELCHAIR
ACCESS (ALSO
WC)

**NEAREST TUBE
STATION**
FARRINGDON

MAP 3

can find vegetable soup, twice-cooked soufflé, a salad of avocado, blood orange and sesame which is surprisingly harmonious and even manages to include a sprinkling of bean sprouts to good effect (this may be a first in the history of catering), Spanish charcuterie and cheese, and meat courses which match a lightly cooked piece of protein with one or two clever vegetable accompaniments. Puddings are, as ever, well considered, as is the drinks list which includes a dozen wines by the glass, sherry, beers and cider. The design is severely modern, with hard surfaces for noise or wrong-footed waiters to bounce off: those disturbed by such a setting may find the new annexe plus seafood bar less unsettling.

THE WINE LIST has expanded since last year, and in a surprising direction, France benefiting at the expense of the New World. As a result, the 1995/6 list looks less tight and modernist than the 1994/5. That said, there is still a good spread of flavours on offer, still a good proportion of halves and of wines available by the glass, and if you want to begin your evening in style the Veuve Clicquot 1988 at £30 is most inviting.

THE STEPPING STONE

123 QUEENSTOWN ROAD SW8   622 0555

'The way restaurants are going'

£24

OPEN
LUNCH SUN–FRI
DINNER MON–SAT

HOURS
12.00–2.30PM
7.00–11.00PM

CREDIT CARDS
AMEX DINER'S
MASTERCARD VISA

SERVICE
OPTIONAL

**SET-PRICE
LUNCH**
£10

FACILITIES
SEATS 56
WHEELCHAIR
ACCESS

**NEAREST BR
STATION**
QUEENSTOWN
ROAD

MAP 2

Emer and Gary Levy, who ran a restaurant in Barnes called The Stable, took over the Battersea site that was previously L'Arlequin to create their next leg-up in the restaurant business, The Stepping Stone. What was a formal, serious French restaurant interior has been completely transformed into a colourful, relaxed space, one half of which is given over to non-smokers. The menu, which changes monthly, has become less ambitious in terms of length than at the outset, and with fewer items offered at two sizes, two prices. But it is a well-thought-out modern list of dishes – two of which are always pasta of the day and fish of the day – and includes tempting vegetarian assemblies, for example ricotta and Swiss chard tart with marinated sweet pepper; braised leeks with a caper, cornichon and hard-boiled egg vinaigrette; wild rice cakes with sautéed field mushrooms and spinach. The side salad features salad leaves from Appledore farm in Kent. Paying attention to the sourcing of ingredients is also apparent in the sausages made in house with organic, free-range pork. Typical meat main courses are rabbit and prune casserole with baked swede and potato; guinea fowl with English spring greens; pan-fried calf's liver. Desserts are made by Emer (Mrs) Levy. The drinks list offers Belgian beers and wines from around the world. The culinary changes in this stretch of Queenstown Road where once two ambitious French restaurants, L'Arlequin and Chez Nico, flourished side by side reflect the way the restaurant business is going – towards affordability on a regular basis.

THE SUGAR CLUB

33A ALL SAINTS ROAD W11   221 3844

'Kiwis back in fashion'

The original Sugar Club was in Auckland, New Zealand, run by the same New Zealanders, Vivienne Hayman and Ashley Sumner, who have started this venture in All Saints Road. Peter Gordon, another Kiwi, is chef. His cooking is modern; it could be said to flesh out descriptions such as eclectic, modern British or – for once accurately – the phrase Pacific rim. Before coming to the UK Gordon travelled widely, and he incorporates into his dishes well-considered techniques and ingredients from South-East Asia. He does it with temperance and enough respect to render the menu, which also offers Mediterranean dishes, harmonious, rather than a rag-bag. Of all the chefs in London currently practising this style – many of them Antipodean – Gordon is, in my view, the best. A list which might include spicy sea trout, quail egg and mint laksa; pan-fried lamb's brains with spicy pear and date chutney on toast; salad of roast pepper, watercress, pine nuts, red onions and pickled gooseberries; grilled turbot on sweet potato and thyme salad; spicy duck coconut curry with scented rice, coriander and pickled plum; pear frangipane tart with whipped cream; Croghan goat's cheese with nectarine relish and home-baked cream crackers requires its perpetrator to have a sense of balance as keen as that of a tightrope walker and this Gordon possesses. Since he is tackling a constantly changing repertoire, not everything succeeds 100%, but enough is delectable at very reasonable prices to make what might strike you as the hazardous walk down All Saints Road eminently worthwhile. The restaurant premises are pretty in a pristine, understated way, with a shining stainless-steel kitchen on view. The short wine list is well chosen. Service is amiable and concerned to get things right.

£26

OPEN
LUNCH SAT–SUN
DINNER EVERY DAY

HOURS
12.30–3.30PM
6.30–11.30PM

CREDIT CARDS
MASTERCARD
SWITCH VISA

SERVICE
OPTIONAL

FACILITIES
SEATS 80
TABLS OUTSIDE
SEAT 26
PRIVATE ROOM
SEATS 10
WHEELCHAIR
ACCESS

**NEAREST TUBE
STATION**
WESTBOURNE
PARK/NOTTING
HILL GATE

MAP 1

LE SUQUET

'Fishing for compliments'

OPEN
EVERY DAY

HOURS
12.30–2.30PM
7.00–11.30PM
SUN
12.30–11.30PM

CREDIT CARDS
AMEX DINER'S
MASTERCARD
SWITCH VISA

SERVICE
OPTIONAL

COVER CHARGE
£1

**SET-PRICE
LUNCH**
£12

FACILITIES
SEATS 70
TABLES OUTSIDE
SEAT 8
PRIVATE ROOM
SEATS 16

**NEAREST TUBE
STATION**
SOUTH
KENSINGTON

MAP 2

Doubtless one or two of the clientele have had recourse to a discreet facelift and this year the long-serving Le Suquet has very sensibly had one itself. New windows installed, pale cream paint, an opening up of the cramped space at the front which used to hold the fish tanks and a change of tablecloth colour from Provençal blue to a soft mulberry render the restaurant lighter and seemingly more spacious. Owner Pierre Martin is too canny to fiddle with the successful formula for food which is shellfish and fish served with a pronounced French accent. For those who resist the rewarding fiddle of tackling the heaped plateau de fruits de mer to start, there are salads, feuilletés, langoustines, scallops, mussels and clams served various ways. Soupe de poissons, crêpe de fruits de mer or harengs pommes à l'huile make a more substantial beginning. Main-course fish dishes of the day might be grilled daurade or sea bass sold per 100 grams; raie à la moutarde; cabillaud Provençale, filet de St Pierre au basilic; salade de homard. Meat dishes are steak or plats du jour of a homely nature; for example, boeuf bourguignon, choucroute garnie or tripes au Muscadet. Desserts tend to the vampish after this quite straightforward approach. Service is well led by Francis Mornay.

SWEETINGS

'A City institution which is fishy with impunity'

OPEN
MON–FRI

HOURS
11.30AM–3.00PM

CREDIT CARDS
NONE

SERVICE
OPTIONAL

FACILITIES
SEATS 60
WHEELCHAIR
ACCESS

**NEAREST TUBE
STATION**
CANNON STREET

MAP 1

A lunch at Sweetings can cost £1 a minute as brisk, efficient Cockney and Italian waiters anxious to turn over as many customers as possible meet with high prices. However, the City folk who flock to this English insitution (est. 1906) are presumably well acquainted with the notion that time is money. In the front part of the room the counter seating is policed by a waiter of a certain age who offers a glass of suave (as in Roger Moore), rather than Soave (as in Italian wine). The room at the back is a faintly grubby, cream-painted dining hall with refectory tables. Women are in short supply but fish on the period-piece menu is plentiful. Dover sole, halibut, turbot, brill, plaice, salmon, scampi and skate can be grilled, fried or poached as is appropriate and it is the freshness and quality of the raw material, not the sauces or garnishes, wherein the excellence lies. Start with environmentally unsound real turtle soup, West Mersea oysters, dressed crab, potted shrimps or fried whitebait. To finish there are savouries or 'sweets' such as baked jam roll, spotted dick or steamed syrup pudding. It is Friday's lunch straight from the nursery which only delights the gents who over a glass of vintage port can dawdle a moment and dream of nanny. Go early or late to avoid queues.

TABAC

46 GOLBORNE ROAD W10   0181-960 2433

'The neighbourhood restaurant of a funky neighbourhood'

Proprietors Pip Wylie (chef) and Bennie Neville (manager) chose the name Tabac for their venture hoping it would convey a lack of restaurant pretension. Opening in the summer of 1994 in the Golborne Road best known for the shops and cafés which serve the local Portuguese community was simply a bold move. But the street now accommodates seamlessly Tabac's minimalist, stagily lit front room and the menu which is distinctive due to no stinting on fine ingredients, superior baking and an assured hand with timing and seasoning. Wylie, a New Zealander, has cooked at The French House Dining Room (q.v.) and The River Café (q.v.), work experience which to some extent can be inferred from the style and content of the dishes. Soups transform ingredients from solid to liquid without losing their essence. A salad Niçoise takes the conventional ingredients but does them bigger and better. Antipasto, a constant on the menu, demonstrates high regard for the constituent parts. Thai spicing might galvanize oyster wontons or marinated chicken breast. Roast leg of lamb served in thick, pink slices is something of a speciality, maybe served with polenta cakes and mint sauce, maybe with salsa rossa and rape broccoli. Two must-haves are the breads and the home-made ice creams. Downstairs at Tabac is a bar, and a dining room with a different atmosphere, ideal for parties. Also worth noting is the Sunday brunch menu which includes items such as cinnamon toast, eggs Benedict, banana pancake with maple syrup and huevos rancheros. Customers often seem to know each other or the owners. In other words, Tabac succeeds as a neighbourhood restaurant, in this case responding to a diverse, funky neighbourhood.

£28

OPEN
LUNCH TUES–SUN
DINNER EVERY DAY

HOURS
11.00AM–11.00PM

CREDIT CARDS
DINER'S
MASTERCARD VISA

SERVICE
OPTIONAL

SET-PRICE LUNCH
£8.50

SUNDAY BRUNCH

FACILITIES
SEATS 80
PRIVATE ROOM
SEATS 40

NEAREST TUBE STATION
WESTBOURNE
PARK/LADBROKE
GROVE

MAP 1

TAMARIND

20 QUEEN STREET W1   629 3561

'From Hollywood to Bollywood'

£30

OPEN
LUNCH SUN–FRI
DINNER EVERY
DAY

HOURS
12.00PM–12.00AM
SAT
6.00PM–12.00AM
SUN
12.00–11.00PM

CREDIT CARDS
AMEX DINER'S
MASTERCARD VISA

SERVICE
12½%

**SET-PRICE
LUNCH**
£13.50

FACILITIES
SEATS 80

**NEAREST TUBE
STATION**
GREEN PARK

MAP 3

What once was Tiberio, an Italian restaurant where you could dance and where Frank Sinatra gave his name to a dish, is now Tamarind, a smart Indian restaurant with a chef, Atul Kochhar, who came directly from the Oberoi Hotel in Delhi. Kochar's cooking is impressive, and the menu has evolved since the early days at the end of 1994. It has become a diverting, manageable assemblage with an important contribution made by the two tandoori ovens on view behind glass at the back of the restaurant. From their torrid depths try phool, a whole cauliflower marinated in spices; malai kebab, breast of chicken softened in cheese, cream, cardamom and mace; or khaas seekh kebab, a particularly alluring minced lamb patty, nutty with chopped cashews. Amongst the appetizers, sunheri khasta, spiced vegetables enclosed in crisp filo-type pastry served with mint chutney, is original and excellent, as is the salad made from tandoori-cooked chicken flavoured with tamarind presented heaped up in a sandcastle shape. From the dishes in sauce – curries – roganjosh is powerful, and murgh adraki, chicken cooked in a karahi, reveals what a difference is made to Indian food when ingredients are high quality. Vegetable dishes are interesting. Try gucchi mattar, a rich mixture of morels (they grow in India) and peas; phal dhari kofta, cheese and vegetable dumplings in a saffron and honey sauce and the opulent, buttery black dal bukhari. Breadmaking in the tandoori is beautifully done and is something of a floor show. Service is all over the place and rarely where you want it. Luckily, the idea of having live music seems to have been abandoned.

LA TANTE CLAIRE

68 ROYAL HOSPITAL ROAD SW3   352 6045

'It all comes together here'

£64

OPEN
MON–FRI

HOURS
12.30–2.00PM
7.00–11.00PM

CREDIT CARDS
AMEX DELTA
DINER'S
MASTERCARD VISA

The elements that contribute to a fine restaurant meal, from the finesse of the food, through the comfort, flattery and diversion in the surroundings, the gavotte of responsive service, the sommelier's style, the people whom you find yourself dining beside, right down to the prettiness of the flowers, are held here in almost ideal balance. Having negotiated a long passage you enter the soothingly sunny primrose-yellow dining room from the back, which sets up an immediate feeling of having arrived somewhere special. The welcome is unstuffy and you can relax knowing that the chef will not be later prowling round the room asking if you are enjoying the food. You can be equally sure that Pierre Koffmann is in the kitchen, the opening hours (Monday to Friday only) allowing him something approaching a normal life and his autocratic behaviour in the kitchen militating against delegation. The à la carte menu changes slowly and sometimes only in details. It reflects to some extent Koffmann's background of growing up in Gascony, an area with which he maintains a passionate relationship, with foie gras given pride of place in the first course – galette de foie gras au Sauternes et échalotes rôties is one of his self-styled specialities – and duck, rabbit, venison, pigeon and pig's trotter putting the farmyard firmly at the centre of the main courses. But whether taking pig's feet or lobster as the starting point, Koffmann's skill and palate are the wand that transforms them. Coquilles St Jacques à la planche sauce encre is a work of art: fantastic scallops in an extraordinarily rich inky sauce painted with feathery brushstrokes of coral. Papillotte d'agneau et couscous à la vapeur has incredible scent and resonance, a staple dish dressed in couture. Desserts are remarkable, especially croustade de pommes caramelisée, soufflé aux pistaches et sa glace and composition autour d'une poire. Although it is extremely agreeable to be able to eat in a three-star Michelin French restaurant at lunch time for £26, I am afraid you don't really get the goods unless you choose à la carte.

IF YOU ARE going to offer 500 exclusively French wines, as La Tante Claire does (an Hungarian Tokay is the sole interloper), then you can do full justice to the classics of the country while being able to rove farther afield, to the Pyrenean south, the Alpine east, and the Riviera. As yet, La Tante Claire has not managed to do this, and a list which offers 79 clarets and only ten reds from the Rhône has a depressingly dated look. Most items are the wine equivalent of haute cuisine, but £20ish will buy you decent things from Alsace (Zind-Humbrecht's splendid 1991 Riesling), the Loire (Baumard's 1992 Clos du Papillon) and the South-West (Plaimont's 1985 Madiran).

SERVICE
INCLUDED

SET-PRICE LUNCH
£26

FACILITIES
SEATS 43

NEAREST TUBE STATION
SLOANE SQUARE

MAP 2

TATE GALLERY RESTAURANT

MILLBANK SW1   887 8877

£30

OPEN
MON–SAT

HOURS
12.00–3.00PM

CREDIT CARDS
DELTA
MASTERCARD
SWITCH VISA

SERVICE
OPTIONAL

FACILITIES
SEATS 100
WHEELCHAIR
ACCESS (ALSO
WC)

**NEAREST TUBE
STATION**
PIMLICO

MAP 1

'Ate in Arcadia, ego'

Rex Whistler cleverly incorporated the entrance into the wall paintings that surround this restaurant and it is perhaps lucky that most people won't realize that the trompe l'oeil stone arch through which they come is known as the Grotto of Gluttons, just one of the little jokes in the mural which is a teasing evocation of a Golden Age, inspired by the temple gardens of Stowe and rich in references to Claude and Tiepolo. The effect, when you are seated, is that of an Arcadian fête champêtre with a background of sylvan glades and Palladian ruins against which an elaborately allusive story unfolds, entitled An Expedition in Pursuit of Rare Meats. Sadly, the finding of them is unlikely to happen in the basically British menu here, which could be executed with more finesse, ensuring that the contents of steak and kidney pie have some more intimate relationship with their pastry; that the underside of a spinach and brie Pithivier is cooked rather than stretched and soggy. There has been praise for gravadlax, the fresh vegetables of the day, the profiteroles with butterscotch sauce and the 'free' glass of champagne (or Chateau Lepine '83) which comes with it, and with all desserts. The waitresses are motherly in an institutionalized sort of way. While the decoration, in a kind of eau-de-nil aspic, preserves the spirit of an age of elegance, the clientele nowadays fails to live up to it. However, after a morning of looking at art, a good bottle (see below) in this singular dining room is still a great treat.

THE CAPITAL'S most famous restaurant wine list? Probably. Deservedly so? Well, probably not. The clarets remain an enjoyable rag-bag, and the practice of offering grand names in lesser vintages and lesser names in top vintages makes for some appealing buys. The same goes for Burgundy, where glittering names like Corton-Charlemagne, Chambertin and Richebourg all turn up in a more affordable guise than you ever thought possible. The developments of the past generation (in the world of wine if not in the world of art) seem to have passed the gallery by, an impression reinforced by the April 1995 'additions' – 21 clarets, ten burgundies, two Californians and a German. But few will complain when they can drink Sonoma-Cutrer Les Pierres 1986, Ch de Beaucastel 1983 and Ch Climens 1983 for a total of less than £100.

TAWANA

3 WESTBOURNE GROVE W2   229 3785

'Thai to die for'

This Thai restaurant near where Queensway meets Westbourne Grove has notably good food at reasonable prices and some dishes seldom offered elsewhere. One is the labour-intensive (to make) first course of moo sarong, balls of minced pork wrapped in a skein of noodles, deep-fried and served with a tangy dipping sauce. Some more good balls to try alongside are those made of grilled beef – look chin ping – with the meat minced so finely and kneaded so throughly that they almost bounce. The chef's recommendation for a prawn dish is goong phad nam prig pow, fried prawns with Thai chilli sauce and spring onion. She also singles out – and so do I – pla pae sa, seasonal fish, usually sea bass, cooked in stock scented with lemon grass, salted plum and celery. The fish served on steamed fragrant rice into which the haunting broth can soak results in a superlatively good dish. The noodle assembly to go for is phad kuay teow kee mow goong, wide rice noodles flavoured with shrimps and basil leaves, which delivers a wonderful mix of textures and flavours, the sauce seductively sweet with the overtones of liquorice that Thai or holy basil contributes. In addition to the main menu, there is an enterprising vegetarian list. The waitresses bring the food with pride.

£23

OPEN
EVERY DAY

HOURS
12.00–3.00PM
6.00–11.00PM

CREDIT CARDS
AMEX DELTA
DINER'S
MASTERCARD
SWITCH VISA

SERVICE
OPTIONAL

**SET-PRICE
LUNCH**
£5.95

**SET-PRICE
DINNER**
£15.95

FACILITIES
SEATS 60
PRIVATE ROOM
SEATS 40

**NEAREST TUBE
STATION**
BAYSWATER/
QUEENSWAY

MAP 1

THAILAND

15 LEWISHAM WAY SE14   0181–691 4040

'Food from the Kingdom of a Million Elephants'

The King and Queen of Thailand survey this small, warmly decorated front room of a restaurant with its tapestry-covered banquettes, red lamps, small tables and illuminated stained-glass panels. Regulars know the calm, smiling woman chef/owner Khamkhong Kambungoet Herman, whose personal stamp on the restaurant is self-evident, not least in the list of Lao specialities. The domestic scale of the operation is reflected not in the menu which, true to Thai convention, is long and varied, but with the care taken in the cooking and the sweetness of service. The first course in a test meal paired Thai fish cakes served with sweet and sour cucumber and shallots with slender transparent Lao rice noodles served cold in a fish sauce in which lemon grass, lime leaves and galangal all played a part. A

£25

OPEN
TUES–SAT

HOURS
6.00–11.00PM

CREDIT CARDS
MASTERCARD VISA

SERVICE
OPTIONAL

**SET-PRICE
DINNER**
£20

FACILITIES
SEATS 25

**NEAREST BR
STATION**
NEW CROSS GATE

MAP 1

dish of North-East Thailand, hot and sour minced chicken, is served with lettuce leaves which you load with the chicken mixture to fashion little packets of flavour. Mussels dominated the hot and sour squid, prawns and mussels and the dish needed the contrast of sticky rice which, when cool enough to handle, can be eaten with the fingers almost like bread and used to mop up juices so perfumed and spiced they must not be left. Green papaya, which is not green in colour but in age, has a cabbage-like texture which adds a fresh, crunchy note. There are chargrilled items to contrast with dishes in sauce and curries to add yet more flavours to the symphony.

TURNER'S

87–89 WALTON STREET SW3   584 6711

'Your mother would like it'

£45

OPEN
LUNCH SUN–FRI
DINNER
EVERY DAY

HOURS
12.30–2.30PM
7.30–11.15PM

CREDIT CARDS
AMEX DELTA
DINER'S
MASTERCARD
SWITCH VISA

SERVICE
10%

SET-PRICE
LUNCH
£9.95

SET-PRICE
DINNER
£23.50

FACILITIES
SEATS 52
WHEELCHAIR
ACCESS

NEAREST TUBE
STATION
SOUTH
KENSINGTON

MAP 2

A reporter who took her French mother to Turner's found that both were seduced by the comfort, the prettiness of the room in Giverny shades of yellow and blue, the excellent service and the finesse of the cooking. From the main menu, boldly priced at £32 for two courses, hure de saumon, sauce à l'aneth, a light champagne-coloured jelly with pieces of freshly poached salmon suspended in it, complemented by a good dill sauce and perfect toasted brioche was deemed gentle in textures and flavours. Kidneys, 'the best ever', were thinly sliced, perfectly pink at the centre, meltingly tender, in a sauce of grainy mustard served with spinach. The banana tarte Tatin was a beautifully glazed, caramel-coloured creation served piping hot. Chef /patron Brian Turner and his chef Jonathan Bibbings are proudest of their carré d'agneau aux herbes de Provence and the wide range of fish dishes, which include brill steak grilled with a covering of tomatoes and golden crumbs and John Dory with a foie gras topping and an artichoke garnish. Most of the ladies who lunch fresh from the hairdresser in their Hermes scarves opt for the truly excellent value set-price deal at £9.95 inclusive for two courses. These might be paysanne salad of smoked fish and goat's cheese followed by breast of chicken on a bed of fennel, or medley of lemon sole, sea bass and salmon with a dill butter sauce followed by apple crumble. In the evening two courses from the menu du jour are £23.50. As each year goes by the slightly antiquated restaurant values of Turner's become rarer and thus more beguiling.

TWENTY TRINITY GARDENS

20 TRINITY GARDENS SW9   **733 8838**

'A neighbourly neighbourhood restaurant'

The correct French food served at this address contrasts with the expectations that the name, area and interior create. The dining room, which is part conservatory, has the look of modern Habitat. Jemima Mann-Baha and her husband Abdelali Baha have recently taken charge of the restaurant her mother founded. She cooks what she calls 'ageless French country food' with youthful enthusiam. He greets and serves with the assumption that you live around the corner and ought to enjoy the evening enough to want to return. The choice of food is fairly short and described with English subtitles: stuffed artichokes; salad of herring and potato; bavette and chips; rabbit with mustard sauce; profiteroles; clafoutis; and a beautiful, buttery but slightly collapsed tarte Tatin. An international impulse adds such things as ravioli of mussels (shaped like wontons and very appealing with a cool tomato sauce) or ceviche of salmon. Steak crops up in several styles, something most of us would find useful in a local restaurant, and the politically correct balance is there too in the form of vegetarian sausages and pasties. The cooking is competent to good, and the atmosphere and moderately priced set menus (cheaper on Mondays and Tuesdays) add to the attraction.

£26

OPEN
MON–SAT

HOURS
7.00–10.30PM
FRI & SAT
7.00–11.00PM

CREDIT CARDS
DELTA
MASTERCARD
SWITCH VISA

SERVICE
OPTIONAL

**SET-PRICE
DINNER**
£12.75–£19.50

FACILITIES
SEATS 54
TABLES OUTSIDE
SEAT 14
WHEELCHAIR
ACCESS

**NEAREST TUBE
STATION**
BRIXTON

MAP 1

TWO BROTHERS FISH RESTAURANT

297–303 REGENT'S PARK ROAD N3   **0181-346 0469**

'A fish and chip Brasserie'

There is a problem with Two Bros, and it is that most of us do not live in N3, otherwise the huge helpings of carefully prepared fish and chips could do marvellous things to our wallets and less desirable things to our waists. The fish is chosen with discrimination and served in huge portions: cod, haddock and skate overlap the plate. Every day the kitchen starts from scratch, cutting chips from Maris Piper potatoes, making batter and changing the groundnut oil. It is worth trying to find space for their mushy peas and new pickled cucumbers, or sampling the crunchy matzo meal coating for a change. Recommended starters are marinated herrings, fish soup, Rosier oysters and a rich dish of Arbroath smokies with cream and cheese that one

£21

OPEN
TUES–SAT

HOURS
12.00–2.30PM
5.30–10.15PM

CREDIT CARDS
AMEX
MASTERCARD
SWITCH VISA

SERVICE
OPTIONAL

FACILITIES
SEATS 90

**NEAREST TUBE
STATION**
FINCHLEY
CENTRAL

of the brothers devised. Grilled sole, sautéed sardines and a daily list which includes more unusual fish dishes are the alternatives to fish and chips, with steak and chicken for unfortunates with a horror of fish. Either Tony or Leon Manzi is usually directing affairs, soothing the queue which forms because there are no bookings or keeping an eye on the incredibly efficient waiting staff. They have designed the place to look like a modern brasserie, and chosen the wines with care. Big spenders like the dry champagne, but Tony Manzi's pride in his Côte de Duras house wine at £8.85 is quite justified.

UNION CAFÉ & RESTAURANT

£28

OPEN
MON–FRI

HOURS
10.00AM–10.00PM

CREDIT CARDS
DELTA
MASTERCARD
SWITCH VISA

SERVICE
OPTIONAL

FACILITIES
SEATS 60
WHEELCHAIR
ACCESS

**NEAREST TUBE
STATION**
BOND STREET

MAP 3

96 MARYLEBONE LANE W1   486 4860

'One worth joining'

Occupying a light and bright corner site in Marylebone Lane near the Cordon Bleu cookery school and round the corner from the American College, this modern refectory run by chef/proprietors Caroline Brett and Samantha Russell is also well poised to serve the BBC in Portland Place and the Condé Nast offices in Hanover Square. Indeed, slimsters from Vogue House may well have followed the pair from their previous place of work, O'Keefe's. Their policy is to source the best ingredients (which don't come cheaply), British if possible, and create a healthy, delicious daily-changing menu, and in this they succeed. Soups are an art form as evidenced by green garlic; orange lentil, lemon and garlic; red onion with goat's cheese croûtons. Salads are carefully assembled, as are the plates of cheese or charcuterie. Fish and meat main courses tend to take their bearings from the grill, as in salmon with marinated fennel and leeks or Heal Farm pork chops with apples, sultanas and mash. The baking arm is strong; apparent in the breads, desserts and pizza bases but also at breakfast when waffles, muffins and fritters are offered. The drinks list is more creative than most, with home-made lemonade, cordials, fresh juices and fruit 'smoothies' offered as well as wines. Lunch times are busy, but I rather like the Edward Hopper atmosphere of evenings.

THE UPPER STREET FISH SHOP

324 Upper Street N1   359 1401

'No small fry'

The Conways have been fryers for three generations, and if you hear Islington people refer to Olga's, Olga Conway, who manages the restaurant, is the reason. Although it looks like a bistro, their 'shop' has kept an old-fashioned conviviality perhaps because a cross section of N1 society meets here while sharing tables. Upper Street is a BYO or STT (stick to tea), so some go so far as to offer to share the wine they have selected at Oddbins. It is hard to tear oneself away from the favourite battered fish with big chips, but the deep-fried shellfish or halibut coated in egg have been enjoyed as substitutes. There is also a heretical impulse to, say, take the moules marinière as a starter instead of the smoked salmon pâté or fish soup. Oh dear, Olga will be disappointed. But we won't hear a word against her authentic English puddings with proper packet custard.

£14 BYO

Open
Lunch Tues–Sat
Dinner Mon–Sat

Hours
12.00–2.00pm
5.30–10.00pm

Credit Cards
None

Service
Optional

Facilities
Seats 50
Wheelchair
access

**Nearest Tube
Station**
Angel/Highbury
& Islington

Map 1

VASCO & PIERO'S PAVILION

15 Poland Street W1   437 8774

'Pitch up for a good Italian meal'

It is possible to infer the pattern of business at this family-run Italian restaurant from the price structure. Lunch time, when it is popular with people who work in the area, there is a cover charge and à la carte list with vegetables separately priced; evenings when regulars, tourists and theatre-goers who wander along from the Palladium have to be relied upon, there is a startlingly reasonable three-course menu with a great deal of choice. At either event the cooking is careful and unclichéd, delivering fresh, clean flavours and notably good pasta dishes such as the home-made sea bass tortelloni; fresh asparagus tortelloni; strangozzi al tartuffo, an Umbrian pasta made with truffles; and black pappardelle with fresh salmon. Cold meats such as thin slices of pink lamb or charcoal-roasted ham make good first courses served with artichokes and rucola. Carasau is an interesting item, paper-thin Sardinian bread served with tomato, basil, rucola and shaved Parmesan; the lightest bruschetta ever. Calf's liver with fresh sage is perfectly cooked and sautéed calamari with chilli, parsley and garlic something of a speciality. Desserts might include white chocolate semifreddo and pannacotta, both made in house.

£28

Open
Mon–Fri

Hours
12.00–3.00pm
6.00–11.00pm

Credit Cards
Amex Diner's
Mastercard
Switch Visa

Service
Optional

Cover Charge
£1.50 (Lunch
only)

**Set-Price
Dinner**
£13.95

Facilities
Seats 85
Private room
seats 35
Wheelchair
access

**Nearest Tube
Station**
Oxford Circus

Map 5

VILLANDRY

89 MARYLEBONE HIGH STREET W1   487 3816

'Noisy nourishment'

£24
OPEN
MON–SAT
HOURS
8.30AM–6.00PM
CREDIT CARDS
AMEX
MASTERCARD
SWITCH VISA
SERVICE
INCLUDED
FACILITIES
SEATS 50
PRIVATE ROOM
SEATS 40
WHEELCHAIR
ACCESS
NEAREST TUBE
STATION
BAKER STREET/
BOND STREET
MAP 3

Apparently plans for expansion at this popular delicatessen with, it is said, the most bizarre selection of pasta and the best eggs in London, have been thwarted for the moment by the plans Sir Terence Conran has for Marylebone High Street. Thus there is pressure on tables, a high level of noise in the puritan dining room at the rear of the premises and at peak time the risk of slow service. However, most agree it is worth putting up with these drawbacks for the sake of the wholesome and also delicious food. The daily-changing menus are without pretension or frills and nearly always include a soup – one of cannellini beans, rosemary and tomato was much liked; a plate of charcuterie served with proper cornichons; an interesting, substantial salad such as warm new potato with radicchio, crispy prosciutto and a poached egg; and bigger dishes such as braised tarragon chicken with noodles and carrots Vichy and best end of lamb with roast vegetables and mint butter, a dish that was cooked perfectly as requested (medium) and served on a bed of ratatouille-inspired vegetables. More shop produce is evident in the selection of cheeses and in the quality of chocolate used in the moist chocolate cake, which came extravagantly served with a soup tureen of cream. The wine selection is good if hardly at bargain prices, but note that prices are fully inclusive of tax and service.

VRISAKI

73 MYDDLETON ROAD N22   0181-889 8760

'Enough to make outsiders Wood Green with envy'

£17
OPEN
MON–SAT
HOURS
12.00–3.00PM
6.00PM–12.00AM
CREDIT CARDS
NONE
SERVICE
10%
SET-PRICE
LUNCH & DINNER
£12.50
FACILITIES
SEATS 120
PRIVATE ROOM
SEATS 18
WHEELCHAIR
ACCESS

London N22 has Cypriot shops, Cypriot banks and, hidden away in a residential terrace, this busy Greek Cypriot kebab house which also serves a munificent meze. The first room is filled by the grills and with seating for those waiting for a takeaway. Behind this are two long rooms very simply furnished. Most of the customers come at 9pm or later, so earlier callers may be told they can't have the set meal of every meze plus grills because an hour and a half is not time enough to get through it – 'It's not nice for us or you if we have to chase you out because we want the table back.' Service throughout is likely to be similarly straightforward. Still, an à la carte order of starters may arrive augmented with saucers of sharp green olives, of beetroot and of stewed dried beans which are not on the menu, and the standard-sounding starters such as taramasalata, tzaziki and hummus are freshly prepared and full of flavour. Fried squid rings and grilled prawns are evidently popular orders, but meat dishes such as lamb kebabs and T-bone steaks make more of an impression. Vrisaki has the appeal of a restaurant that concentrates on doing a few things well, and not charging too much for them.

NEAREST TUBE
STATION
WOOD GREEN/
BOUNDS GREEN

WAGAMAMA

4 STREATHAM STREET WC1   323 9223

'Necessary noodles from the Wagamamas of Invention'

Policemen, school teachers and dinner-ladies would do well to study the Wagamama methods of discipline and crowd control. With over a hundred people squashed up at long refectory tables, the staff here give orders as readily as they take them, the latter activity accomplished with the use of electronic ordering pads which send a radio signal to the appropriate station in the kitchen or bar. Queuing for a seat is the usual preliminary but the queue moves quickly as the menu is designed for quick, nourishing eating. There are no first courses but the main dishes, based on noodles served either in soup with garnishes or pan-fried with garnishes, or based on rice, can be accompanied by side dishes of gyoza (dumplings), deep-fried prawns in breadcrumbs, marinated deep-fried chicken wings, salad or freshly steamed green soya beans. The noodle soups are beautifully composed and flavoured, lit from within by the glowing colour of the vegetables swirling in the translucent broth, each steaming bowl looking like a photograph from a Sunday magazine. A customer who was presented with her chilli chicken ramen and a pair of disposable chopsticks thought that the prospect of eating the soup with chopsticks alone entirely consistent with the character-building nature of this restaurant – expressed in drink form by raw juices – but a spoon was brought. Sake, wine, including organic wines, Sapporo and Asahi beers, calpico, a yogurt-based drink, soft drinks and free Japanese tea are also available. The value for money combined with the healthiness of the food is an unbeatable combination. Though more Wagamamas are planned it seems evidence of their policy of *kaizen* – meaning continuous improvement – that expansion has not been rushed into.

£18

OPEN
EVERY DAY

HOURS
12.00–11.00PM
SAT
12.30–11.00PM
SUN
12.30–10.00PM

CREDIT CARDS
DELTA SWITCH

SERVICE
OPTIONAL

SET-PRICE
LUNCH & DINNER
£6.80

FACILITIES
SEATS 104

NEAREST TUBE
STATION
TOTTENHAM
COURT ROAD

MAP 4

THE WATERLOO FIRE STATION

£22

OPEN
MON–SAT

HOURS
12.00–3.30PM
6.30PM–12.00AM

CREDIT CARDS
AMEX DINER'S
SWITCH VISA

SERVICE
OPTIONAL

FACILITIES
SEATS 100
PRIVATE ROOM
SEATS 70
WHEELCHAIR
ACCESS (ALSO
WC)

**NEAREST TUBE
STATION**
WATERLOO

MAP 3

150 WATERLOO ROAD SE1   620 2226

'Bring your own brigade to be sure of a table'

It is all go at the fire station turned feeding station: the
kitchen is integral so you can watch the service progress (or
digress or regress) and as there are no bookings total strangers
try to share tables, leading to some interesting interaction. The
place is noisy, barely decorated, and busy. What those working
around Waterloo, or passing through, seem to appreciate is
exciting food, generously served at fair prices, plus the fact that
almost half the space operates as a bar, also competitively
priced. What was not appreciated recently was the way dishes
were falling like runners in the Grand National and everything
fancied seemed to vanish in a puff of chalk dust (choices are
chalked up on a blackboard). The commentary on: fish soup;
green herb and watercress salad; artichoke, poached egg and
Parmesan salad; Parma ham with figs and pickles; chargrilled
mackerel and fattoosh (herb and bread salad); and chump of
lamb with spinach deserves the tones of Peter O'Sullivan.
Unfortunately the going can get the better of the kitchen's
judgement at times: the limpid character of poached char is
never going to match garlic greens and it is a mistake to offer
Bearnaise sauce (to go with asparagus) if the sauce can not be
given sufficient attention. Fewer sauces and more concentration on what goes with what seem called for. It would be a
shame if, minus the mercurial but talented Dan Evans,
standards slip.

WEST ZENDERS

£26

OPEN
EVERY DAY

HOURS
12.00–4.30PM
6.00–11.30PM

CREDIT CARDS
AMEX DELTA
DINER'S
MASTERCARD
SWITCH VISA

SERVICE
12½%

4A UPPER ST MARTIN'S LANE WC2   497 0376

'Another day, another pun'

The last time this address was reviewed the restaurant was
called Now & Zen, but with these Chinese owners
another day is just another pun and now, with some regrettable
alterations to architect Rick Mather's original pristine design,
complete with what one felt was irreproachable feng shui, a new
concept is up and running. One compensation for the absence
of the waterfall and the illuminated glazed bridge over untrou-
bled tables is newly created space for seating on the entrance
floor. Menus are presented as a carte or a booklet entitled The
Zen Experience from which customers can choose as many

dishes as they want for a fixed price of £18.80 (plus 12½%
service). There is a certain amount of overlap between the two,
making The Zen Experience a potential bargain if armed with
the requisite appetite. Eating à la carte, first courses to try
include spring onion cake, crisp plump discs of dough laced
with the scallions; grilled Peking dumplings seemingly freshly
made; five spiced beef slices, cold meat imbued with haunting
flavours; minced chicken in lettuce wrap from which you can
make a soft parcel with crunchy, fresh packaging. Half a tea-
smoked chicken with supreme soya makes an excellent centrepiece dish, a change from duck or sea bass. Other slightly
unusual main courses are sautéed venison with coriander leaves
and celery; braised ox tongue; prawns sautéed with Cointreau
and Ma Pa tofu. Service is friendly and deft and well led by
Antony Au Lung. Closer to clubland than Chinatown in feel,
West Zenders is ideal for after theatre or the movies.

SET-PRICE
LUNCH
£10.80
SET-PRICE
DINNER
£18.80
FACILITIES
SEATS 200
PRIVATE ROOM
SEATS 30
WHEELCHAIR
ACCESS
NEAREST TUBE
STATION
LEICESTER
SQUARE
MAP 5

THE WHITE TOWER

1 PERCY STREET W1   636 8141

'Changes are afoot'

£34
OPEN
LUNCH MON–FRI
DINNER SAT
HOURS
12.30–2.30PM
SAT
6.30–10.30PM
CREDIT CARDS
AMEX DINER'S
MASTERCARD VISA
SERVICE
OPTIONAL
COVER CHARGE
£2
FACILITIES
SEATS 80
PRIVATE ROOM
SEATS 16
WHEELCHAIR
ACCESS
NEAREST TUBE
STATION
GOODGE STREET/
TOTTENHAM
COURT ROAD
MAP 4

George Metaxas and Mary Dunne ('Miss Mary') have
worked at this venerable Greek/Cypriot restaurant for 43
and 37 years respectively. In recent years they became the
owners – Miss Mary is the niece of the founder, the late John
Stais – but their wholly understandable wish for at least a
Saturday night off has this year seen the sale of The White
Tower to the Restaurant Partnership, the same outfit which
now owns two other Soho and Fitzrovia institutions, The Gay
Husssar (q.v.) and Elena's L'Étoile (q.v.). Such is the affection
in which The White Tower is held by its many regulars in the
worlds of politics, publishing and the media – including me –
that changes are bound to be resented. New staff at managerial
level seem to have the wrong temperament for this gentle place
and, to my mind, the loquacious menu has not been improved
by rationalization. The last straw was seeing an ad in my local
paper, *The Camden New Journal,* offering a free course at The
White Tower with the purchase of Odeon Cinema tickets.
Consolation can be found in the continuing presence most of
the time of George and Miss Mary; the pictures of Greek
heroes vying for space with old decorative plates on the walls;
the taramasalata, pâté Diana and the duckling farci à la
Cypriote which have not been ousted from the menu.

WILSON'S

'Scotch house meets Scotch broth'

£25
OPEN
MON–SAT
HOURS
7.30–10.30PM
CREDIT CARDS
AMEX
MASTERCARD VISA
SERVICE
OPTIONAL
**SET-PRICE
DINNER**
£9.75
FACILITIES
SEATS 44
WHEELCHAIR
ACCESS
**NEAREST TUBE
STATION**
OLYMPIA/
SHEPHERD'S
BUSH/GOLDHAWK
ROAD
MAP 1

Tartan curtains, tartan tablecloths and stacks of books on Scottish subjects such as Mary Queen of Scots to leaf through if conversation flags alert you to the theme of this homely restaurant which offers very good value. Mercifully, the menu is not self-consciously ethnic and although haggis, helpfully described by the flamboyant owner as 'like a hot pâté with oatmeal', served with mashed neeps and tatties makes an appearance – as does Finnan haddock pudding and Athol brose – Scottish culinary links are not stretched beyond their loadbearing capacity. First courses might include cream of wild mushroom soup; fresh steamed cockles with balsamic vinegar; rare roast beef with céleri rémoulade; grilled field mushroom with spinach and mozzarella; Stilton and pear tartlet. Main courses enjoyed this year were the aforementioned haggis, a rewarding version, and duck and spring onion sausages served with sauerkraut, which featured two robust sausages with the contributing flavours distinct but well matched and happily married to the piquant cabbage. A rich, smooth and slightly tart rhubarb fool and an old-fashioned blackcurrant trifle concluded a meal without pretension in a place with its own pronounced personality. The wine list is short, but there is a selection of single malt whiskies to browse through.

WILTONS

'There'll always be an England.
Not sure when. Not sure why'

£50
OPEN
SUN–FRI
HOURS
12.00–2.30PM
6.00–10.30PM
CREDIT CARDS
AMEX DINER'S
MASTERCARD
SWITCH VISA
SERVICE
OPTIONAL
COVER CHARGE
£1
**SET-PRICE
LUNCH**
19.75 (SUN ONLY)

The waitresses here in their absurd white nursery overalls, nowadays softened and trimmed with blue, have been described as wearing expressions of great sympathy and maniacal certainty comparable to those who believe the world is due to end on a certain, given date. Except for a privileged few, the world Wiltons represents has ended. Here is the universe, decorated in this instance with velvet banquettes and bevelled glass screens, P.G. Wodehouse peopled, but on view – as is Madame Tussaud's – to anyone with the price of admission. It is a high price but, on the whole, delivers excellent ingredients, particularly fish and game, which are not mucked about. A typical meal at Wiltons will begin with oysters or, out of oyster season (May to August), lobster cocktail served in a wine glass with a sauce attributable to Aunt Mary Rose, or perhaps potted shrimps, followed by plainly cooked fish such as turbot or halibut, or grilled meat or game in season with crème brûlée, a crumble or fresh berries to finish. Four savouries are also offered. Garnishes are not always all they should be. Chips, it was noted, were fried in old oil. Casual visitors are almost never given the privilege of sitting in the booths known as Pullmans. Regulars, usually with a title to their name, 'earned' as well as inherited, get those. Most days the customers are a mixture of regulars and tourists. Sunday lunch with its set menu at £19.75 for three courses is the one time you could eat here relatively reasonably, but the point of the place will be at their country houses or estates.

FACILITIES
SEATS 90
PRIVATE ROOM
SEATS 18
WHEELCHAIR
ACCESS

**NEAREST TUBE
STATION**
GREEN PARK

MAP 3

WÓDKA

12 ST ALBANS GROVE W8   937 6513

'Full of Polish spirit'

Jan Woroniecki opened Wódka in 1989 on the site of his father's restaurant, Chez Krysztof, a key Polish emigré hangout in the Fifties and Sixties. Since then the restaurant has expanded horizontally and now comprises two rooms, one decorated in the tiles which were there when the premises was a dairy at the turn of the century. Both rooms are sparse and purposeful in look: this is a place for serious drinking from a list of 30 vodkas and eaux de vie and for exhibiting a certain amount of solidarity with the Polish food prepared by chef Mirek Golos. The obvious partner for shots or half-litre carafes of vodka are blinis, which are served with a variety of accompaniments: herring; smoked salmon; aubergine purée; Sevruga caviar; keta (salmon eggs). Alternatively, you might want to build the foundations of an evening on a hearty soup such as krupnik (barley) or barszcz with pasztecik (borscht with meat-filled roll) or pierogi, dumplings filled with veal and wild mushrooms plus soured cream. There are salads for the faint-hearted. In the main course, dishes praised this year include kaczka, roast duck; golabki, cabbage stuffed with pork and wild rice with a berry sauce and a side order of lentils. The standard of cooking is creditable, a fact that sometimes risks going unappreciated during evenings towards the end of the week when spirits are high and noise is deafening.

£26

OPEN
LUNCH MON–FRI
DINNER
EVERY DAY

HOURS
12.30–3.30PM
7.00–12.30PM

CREDIT CARDS
AMEX DINER'S
MASTERCARD
SWITCH VISA

SERVICE
OPTIONAL

FACILITIES
SEATS 62
PRIVATE ROOM
SEATS 30
WHEELCHAIR
ACCESS

**NEAREST TUBE
STATION**
HIGH STREET
KENSINGTON

MAP 2

YOISHO

£18

OPEN
MON–SAT

HOURS
6.00–11.00PM

CREDIT CARDS
NONE

SERVICE
10%

FACILITIES
SEATS 60
TABLES OUTSIDE
SEAT 8

**NEAREST TUBE
STATION**
GOODGE STREET

MAP 4

33 GOODGE STREET W1   323 0477

*'For the simple pleasures of kimchi with
everything or offal on skewers'*

To enter Yoisho in the early evening is to step into a strange world where single Japanese men come to eat at the bar and take up conversations left off the day before yesterday. In this way the place resembles an old-fashioned pub at a similar hour, offering in place of pork scratchings bowls of vegetables or some chicken gizzards hot off the grill. Kimchi, a sort of sauerkraut dressed with soy sauce, garlic and chilli usually associated with Korea, crops up several times on the menu and should be sampled, as it is well made. Quibbles about quality here seem unjustified or out of date: the cooking is better than others of the type. Snack dishes or starters are cheap and quite generous. Bar customers are perched around the grill on which little kebabs of chicken or whole fish cook, and a starter and a skewer or two are probably all that will be required for a casual call. There is proper dining space and options such as sashimi (not sushi) and rice porridge dishes for those wanting a full meal.

ZAFFERANO

£28

OPEN
TUES–SAT

HOURS
12.00–2.30PM
7.00–11.00PM

CREDIT CARDS
AMEX
MASTERCARD VISA

SERVICE
OPTIONAL

**SET-PRICE
LUNCH**
£13.50 & £16.50

**SET-PRICE
DINNER**
£15.50 & £18.50

FACILITIES
SEATS 50
TABLES OUTSIDE
SEAT 15
WHEELCHAIR
ACCESS

15 LOWNDES STREET SW1   235 5800

'Italian restaurant of the year'

Giorgio Locatelli, chef/proprietor of this Knightsbridge Italian restaurant which opened early in 1995, has worked at Olivo (q.v.) and helped launch The Red Pepper (q.v.), but he has also worked in Paris at the two-star Michelin Laurent. It has to be said that something, and it is most probably the Parisian interlude, lifts his cooking above that of most of his compatriots. The menu, which strikes one as eminently reasonable for the area, presents many temptations: chargrilled cuttlefish salad; layered potatoes and pancetta with fontina cheese; fazzoletti, a herb pasta layered with spring vegetables and basil purée; pappardelle with broad beans and rocket; ravioli of ossobucco with a saffron sauce; nettle risotto; roast rabbit with Parma ham and polenta; chargrilled sliced lamb's leg with white beans and aubergine; cod with lentils; and I could go on. It is Italian food attached to no particular region but on which creativity, an alert palate and well-honed cooking skills have been focused. Desserts are also unusually fine. The Zafferano version of tiramisu, served in a biscuit cup surrounded by a lake of espresso sauce follows, a tradition started at The Halkin Hotel (q.v.) and continued at The Red Pepper (q.v.). Lemon and mascarpone tart and saffron (the meaning of Zafferano) brioche with apples, candied fruit and ice cream have been much liked. The coffee served is also notable. Apart from champagne, the wine list is completely Italian, ranging from house wines at £8.50 to a single vineyard Barbaresco and Barolo from the family firm of Gaja at £115. The agreeably plain rooms decorated in a colour that bears out the restaurant's name contain some annoyingly small tables.

NEAREST TUBE STATION
KNIGHTSBRIDGE
MAP 2

ZEN CENTRAL

20 QUEEN STREET W1   629 8089

'Upmarket Chinese food and prices'

Think of this as a Mayfair dining experience rather than going out for a Chinese meal and the price will seem less shocking. It is tempting to explore, by ordering at least one dish, most of the sections on the well-organized menu, but a dumpling here, a dumpling there, perhaps some steamed scallops, a luxurious centrepiece dish such as lobster with tangerine peel and crushed garlic, or steamed sea bass with black bean sauce, plus some main courses, rice and vegetables, can mount up to a serious total. My approach is to home in on the less unfamiliar dishes which anyway tend to reveal the talents of the kitchen and also remove the temptation to think things like, 'Sesame prawn toast for £7.50? That's outrageous.' Deep-fried crispy beef fingers; pan-fried Pekingese dumplings; pig's trotter slices; Ching Dynasty beef broth with mashed spinach; dragon prawn and sea-spice prawn sautéed with scallops; veal cutlets in black pepper sauce; hand-cut pork with dried shredded scallops; baked rice with duck and shrimps in lotus leaf are relatively reasonably priced and recommended. For those seeking the Chinese banquet experience the appropriately expensive ingredients such as shark's fin and abalone are offered, and suckling pig can be ordered in advance. Service, which is young, professional and friendly, adds to the enjoyment of a meal here, as does Rick Mather's sleek interior.

£40

OPEN
EVERY DAY

HOURS
12.00–2.30PM
& 6.30–11.30PM

CREDIT CARDS
AMEX DELTA
DINER'S
MASTERCARD
SWITCH VISA

SERVICE
OPTIONAL

COVER CHARGE
£1

SET-PRICE
LUNCH
£28

SET-PRICE
DINNER
£35 & £42

FACILITIES
SEATS 90
WHEELCHAIR
ACCESS

NEAREST TUBE STATION
GREEN PARK
MAP 3

ZENW3

£26

OPEN
EVERY DAY

HOURS
12.00–3.00PM
6.00–11.30PM

CREDIT CARDS
AMEX DELTA
DINER'S
MASTERCARD
SWITCH VISA

SERVICE
12½%

**SET-PRICE
LUNCH**
£10.50

**SET-PRICE
DINNER**
£28.50

FACILITIES
SEATS 140
PRIVATE ROOM
SEATS 24
WHEELCHAIR
ACCESS (ALSO
WC)

**NEAREST TUBE
STATION**
HAMPSTEAD

MAP 1

83–84 HAMPSTEAD HIGH STREET   794 7863/4

'Another aspect of Hampstead's arts and crafts'

Pure enlightenment about Chinese food seems most likely at this Hampstead branch of the Zen Garden group where the chef, Kwok Lee Tang, is allowed to express his culinary creativity in a list of seasonal suggestions. Regulars, who have many times combed their way through the well-organized booklet which contains the main menu, turn with pleasure to items such as quick-fried scallop stuffed with mashed shrimp in peppercorn salt; fillet of venison with preserved vegetable; steamed minced pork with dried scallop and water chestnut; fish fillet in sour curry sauce; sliced lamb with spiced honey sauce; and Zen fried rice with diced seafood and duck meat. A stylish healthy first course is Zen wrapping platter. Slices of barbecued beef, chicken and prawn, a heap of rice noodles, and a julienne of spring onion and cucumber are the ingredients which the waiter deftly wraps in skins of softened rice paper, making little packages ready for dipping into a piquant sauce. Along the same lines, the cold tossed salad of shredded chicken, roast duck and jellyfish with spring onion and cucumber (from the main menu) is clean and light. Pan-fried king prawns in soya sauce (seasonal dish) are huge creatures excitingly scorched. The sliced lamb with spiced honey sauce has the allure of being sweet and yet chilli hot. Generally the food here has an unusually lively straight-from-the-wok feel. Rick Mather's lucent design, where the mezzanine floor seems to float in space, stands the test of time. Staff are ready to smile.

INDICES

GREEK

Beoty's WC2
Café O SW3
Kalamaras Mega &
  Micro W2
Kleftiko W4
Lemonia NW1
Vrisaki N22
The White Tower W1

GRILLS

Café Med W11
Clarke's W8
Christopher's American
  Grill WC2
The Connaught W1
Dorchester Grill W1
Museum Street Café
  WC1
Porto Bello W10
Quaglino's SW1
The River Café W6
The Savoy Grill WC2

INDIAN

Babur Brasserie SE23
Bengal Clipper SE1
Bodali N5
Bombay Brasserie SW7
Chutney Mary SW10
Lahore Kebab House
  E1
Ma Goa SW15
Malabar W8
Namaste E1
Old Delhi W2
Ragam W1
Salloos SW1
Shree Krishna SW17
Star of India SW5
Tamarind W1

INDIAN VEGETARIAN

Chutneys NW1
Kastoori SW17
Mamta SW6
Mandeer W1
Ragam W1
Rasa N16
Shree Krishna SW17

ITALIAN

L' Accento W2
Alba EC1
Al San Vincenzo W2
Arts Theatre Café WC2
La Capannina W1
Caraffini SW1
Cibo W14
Daphne's SW3
Del Buongustaio SW15
Dorchester Hotel Bar
  W1
Enoteca SW15
La Famiglia SW10
Florians N8

Formula Veneta SW10
Il Goloso SW10
The Halkin Hotel
  Restaurant SW1
L'Incontro SW1
Olivo SW1
Orsino W11
Orso WC2
Osteria Antica Bologna
  SW11
The Red Pepper W9
Riva SW13
The River Café W6
San Lorenzo Fuoriporta
  SW19
Vasco & Piero's Pavilion
  W1
Zafferano SW1

JAPANESE

Arisugawa W1
Gonbei WC1
Inaho W2
Isohama SW1
Mitsukoshi SW1
Moshi Moshi Sushi EC2
Wagamama WC1
Yoisho W1

KOREAN

Bu San N7

LEBANESE

Al Bustan SW1
Al Hamra W1

MEDITERRANEAN

Avenue West Eleven
  W11
Bistrot 190 SW7
Café dell'Ugo SE1
The Eagle EC1
Granita N1
The Lansdowne NW1
The Peasant EC1
Snows on the Green
  W6

MODERN BRITISH

Alastair Little W1
Andrew Edmunds W1
Atelier W1
The Belvedere W8
Bibendum Restaurant
  SW3
Blue Print Café SE1
The Capital Hotel SW3
Le Caprice W1
Chesterfield Hotel –
  Butler's Restaurant
  W1
The Cow W2
The Engineer NW1
Frocks E9
Fulham Road SW3
Halcyon Hotel – The
  Room W11

The Ivy WC2
Kensington Place W8
Launceston Place W8
Leith's W11
The Lexington W1
Le Metro SW3
Museum Street Café
  WC1
Nicole's W1
192 W11
The Peoples Palace SE1
Pied à Terre W1
Le Pont de la Tour SE1
Quaglino's SW1
Quincy's NW2
Ransome's Dock SW11
Shaw's SW7
Sonny's SW13
The Square SW1
Stephen Bull W1
The Stepping Stone
  SW8
Union Cafe &
  Restaurant W1
Villandry W1
The Waterloo Fire
  Station SE1

NEPALESE

Great Nepalese NW1

NORTH AFRICAN

Laurent NW2

PORTUGUESE

Porto Bello W10

PUBS

The Abingdon W8
The Cow W2
The Eagle EC1
The Engineer NW1
The French House
  Dining Room W1
The Lansdowne NW1
The Peasant EC1
Prince Bonaparte W2

SCANDINAVIAN

Anna's Place N1

SCOTTISH

Wilson's W14

SPANISH

Albero & Grana SW3
Rebato's SW8

SRI LANKAN

Prince of Ceylon NW4

THAI

Bahn Thai W1
Blue Elephant SW6
Chada Thai SW11
Mantanah Thai Cuisiue
  SE25

Thailand SE14
Tawana W2

TURKISH

Istanbul Iskembecisi
  N16
Sofra W1 & WC2

**RESTAURANTS
BY AREA**

**BARBICAN/
FARRINGDON**

Alba
Bleeding Heart
Le Café du Marché
The Eagle
Quality Chop House
The Peasant
St John
Stephen Bull's Bar &
  Bistro

BARNES

Riva
Sonny's

BATTERSEA

Chada Thai
Joy Luck
Osteria Antica Bologna
Ransome's Dock
The Stepping Stone

BAYSWATER

L'Accento
Four Seasons
Inaho
Kalamaras Mega &
  Micro
Mandarin Kitchen
Royal China
Tawana

BELGRAVIA

Al Bustan
The Halkin Hotel
  Restaurant
Salloos

BLOOMSBURY

Alfred
Arisugawa
Chiaroscuro
Chez Gerard
Elena's L'Étoile
Interlude de Chavot
Mandeer
Museum Street Café
Pied à Terre
Ragam
Wagamama
The White Tower
Yoisho

BRIXTON

Twenty Trinity Gardens

Fina Estampa
The Peoples Palace
Le Pont de la Tour
RSJ
The Waterloo Fire
Station

SOUTH KENSINGTON
Bibendum
Bibendum Oyster Bar
Bistrot 190
Bombay Brasserie
Café O
Chez Max
Daphne's
Gilbert's
Hilaire
Lou Pescadou
Ognisko Polskie
Shaw's
Star of India
Le Suquet

SOUTH NORWOOD
Mantanah Thai Cuisine

STOKE NEWINGTON
Istanbul Iskembecisi
Rasa

TWICKENHAM
McClement's Bistro

VAUXHALL
Rebato's

WANDSWORTH/
TOOTING
Brady's
Chez Bruce
Kastoori
Le P'tit Normand
Shree Krishna
Smokey Joe's Diner

WESTMINSTER
The Atrium
Isohama
Tate Gallery

WIMBLEDON
San Lorenzo Fuoriporta

WOOD GREEN
Vrisaki

**RESTAURANTS
WITH LAST
ORDERS AFTER
11.30PM**

The Atlantic Bar &
Grill W1 (12.30am
restaurant, 2.30am bar)
Bistrot 190 SW7
(12.00am)
Bombay Brasserie SW7
(12.00am)

Le Caprice SW1
(12.00am)
China City WC2
(11.45pm)
Christopher's American
Grill WC2 (11.45pm)
dell'Ugo W1 (12.15am
restaurant)
Dorchester Bar W1
(11.45pm)
Elena's Étoile W1
(12.00am)
La Famiglia SW10
(11.45am)
Istanbul Iskembecisi
N16 (4.30am)
The Ivy WC2
(12.00am)
Kalamaras Mega &
Micro W2 (12.00am)
Kensington Place W8
(11.45pm)
Lahore Kebab House
E1 (12.00am)
London Hilton on Park
Lane – Trader Vic's
W1 (11.45am)
Lou Pescadou SW5
(12.00am)
Ming W1 (11.45pm)
Mr Kong WC2
(1.45am)
Le Palais du Jardin
WC2 (12.00am)
Poissonerie de l'Avenue
SW3 (11.45pm)
Prince of Ceylon NW4
(12.00am)
Ransome's Dock SW11
(12.00am)
Rasa N16 (11.45pm)
Shree Krishna SW17
(12.00 Fri–Sat)
Sofra W1 (12.00am)

**RESTAURANTS
THAT BAN
SMOKING, OR
WITH NO-
SMOKING ROOMS**

Al Bustan SW1
The Atrium SW!
Beoty's WC2
La Capannina SW1
Chesterfield Hotel W1
Chez Gerard W1
Clarke's W8
La Famiglia SW10
London Hilton on Park
Lane – Trader Vic's
W1
Mandeer W1
McClement's Bistro
TW1
Mijanou SW1

Moshi Moshi Sushi
EC2
Museum Street Café
WC1
Rasa N16
St James's Court Hotel –
Auberge de Provence
SW1
Stepping Stone SW8
The Sugar Club W11
Twenty Trinity Gardens
SW9
Villandry W1
Wagamama WC1

**RESTAURANTS
WITH TABLES
OUTSIDE**
(* = Restaurant has a
garden/courtyard,
rather than tables on
the pavement)

The Abingdon W8
Al Bustan SW1
Alfred WC2
Al Hamra W1
Andrew Edmunds W1
Anna's Place* N1
The Atrium* SW1
L'Aventure*
Bahn Thai W1
The Belvedere* W8
Bleeding Heart
Restaurant and Wine
Bar* EC1
The Blenheim NW8
Blue Print Café SE1
The Brackenbury W6
Brasserie du Marché aux
Puces W10
Butlers Wharf Chop
House SE1
Café Fish SW1
Café Med W11
Café O SW3
Caraffini SW1
Chez Gerard W1
Chez Max* SW10
Chiaroscuro WC1
Chinon W14
The Chiswick W4
Cibo W14
Daphne's* SW3
dell'Ugo W1
La Dordogne W4
The Eagle EC1
Elena's L'Étoile W1
The Engineer* NW1
La Famiglia* SW10
Florians N8
Formula Veneta* SW10
Frocks* E9
Geales W8
Gilbert's SW7
Il Goloso SW10

Halcyon Hotel – The
Room* W11
Jimmy Beez W10
Kalamaras Mega &
Micro* W2
Kleftiko W4
The Lansdowne Public
House* NW1
Lemonia* NW1
Lou Pescadou* SW5
Mijanou* SW1
Ming W1
Mon Petit Plaisir W8
Namaste E1
Odette's NW1
Ognisko Polskie* SW7
Olivers Island W4
192 W11
Osteria Antica Bologna
SW11
Overton's* SW1
Le Palais du Jardin
WC2
Le Pont de la Tour SE1
Porto Bello W10
Ransome's Dock* SW11
Rasa* N16
Red Pepper W9
The Ritz* W1
Riva SW13
River Café* W6
RSJ SE1
San Lorenzo
Fuoriporta* SW19
Shaw's SW7
Singapore Garden NW6
Sofra W1
St John* EC1
The Sugar Club* W11
Le Suquet SW3
Twenty Trinity Gardens
SW9
Yoisho W1
Zafferano SW1

**RESTAURANTS
WITH LIVE MUSIC**
(This is often occasional.
Please telephone
restaurants for details.)

The Atlantic Bar &
Grill W1
The Atrium SW1
Bengal Clipper SE1
Bombay Brasserie SW7
Le Café du Marché
EC1
Café Fish SW1
Le Caprice SW1
Chesterfield Hotel W1
Dorchester Hotel Bar
W1
L'Escargot Brasserie W1
Four Seasons Hotel –
Four Seasons

Restaurant W1
The Halkin Hotel
Restaurant SW1
London Hilton on Park
Lane – Trader Vic's
W1
L'Incontro SW1
Jimmy Beez W10
Kalamaras Mega W2
The Lansdowne Public
House NW1
The Lexington W1
The Lobster Pot SE11
Le Pont de la Tour SE1
Prince of Ceylon NW4
Quaglino's SW1
Rebato's SW8
The Ritz – Louis XVI
Restaurant W1
St James Court Hotel –
Auberge de Provence
SW1
Sofra W1
Star of India SW5
Tamarind W1
Wilson's W14

UNDER £20 PER PERSON

Ali Baba NW1 £14
Bodali N5 £16
Brady's SW6 £15
Calabash WC2 £17
Chutneys NW1 £16
Geale's Fish Restaurant W8 £17
Il Goloso SW10 £18
Great Nepalese NW1 £18
Istanbul Iskembecisi N16 £18
Kalamaras Micro W2 £18
Kastoori SW17 £16
Lahore Kebab House E1 £9
Laurent NW2 £17
Ma Goa SW15 £18
Mandeer W1 £18
Moshi Moshi Sushi EC2 £14
Porto Bello W10 £16
Ragam W1 £18
Rasa N16 £17
Shree Krishna SW17 £15
Smokey Joe's Diner SW18 £12
Upper Street Fish Shop N1 £14
Vrisaki N22 £17
Wagamama WC1 £18
Yoisho W1 £18

£20–£40 PER PERSON

The Abingdon W8 £25
L'Accento W2 £26
Alba EC1 £26
Albero & Grana SW3 £37
Al Bustan SW1 £30
Alfred WC2 £24
Al Hamra W1 £26
Al San Vincenzo W2 £34
Arisugawa W1 £40
Andrew Edmunds W1 £24
Anna's Place N1 £26
Arts Theatre Café WC2 £20
Les Associés N8 £28
Atelier W1 £34
Atlantic Bar & Grill W1 £33
The Atrium SW1 £25
Aubergine SW10 £40
Avenue West Eleven W11 £30
L'Aventure NW8 £32
Babur Brasserie SE23 £20
Bahn Thai W1 £29
Belgo Centraal WC2 £20
Belgo Noord NW1 £20
The Belvedere W8 £28
The Bengal Clipper SE1 £28
Bentley's W1 £36
Beoty's WC2 £26
Bibendum Oyster Bar SW3 £24
Bistrot Bruno W1 £30
Bistrot 190 SW7 £24
Bleeding Heart Restaurant & Wine Bar EC1 £26
The Blenheim NW8 £24
Blue Elephant SW6 £33
Blue Print Café SE1 £30
The Bombay Brasserie SW7 £32
The Brackenbury W6 £24
Brasserie du Marché aux Puces W10 £24
Bu San N7 £26
Butlers Wharf Chop House SE1 £30
Café dell'Ugo SE1 £23
Café du Marché EC1 £30
Café Fish SW1 £28
Café Med W11 £28
Café O SW3 £25

La Capaninna W1 £26
Le Caprice SW1 £30
Caraffini SW1 £26
Caviar House – La Brasserie W1 £36
Chada Thai SW11 £26
Chez Bruce SW17 £28
Chez Gerard W1 £28
Chez Max SW10 £32
Chez Moi W11 £32
Chiaroscuro WC1 £29
China City WC2 £20
Chinon W14 £30
The Chiswick W4 £25
Christopher's American Grill WC2 £36
Chutney Mary SW10 £30
Cibo W14 £30
Clarke's W8 £40
Coast W1 £40
The Cow W2 £25
Cucina NW3 £24
Daphne's SW3 £30
Del Buongustaio SW15 £30
Dell'Ugo W1 £26
Dorchester Hotel Bar W1 £35
La Dordogne W4 £30
The Eagle EC1 £20
Elena's L'Étoile W1 £30
The Engineer NW1 £22
Enoteca SW15 £25
L'Escargot Brasserie W1 £36
L'Estaminet WC2 £28
La Famiglia SW10 £30
Feng Shang Floating Restaurant NW1 £30
Fifth Floor Restaurant SW1 £35
Fina Estampa SE1 £24
Florians N8 £28
Formula Veneta SW10 £30
Four Seasons (Queensway) W2 £23
The French House Dining Room W1 £25
Frocks E9 £22
Fulham Rd SW3 £35
Fung Shing WC2 £28
The Gate W6 £20
Gaucho Grill W1 £30
The Gay Hussar W1 £30
Gilbert's SW7 £26
Il Goloso SW10 £27
Gonbei WC1 £22
Gourmet Garden NW4 £20
Granita N1 £25
The Greenhouse W1 £35
Green's Restaurant & Oyster Bar SW1 £40

The Green Street Restaurant W1 £26
Grill St Quentin SW3 £27
Halcyon Hotel – The Room W12 £34
The Halkin Hotel Restaurant SW1 £40
Hilaire SW7 £39
Imperial City EC3 £32
Inaho W2 £28
L'Incontro SW1 £38
Interlude du Chavot W1 £35
Isohama SW1 £28
The Ivy WC2 £34
Jade Garden W1 £24
Jason's W9 £30
Jimmy Beez W10 £24
Jones WC2 £28
Joy Luck SW11 £22
Kalamaras Mega W2 £22
Kensington Place W8 £34
Kleftiko W4 £20
The Lansdowne Public House NW1 £20
Launceston Place W8 £33
Leith's W11 £36
Lemonia NW1 £20
The Lexington W1 £27
The Lobster Pot SE11 £35
London Hilton – Trader Vic's W1 £35
Lou Pescadou SW5 £24
Magno's Brasserie WC2 £32
Malabar W8 £24
Mamta SW6 £20
Mandarin Kitchen W2 £26
Mantanah Thai Cuisine SE25 £22
McClements Bistro Twickenham £25
Le Metro SW3 £23
Ming W1 £25
Mr Kong WC2 £25
Mon Petit Plaisir W8 £28
Mon Plaisir WC2 £32
Le Muscadet W1 £34
Museum Street Café WC1 £30
Namaste E1 £22
Nicole's W1 £35
Odette's NW1 £32
Ognisko Polskie SW7 £26
Old Delhi W2 £26
Olivers Island W4 £25
Olivo W1 £30
192 W11 £28
Orsino W11 £26

Orso WC2 £28
Oslo Court NW8 £32
Osteria Antica Bologna SW11 £25
Overtons SW1 £33
Le Palais du Jardin WC2 £26
Pearl SW1 £35
The Peasant EC1 £24
The Peoples Palace SE1 £28
Le Petit Max Hampton Wick £25.50 BYO
Le P'tit Normand SW18 £28
Poissonerie de L'Avenue SW3 £38
Le Pont de la Tour SE1 £40
Poons WC2 £20
Prince Bonaparte W2 £20
Prince of Ceylon NW4 £20
Quaglino's SW1 £34
The Quality Chop House EC1 £25
Quincy's NW2 £33
Ransome's Dock SW11 £26
Rebato's SW8 £28
Red Pepper W9 £20
Riva SW13 £28
River Café W6 £40
Royal China W2 £28
RSJ SE1 £27
Rules WC2 £28
Salloos SW1 £35
San Lorenzo Fuoriporta SW19 £35
St James's Court Hotel – Auberge de Provence SW1 £40
St John EC1 £25
St Quentin SW3 £34
Sec's and Checks SW3 £30
Shaw's SW7 £40
Singapore Garden NW6 £26
Snows on the Green W6 £28
Sofra WC2 £24
Sonny's SW13 £28
Star of India SW5 £28
Stephen Bull W1 £32
Stephen Bull's Bistro EC1 £25
The Stepping Stone SW8 £24
The Sugar Club W11 £26
Le Suquet SW3 £34
Sweetings EC4 £32
Tabac W10 £28
Tamarind W1 £32

Tate Gallery Restaurant SW1 £30
Tawana W2 £23
Thailand SE14 £25
Twenty Trinity Gardens SW9 £26
Two Brothers Fish Restaurant N3 £21
Union Cafe & Restaurant W1 £28
Vasco & Piero's Pavilion W1 £28
Villandry W1 £24
The Waterloo Fire Station SE1 £22
West Zenders WC2 £26
White Tower W1 £34
Wilson's W14 £25
Wódka W8 £26
Zafferano SW1 £28
ZENW3 NW3 £26

OVER £40 PER PERSON

Alastair Little W1 £42
Bibendum SW3 £45
Café Royal Grill Room W1 £48
Capital Hotel SW3 £50
Connaught Hotel W1 £50
Dorchester Grill W1 £45
Four Seasons Hotel – Four Seasons Restaurant W1 £50
Hyde Park Hotel – The Restaurant SW1 £85
Inter-Continental Hotel – Le Soufflé W1 £44
Le Gavroche W1 £75
Mijanou SW1 £42
Mitsukoshi SW1 £50
Monkeys SW3 £45
Pied à Terre W1 £52
The Ritz – Louis XVI Restaurant SW1 £62
Les Saveurs W1 £55
The Square SW1 £45
La Tante Claire SW3 £64
Turner's SW3 £45
Wiltons SW1 £50

RESTAURANTS SERVING SUNDAY BRUNCH

The Belvedere W8
Bistrot 190 SW7
Blue Elephant SW6
Bombay Brasserie SW7
Butlers Wharf Chop House SE1

Café Med W11
Le Caprice SW1
Chada Thai SW11
Chiaroscuro WC1
Christopher's American Bar & Grill WC2
Cucina NW3
Daphne's SW3
Feng Shang Floating Restaurant NW1
Fina Estampa SE1
Florians N8
Formula Veneta SW10
Frocks E9
The Greenhouse W1
Green's SW1
Halcyon Hotel – The Room W12
Jimmy Beez W10
Kleftiko W4
Odette's NW1
Le Pont de la Tour SE1
Le P'tit Normand SW18
The Quality Chop House EC1
Ransome's Dock SW11
Royal China W2
San Lorenzo Fuoriporta SW19
Shaw's SW7
Snows on the Green W6
The Sugar Club W11
Tabac W10

RESTAURANTS WITH WHEELCHAIR ACCESS
(including access to WC)

The Atrium SW1
Bahn Thai W1 (Men's only)
Belgo Centraal WC2
Belgo Noord NW1
Beoty's WC2
Bistrot 190 SW7
Blue Elephant SW6
Blue Print Café SE1
Butlers Wharf Chop House SE1
Café dell'Ugo SE1
Café Royal Grill Room W1 (Women's only)
Caraffini SW1
Chesterfield Hotel W1
The Chiswick W4
Connaught Hotel W1
Dorchester Hotel Grill W1
La Dordogne W4
Fifth Floor SW1
Florians N8
Formula Veneta SW10

Four Seasons Hotel – Four Seasons Restaurant W1
Fulham Road SW3
Geales W8
The Halkin Hotel Restaurant SW1
Hyde Park Hotel – The Restaurant SW1
Imperial City EC3
Inaho W2
Inter-Continental Hotel Le Soufflé W1
Jason's W9
Kastoori SW17
Kensington Place W8
Kleftiko W4
Lemonia NW1
London Hilton on Park Lane– Trader Vic's W1 (Women's only)
Museum Street Café WC1
Olivers Island W4
Le Palais du Jardin WC2
The Peasant EC1
Le P'tit Normand SW18
The Peoples Palace SE1
Le Pont de la Tour SE1
Prince of Ceylon NW4
Quaglino's SW1
Ragam W1
Ransome's Dock SW11
Rasa N16
The Ritz – Louis XVI Restaurant W1
The River Café W6
Salloos SW1
St John EC1
The Square SW1
Shree Krishna SW17
Stephen Bull's Bistro EC1
Tate Gallery Restaurant SW1
The Waterloo Fire Station SE1
ZENW3 NW3